# PICTURES OF PERSONALITY™

# Also from Typology

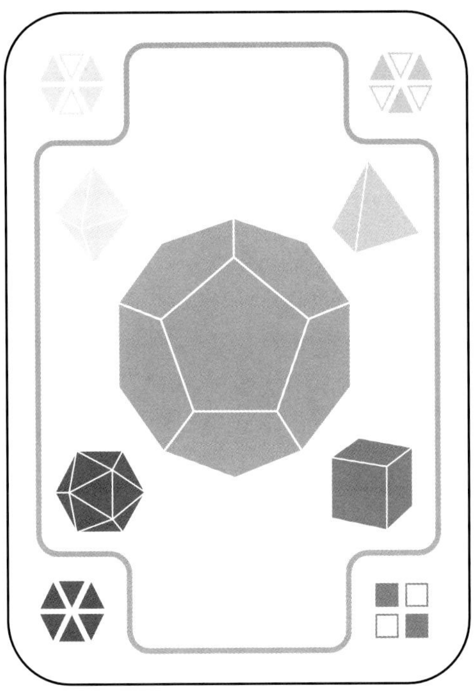

*Pictures of Personality™ Symbol Cards*
(55 cards in color)

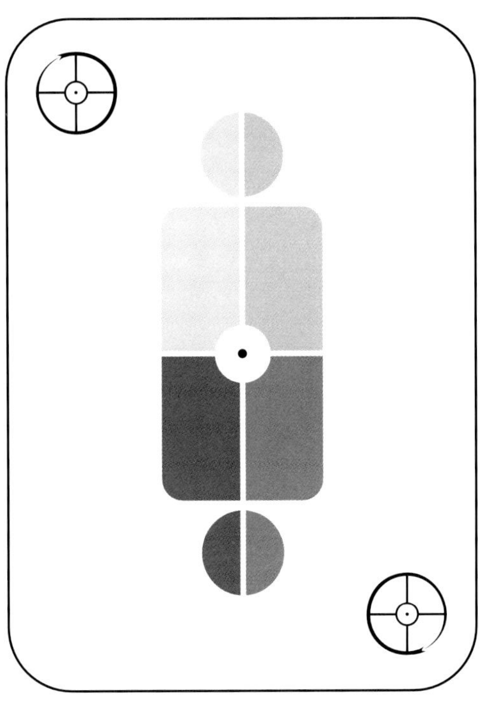

*Pictures of Personality™ Icon Cards*
(55 cards in color)

# PICTURES OF PERSONALITY™

*Guide to the Four Human Natures*

Designed and Written
by
JOHN LOPKER

TYPOLOGY
Los Angeles

FIRST EDITION

Published in 2000 by
TYPOLOGY
Los Angeles
SAN 253-5572
1-800-TYPOLOGY
www.Typology.Net

Opposite Eve's Dream: *The Ascent of the Mountain of Purgatory* (1824–1827)
by William Blake (1757–1827). Illustrations to Dante's *Divine Comedy (Purgatorio IV)*
Pencil, pen, and watercolor. Copyright © Tate, London. Reproduced by permission of the Tate.

Opposite Eve's Awakening: *The Spiral Stairway* (1824–1827)
by William Blake (1757–1827). Illustrations to Dante's *Divine Comedy (Paradiso)*
Pencil. Copyright © The British Museum. Reproduced by permission of the British Museum.

Jung, Carl Gustav, *The Collected Works of C. G. Jung*,
Volumes 5, 6, 7, 8, 9i, 9ii, 10, 11, 12, 13, 14, 15, 16, 17, 18.
Copyright © 1977 by Princeton University Press. Reprinted by permission of Princeton University Press.



Cover and book design by John Lopker
Printed in Singapore by Imago on acid-free paper

1 3 5 7 9 8 6 4 2

Publisher's Cataloging-in-Publication
(Provided by Quality Books, Inc.)

Lopker, John.
Pictures of personality : guide to the four human natures /
designed and written by John Lopker.
– 1st ed.
p. cm.
Includes index.
LCCN 00-109974
ISBN 0-9705810-0-9

1. Typology (Psychology). 2. Temperament. 3. Myers-Briggs Type Indicator.
4. Jung, C. G. (Carl Gustav), 1875–1961. I. Title.

BF698.3.L67 2000 155.2'64 QBI00-937

# CONTENTS

Watercolor by William Blake. © Tate, London

# Eve's Dream

Eve awoke inside a riddle, the condensation of a misty dream. What is human nature? She forgot the dream, but not the question. Only common questions come and go. The good ones stay. They saturate. Make our fate.

Eve decided to search for the secret of human nature in the most obvious place: nature. After a long journey, she found a hidden paradise far from the clamor of civilization. Eve loved her new life, so primitive and primary. She rose every morning in the yellow glow of the moist dawn air to roam the emerald hills and bathe in the cool blue lagoons. Every evening, the sun's red rays arched over the mountains and slowly disappeared as Earth's silent shadow blended with the brilliant night sky.

Eve searched every day and every night for one year. Fall seized her summer, and winter overcame her fall. Spring broke her winter, and summer engulfed her spring. After one spiral of seasons, she had found nothing and gave up all hope. And then the four secrets found Eve.

*Unity.* Water solves the first, in totality.

*Clarity.* Air reveals the second, quite transparently.

*Activity*. Fire generates the third, so energetically.

*Stability.* Earth establishes the fourth, most definitely.

On her last night, Eve rested in a soft field. A gentle breeze carried the original scent of night across the land. She felt so alone and yet so alive. One tear fell down her cheek into the fertile soil below. Above, ten thousand stars sparkled in the black heavens until concealed by the radiance rounding the horizon, once again, once upon a time . . . .

# The Five Point Survey™

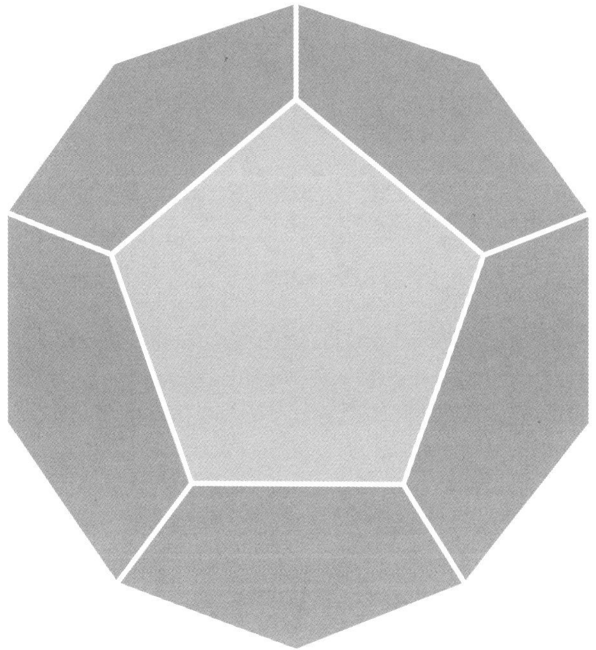

*The real voyage of discovery consists not in seeking new lands but seeing with new eyes.*

Marcel Proust

# What Is My Nature?

## Clarifier

*Air's Clarity*

10%

Confidence, but.
Adapts Strategically
Distinctions

I have bounded confidence, as in: "I can do that which I understand." Naturally, I want to expand the boundaries of my confidence by clarifying. I seek confidence through my own individual insights. My bounded confidence steers my focus to distinctions. Like prepositions, I identify positions. I reveal boundaries and catalyze change. I want to conceive the most efficient means to an end based on logic. Independent, I must attain autonomy. For me, life is a question.

## Activator

*Fire's Activity*

35%

Confidence
Structures Tactically
Opportunities

I have boundless confidence, as in: "I can do that." Naturally, I want to express my boundless confidence through action. I have confidence in my own individual instincts. My boundless confidence steers my focus to opportunities. Like verbs, I structure by action. I melt boundaries and cause change. I want the most expedient means to an end. Independent, I must remain unrestrained. For me, life is to live.

## Unifier

*Water's Unity*

10%

Trust
Adapts Diplomatically
Similarities

We have boundless trust, as in: "We can trust others." Naturally, we want to express our boundless trust by unifying. We trust universal human affinity. Our boundless trust steers our focus to similarities. Like conjunctions, we identify connections. We blend boundaries and nurture change. We want to conceive the most meaningful means to an end based on value. Interdependent, we must attain accord. For us, life is a quest.

## Stabilizer

*Earth's Stability*

45%

Trust, but.
Structures Procedurally
Priorities

We have bounded trust, as in: "We can trust others in our group." Naturally, we want to solidify the boundaries of our trust by stabilizing. We seek trust in group affiliation. Our bounded trust steers our focus to priorities. Like nouns, we structure by naming. We establish boundaries and resist change. We want the most reliable means to an end. Interdependent, we must maintain authority. For us, life is to survive.

# What Is My Attitude?

**External Attitude**
*Extraversion*

Object Attraction
Expends Energy and Expands
Fascinated by the Objective World
Outer Directed and Externally Motivated
My internal world serves the external world.

**Internal Attitude**
*Introversion*

Subject Attraction
Conserves Energy and Contracts
Fascinated by my Subjective World
Inner Directed and Internally Motivated
The external world serves my internal world.

# What Is My Role?

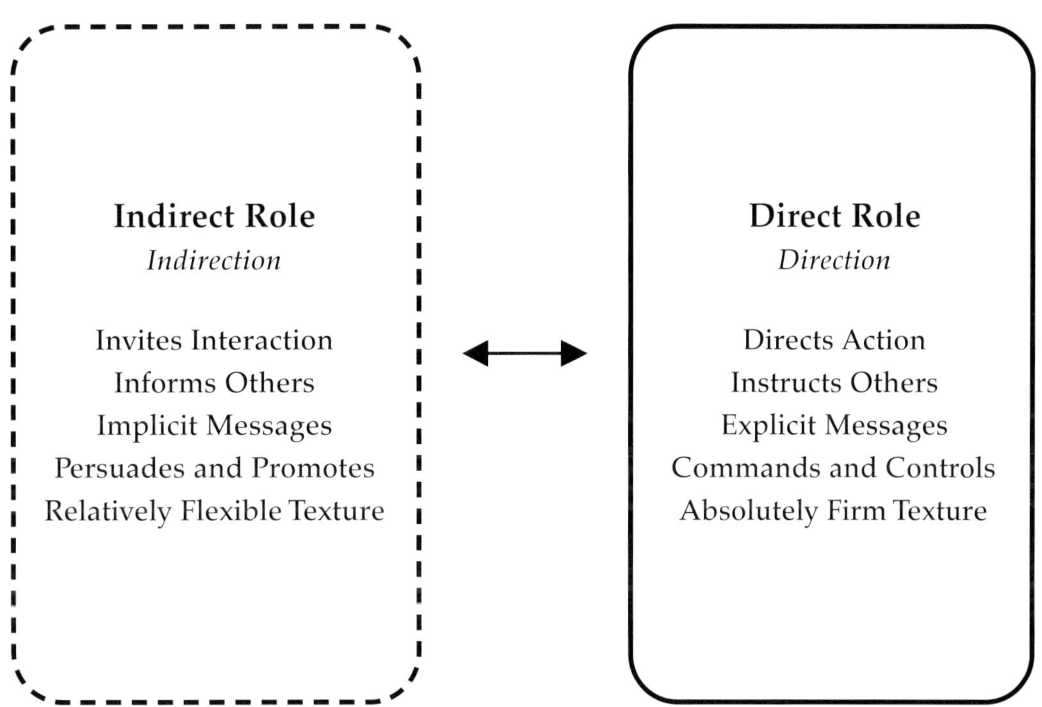

# How Do I Perceive?

**The Actual: Attention**
**Experience the Object**

I sense the actual *Content* of the present, experiencing everything with attention open to the known variables and emerging opportunities.

## OPEN PERCEPTION?

**The Novel: Options**
**Decipher the Object**

I conceive the novel *Context* of the present, deciphering everything with awareness open to the unknown variables and evolving options.

↕

**My Priorities: Continuation**
**My Subjective Impressions**

I sense past *Content*, my impressions of what was, closing out all that does not support the continuation of my priorities.

## CLOSE PERCEPTION?

**My Plans: Anticipation**
**My Subjective Interpretations**

I conceive future *Context*, my interpretations of what will be, closing out all that does not comport with the anticipation of my plans.

**Content.** To perceive *inside* the container of the five senses.

**Context.** To perceive *outside* the container of the five senses.

# How Do I Decide?

**My Ideals: Perfection**
**My Subjective Evaluation**

I *Harmonize* experientially, refining my ideals by my evaluation of natural human values and their perfect expression.

## REFINE DECISIONS?

**My Ideas: Precision**
**My Subjective Contemplation**

I *Organize* experientially, refining my ideas by my contemplation of natural logical principles and their precise expression.

**The Customs: Relations**
**The Objective Conventions**

I *Harmonize* systematically, confined to the customs and conventions prescribed by the general rules of human relations.

## CONFINE DECISIONS?

**The Methods: Causation**
**The Objective Formulas**

I *Organize* systematically, confined to the methods and formulas prescribed by the general rules of logical causation.

**Harmonize.** To decide based on *value*: more or less.

**Organize.** To decide based on *logic*: true or false.

## Global: Variation

I naturally Globalize: open perception and refine decisions. I perceive objectively (The Actual and The Novel) and decide subjectively (My Ideals and My Ideas). I want freedom of choice. I want the freedom to explore life's abundant variation. I am not shackled to a few themes in life. Strict themes imprison me by limiting my choices. I want to experience all of life as it develops and respond spontaneously to the whole changing present situation. I agree with Charles Dickens: "I ask only to be free. The butterflies are free."

## Local: Theme

I naturally Localize: close perception and confine decisions. I perceive subjectively (My Priorities and My Plans) and decide objectively (The Customs and The Methods). I want freedom from choice. I want the freedom to pursue a few chosen themes. I am not shackled to an endless search for life's variety. Unbridled variation imprisons me by compelling unending choices. I want to advance step by step, part by part, from my past to my future in a sequential and systematic progression. I agree with Edmund Burke: "Liberty must be limited in order to be possessed."

# PART I

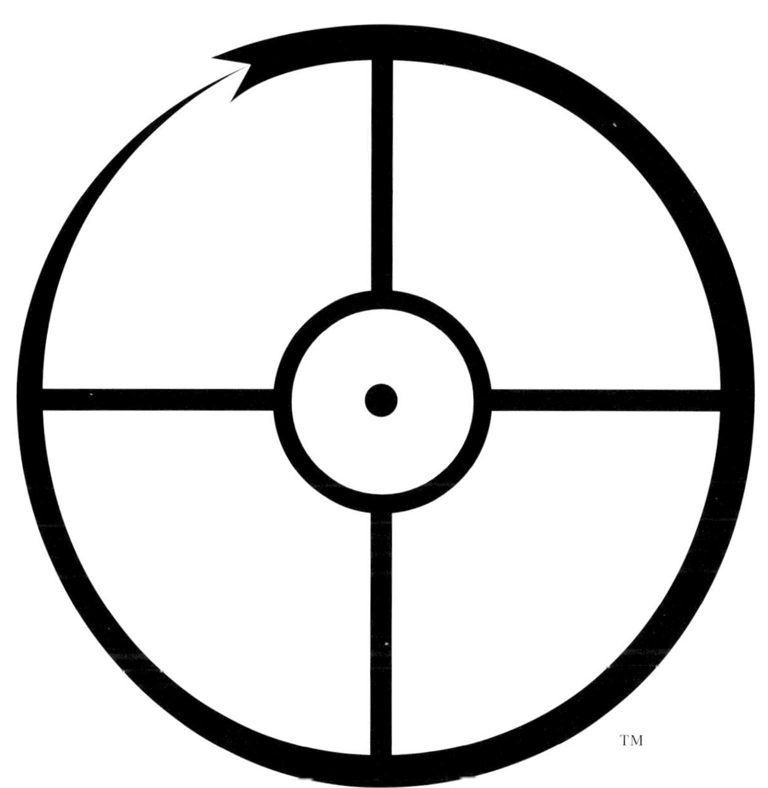


## The Four Natures: Faith and Focus

## The Original Compass

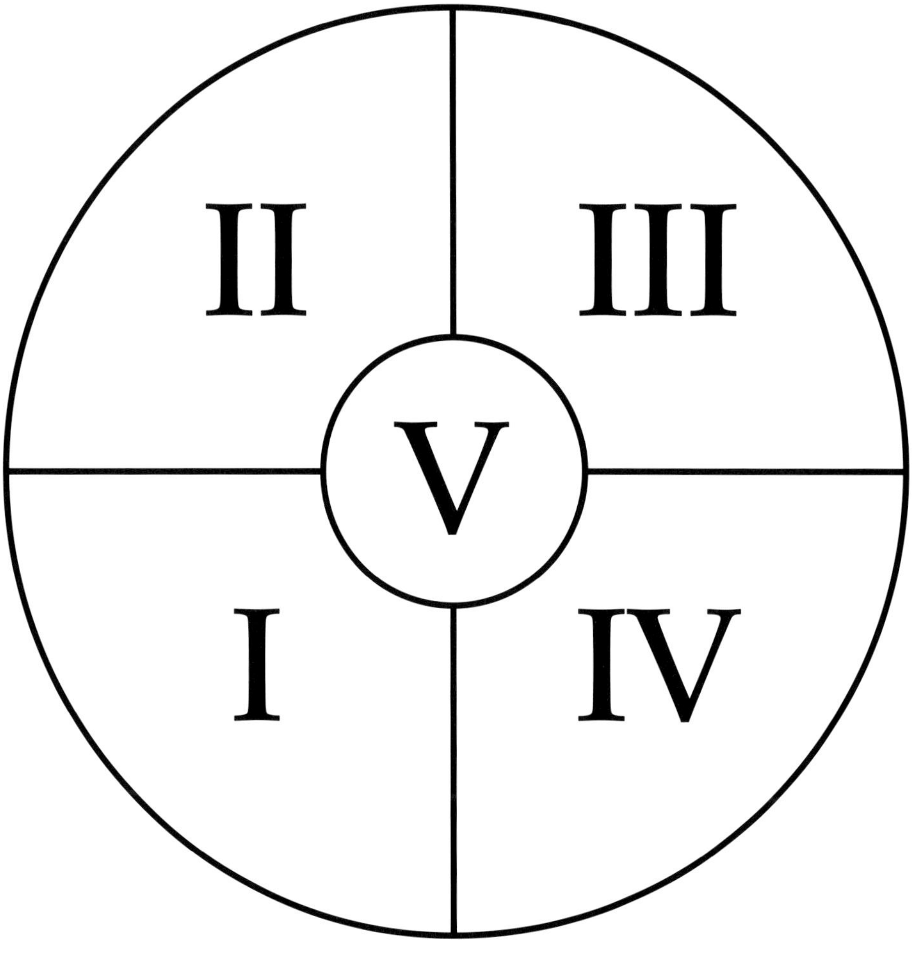

II III

V

I IV

## Chapter 1

# The Original Compass

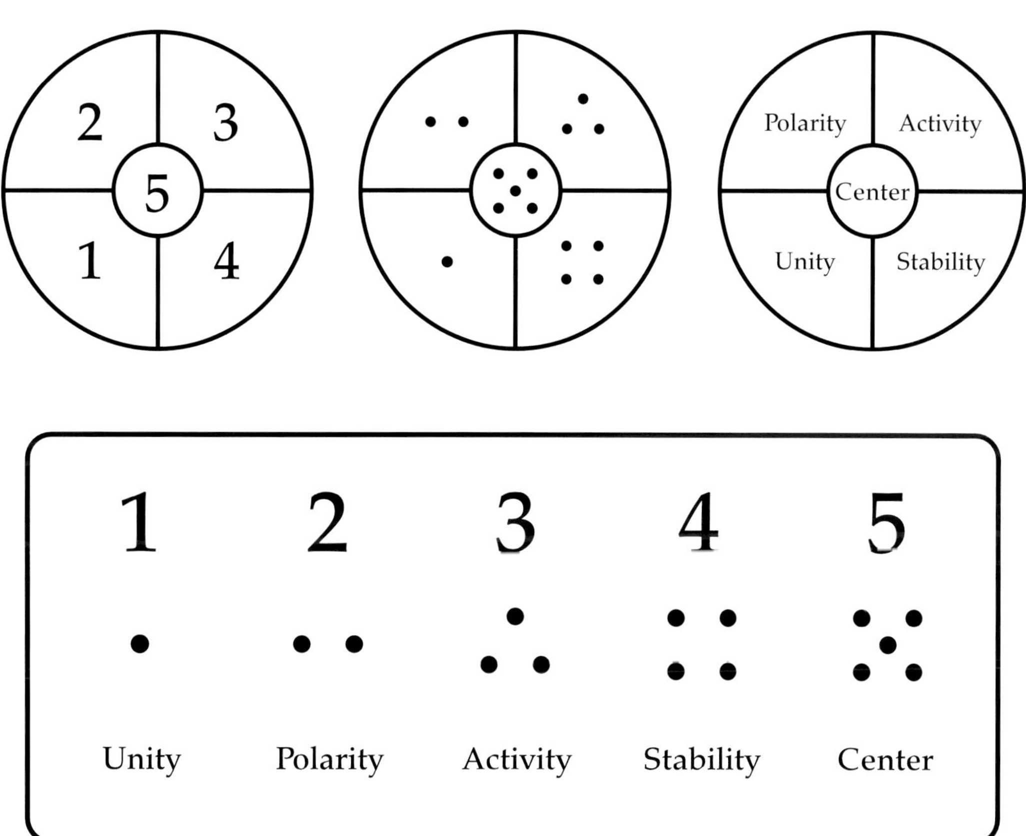


The first four natural numbers mold our perception of the Four Human Natures.

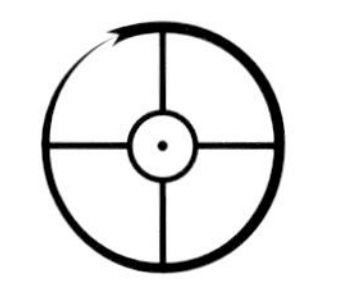

## The Original Compass

1 2 3 4 5 6 7 8 9

1 2 3 4

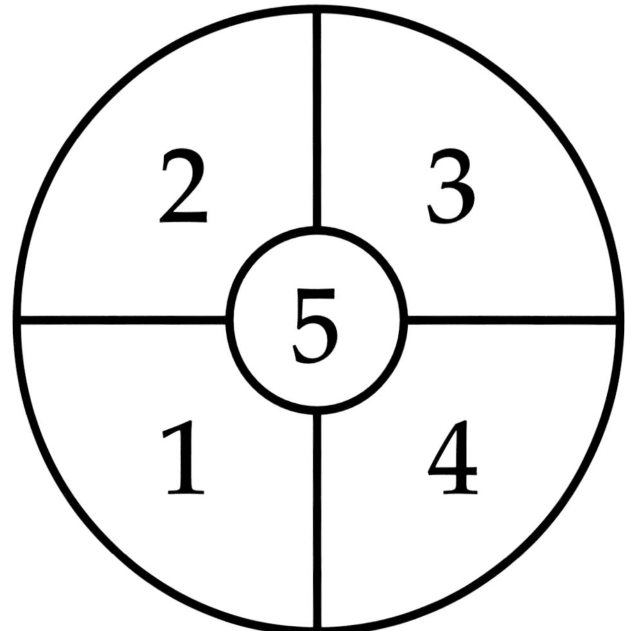


**The Original Compass orients our perception of the Four Human Natures.**

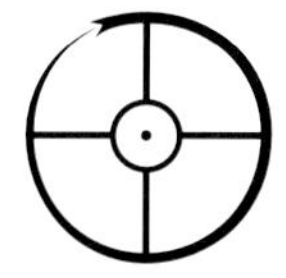

# The Original Compass

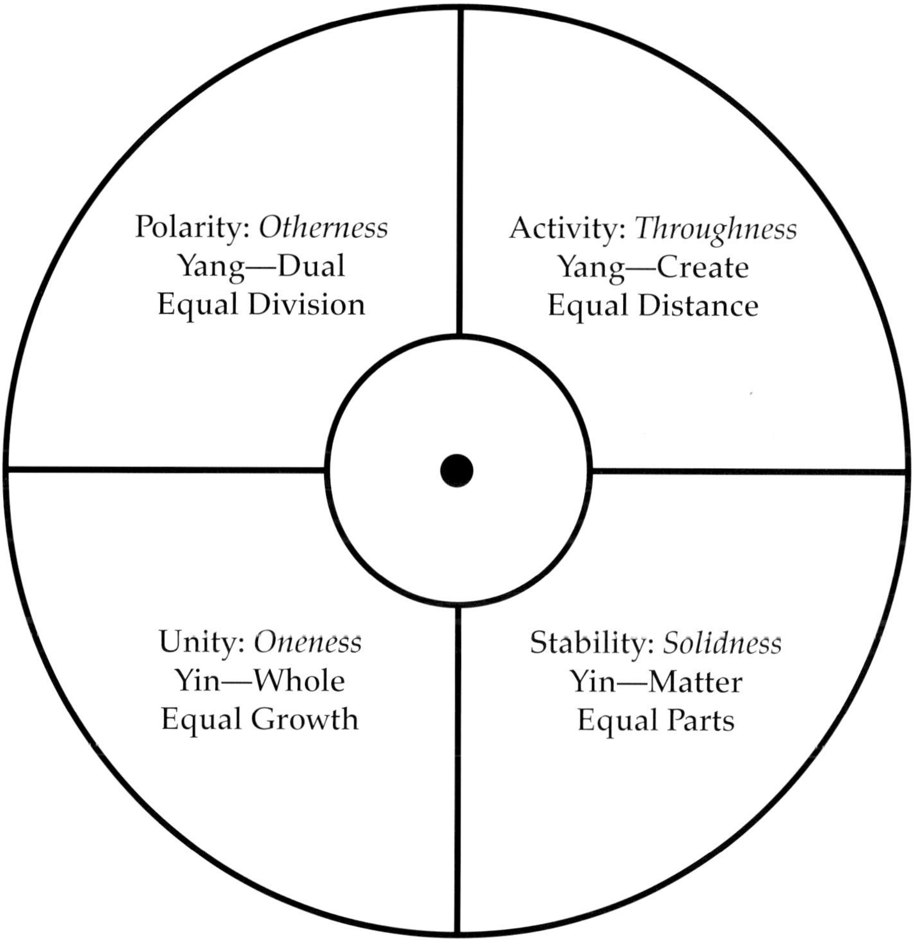

Polarity: *Otherness*
Yang—Dual
Equal Division

Activity: *Throughness*
Yang—Create
Equal Distance

Unity: *Oneness*
Yin—Whole
Equal Growth

Stability: *Solidness*
Yin—Matter
Equal Parts

# The Original Compass

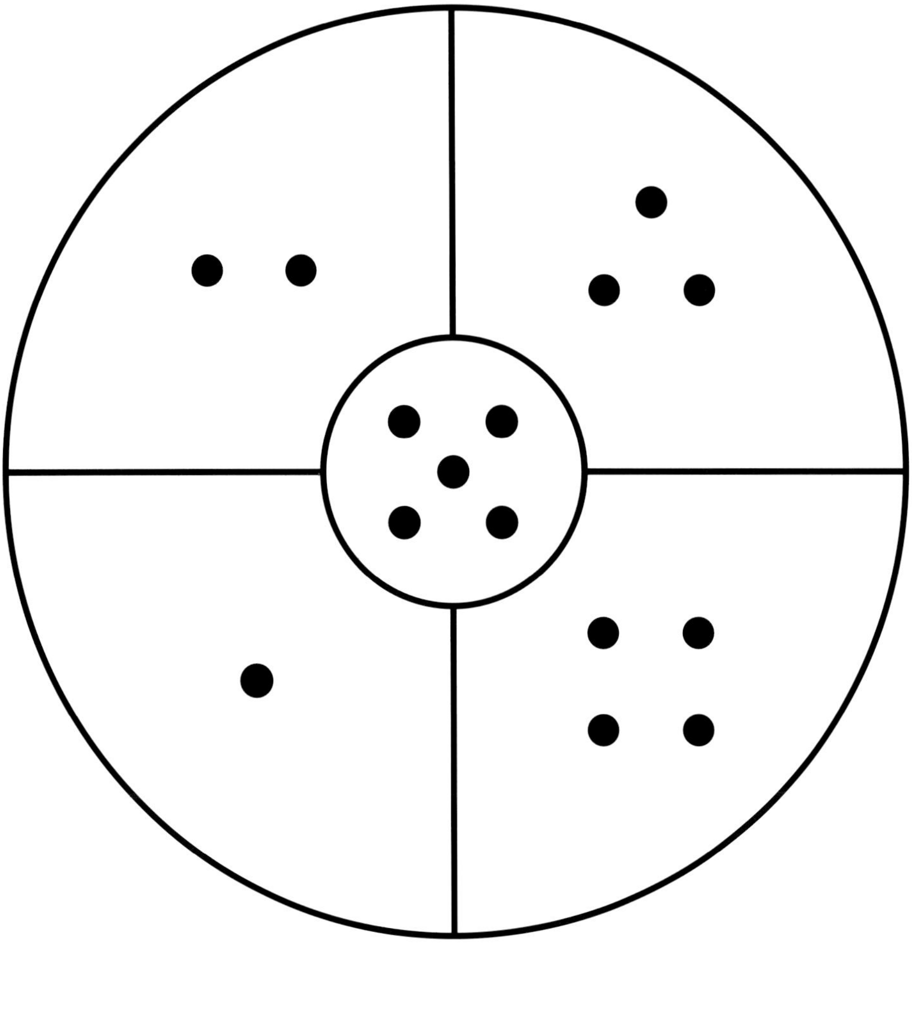

# The Original Compass

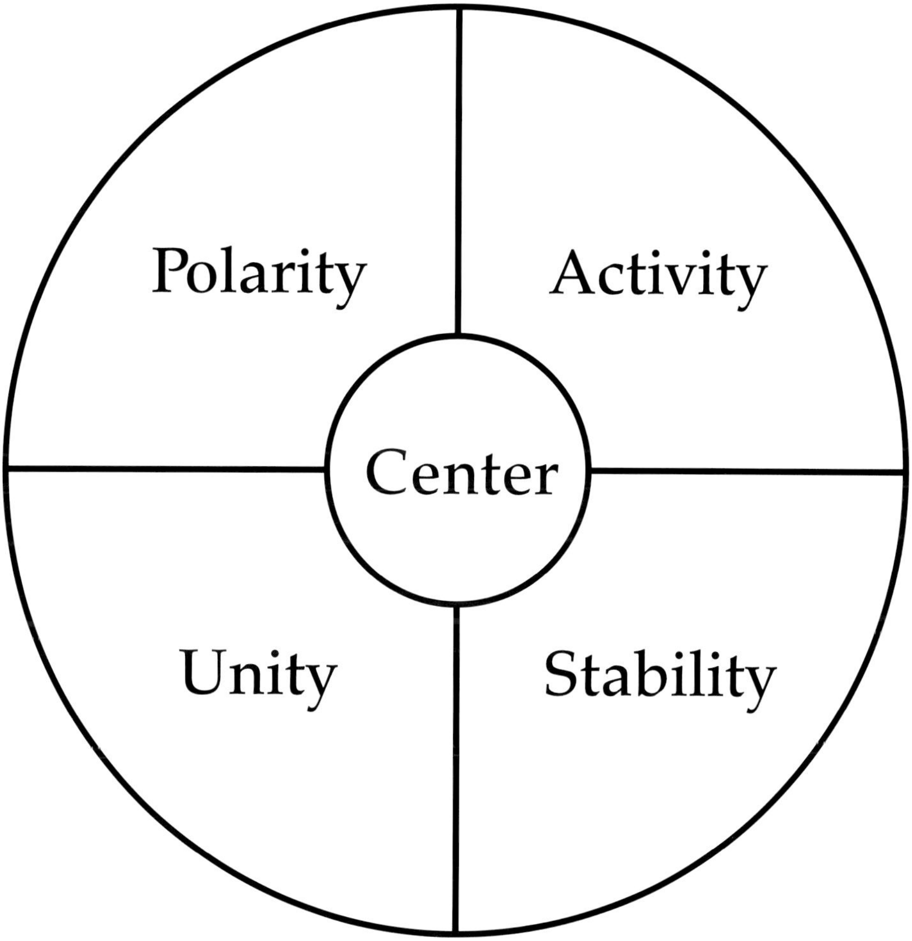

Polarity
Activity
Center
Unity
Stability

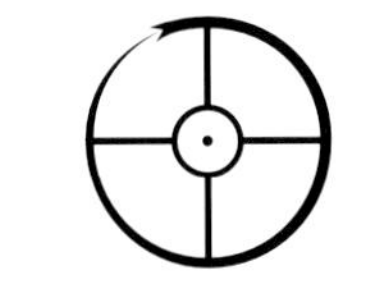

## The Original Compass

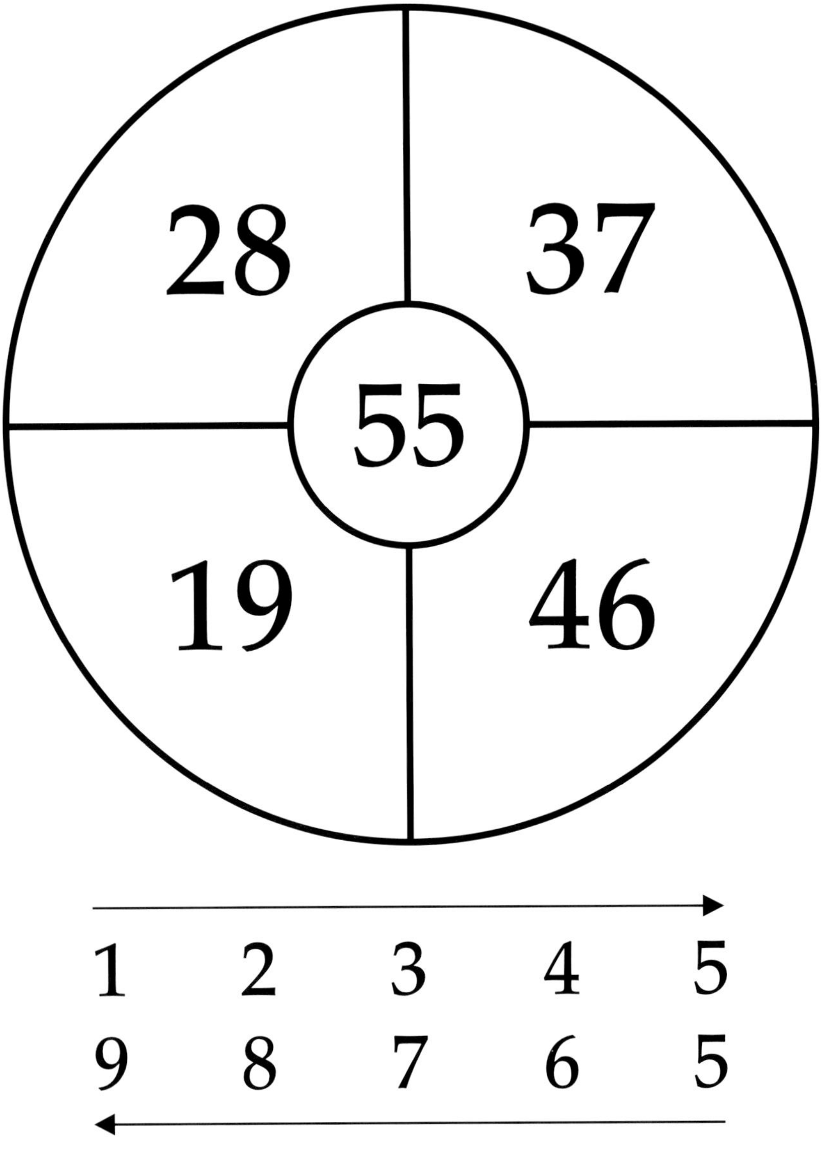

28 37

55

19 46

→

1 2 3 4 5

9 8 7 6 5

←

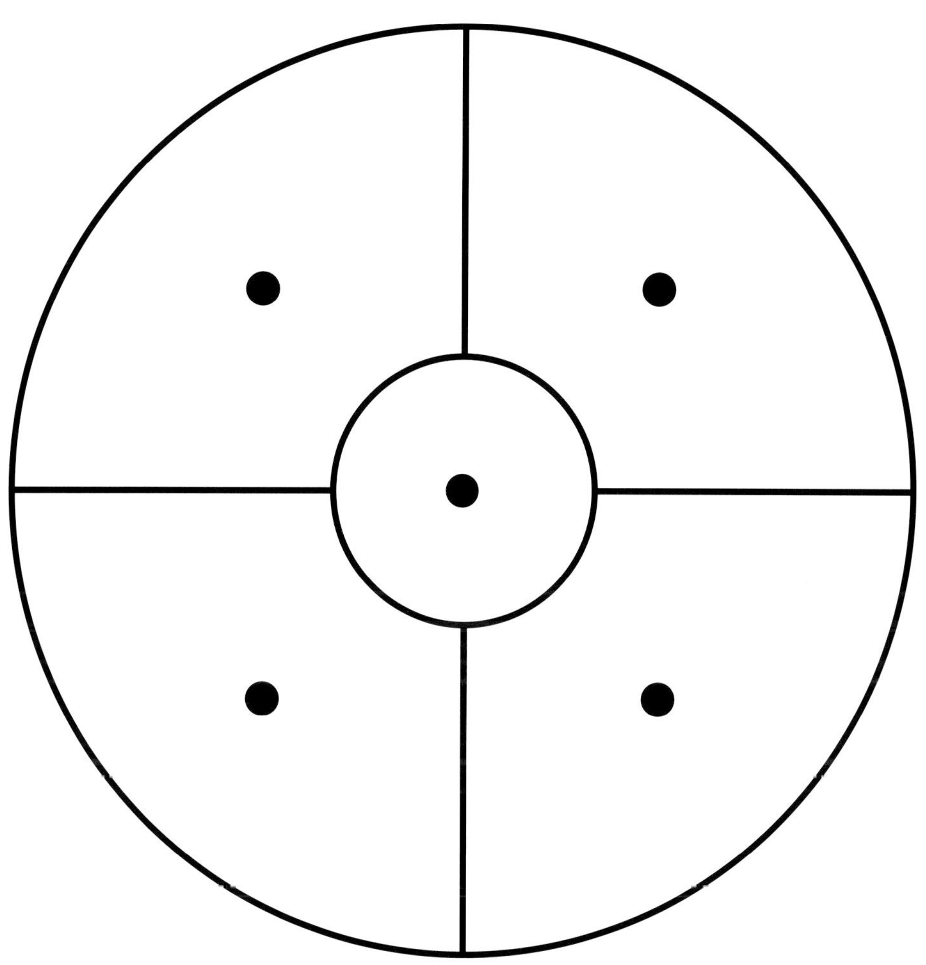

*When thou hast made the quadrangle round,*
*then is all the secret found.*

George Ripley (1415–1490)

## Chapter 2

# The Elements and Forces

On January 31, 2000, an Alaskan jet crashed in the coastal waters of California killing all 88 persons aboard. On the evening news, one sad son struggled to portray his mother and father in a simple television sound bite. Finally, he said that one was the family's fire, and the other its foundation. We all understood.

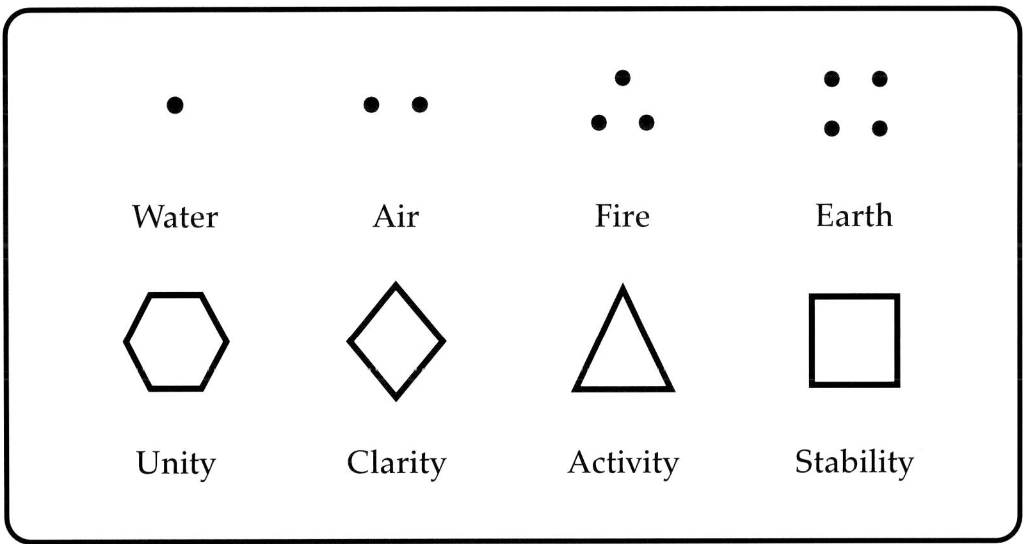


The Four Elements mold our perception of the Four Human Natures.

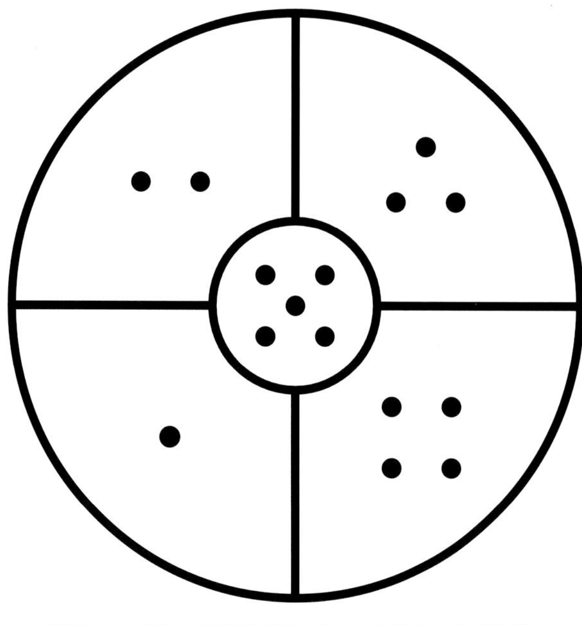

**The Original Compass Reveals the Compass of Elements**

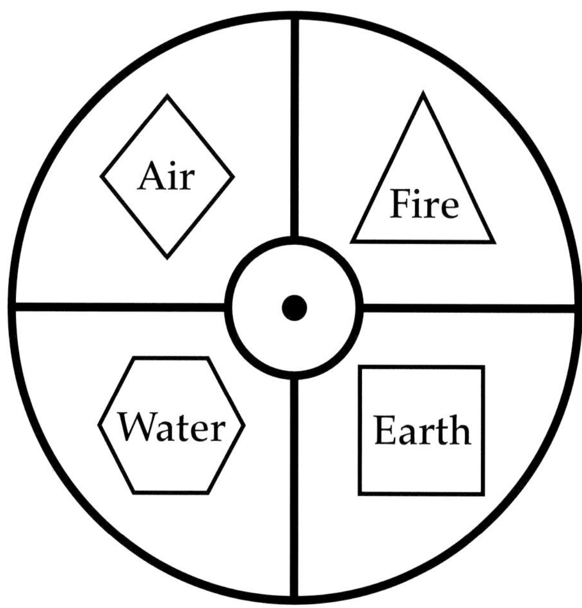

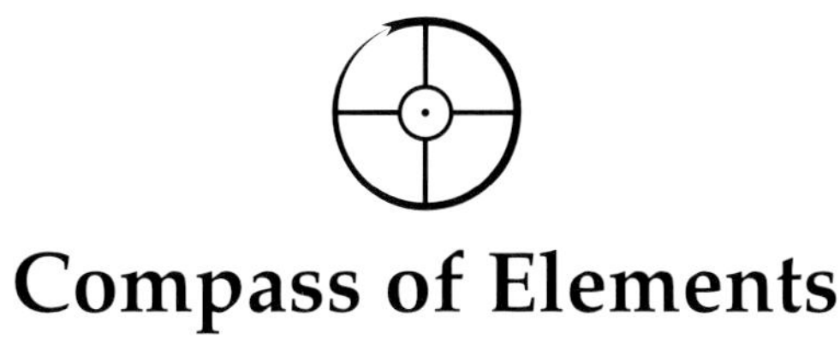

# Compass of Elements

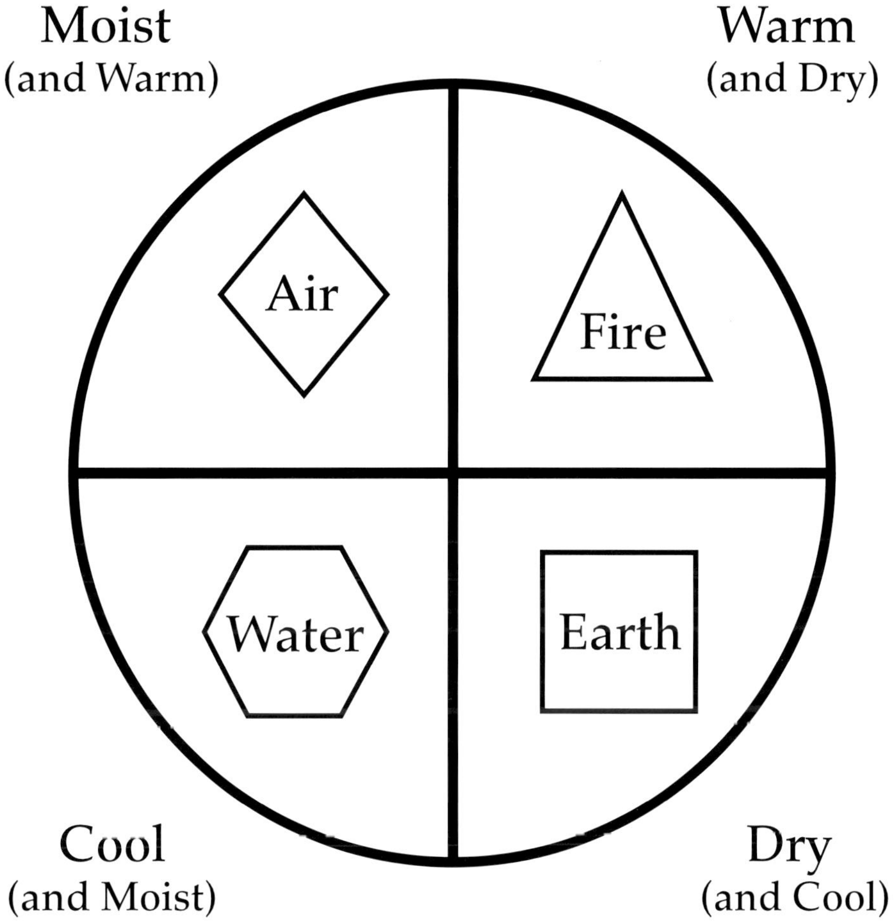

Moist
(and Warm)

Warm
(and Dry)

Air

Fire

Water

Earth

Cool
(and Moist)

Dry
(and Cool)

Fire is Absolutely Light
Air is Relatively Light
Water is Relatively Heavy
Earth is Absolutely Heavy

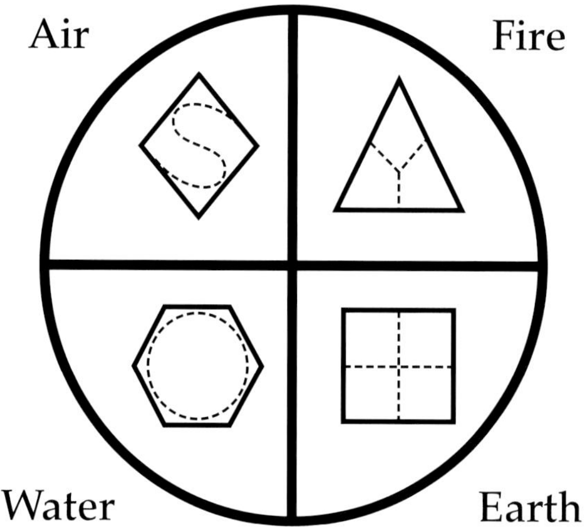


**The Compass of Elements**
**Reveals**
**the Compass of Forces**

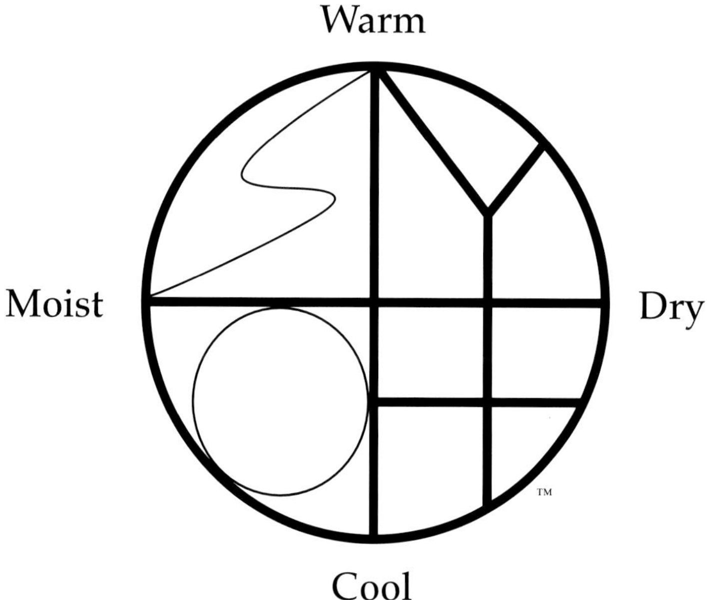

## Compass of Forces

WARM
Expands: Separates
Centrifugal (Center Fleeing)
Light and Fast

MOIST
Conforms: Adapts
Relative and Flexible
Context (White Space)

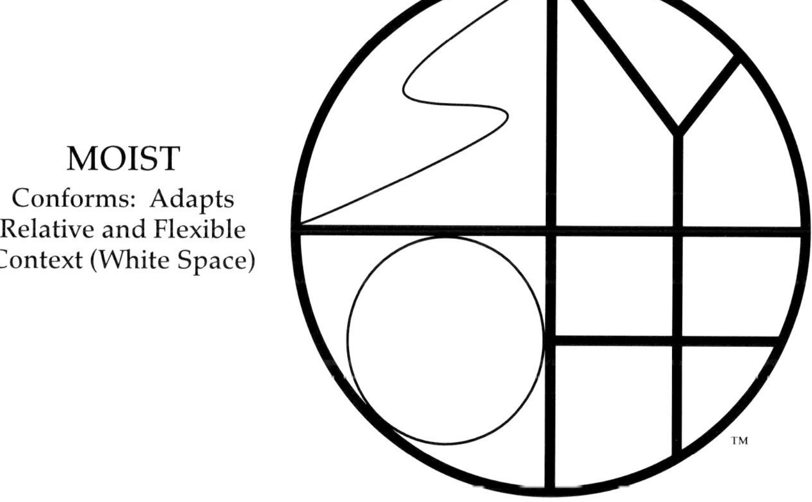

DRY
Forms: Structures
Absolute and Fixed
Content (Black Lines)

COOL
Contracts: Unites
Centripetal (Center Seeking)
Heavy and Slow

## Compass of Forces

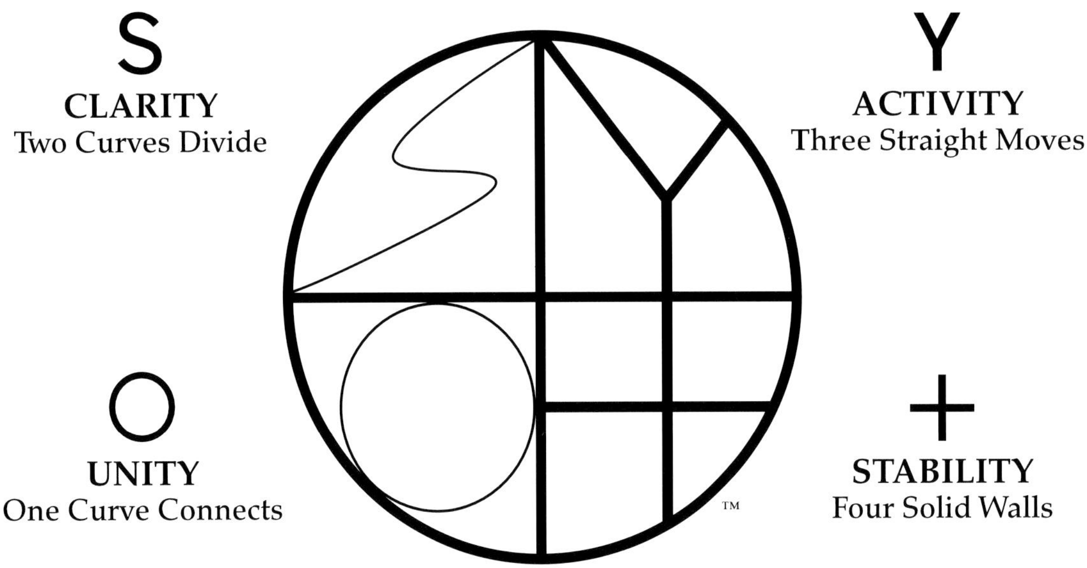

**Activity.** "Y" combines Warm plus Dry in a 3/1 ratio. Warm melts two opposites to create something new: a Third. Warm actively structures two straight (Dry) lines into a third straight (Dry) line. The energetic action and reaction between Yin and Yang moving together creates a Third. Three resolves the tension between Two, and recreates the lost unity of One in an actual form that is recognizable to the five senses. Fire is absolutely light and fixed. "Y" looks like a spark of fire.

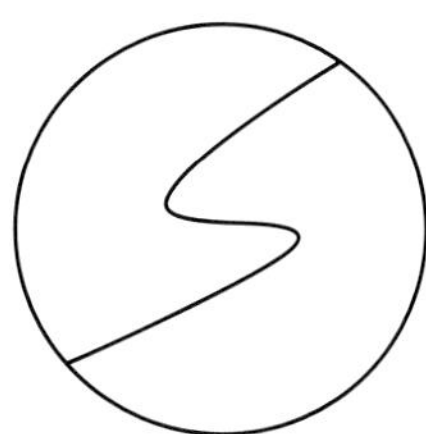

**Clarity.** "S" combines Moist plus Warm in a 3/1 ratio. Moist adapts, curving the line twice, flexing and conforming to form, revealing boundaries between opposites: Yin and Yang. Warm expands the line, separating like things with like things: Yin with Yin and Yang with Yang. As with all polarities, the two halves make one whole. The "S" both divides and joins the two sides which alternate between attraction and repulsion, in perpetual polar tension. Air is relatively light and flowing. "S" looks like a scarf floating in the air.

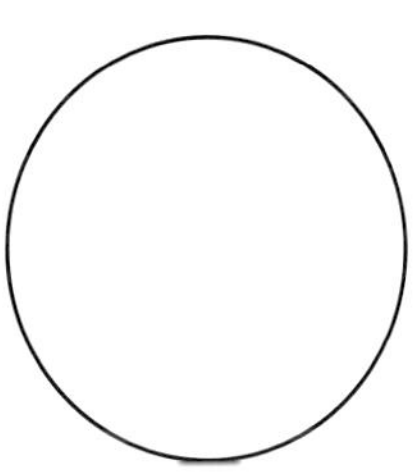

**Unity.** "O" combines Cool plus Moist in a 3/1 ratio. Cool connects the curve and contracts all things toward one center to blend and unite everything as one. Moist adapts, curving the line once, flexing and conforming to form, dissolving all boundaries. Of all shapes, the circle encloses the largest area with the shortest perimeter (maximizing enclosure while minimizing exposure). Water is relatively heavy and flowing. "O" looks like a pond of water.

**Stability.** "+" combines Dry plus Cool in a 3/1 ratio. Dry structures two straight lines into a cross that establishes the firm boundaries of four quadrants. Cool contracts and unites the things within each quadrant. Cool also contracts the four quadrants around one central intersection which forms the center of a continuous spiral. Earth is absolutely heavy and fixed. "+" looks like the four quarters of the Earth.

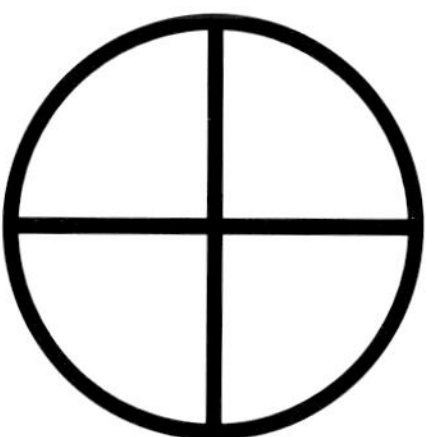

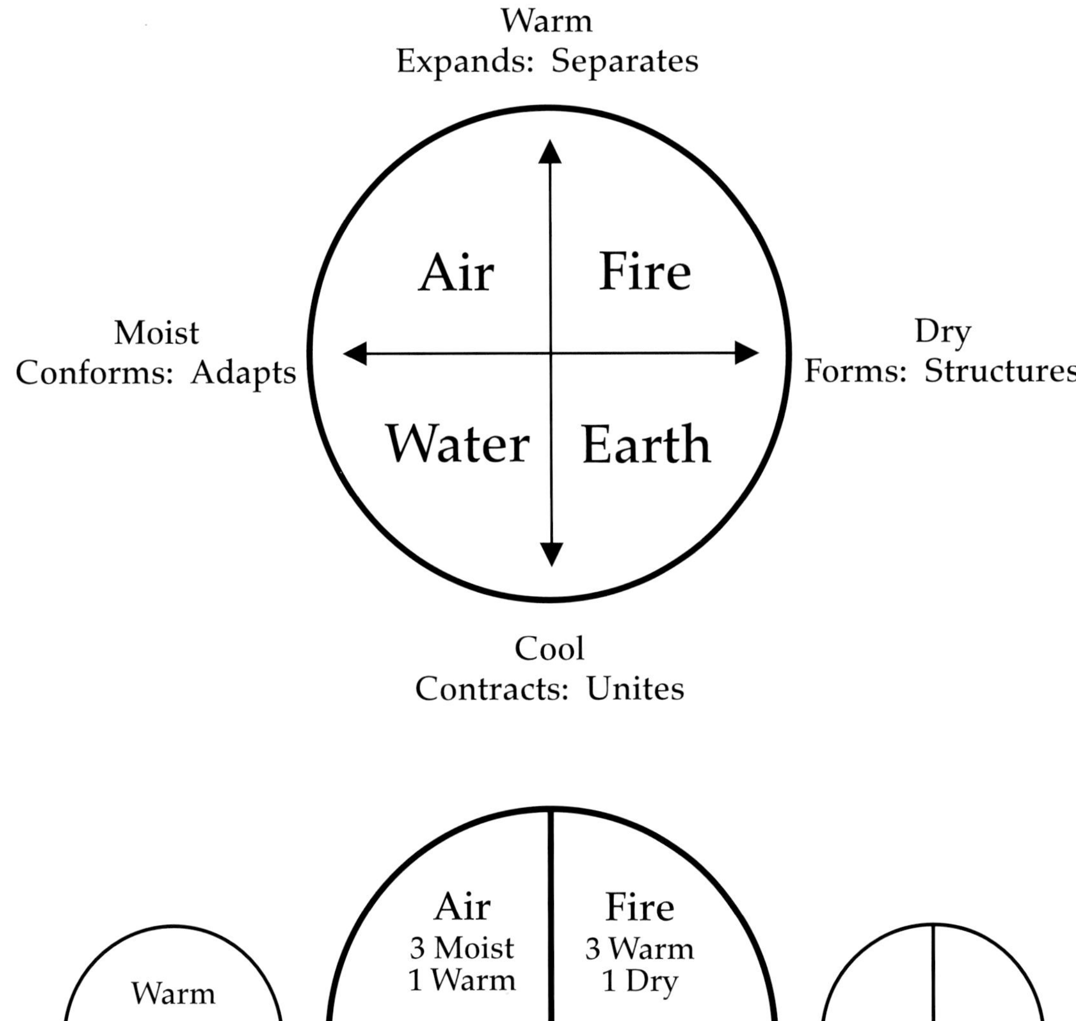


Each Element combines two of the Four Forces in a 3/1 ratio.

## Active Forces: Warm and Cool

### Warm Expands: Separates

Light and fast, Warm pushes out towards many points, fleeing the center. Warm causes things of the same kind to join together by separating things of different kinds. Warm radiates, rising to the north.

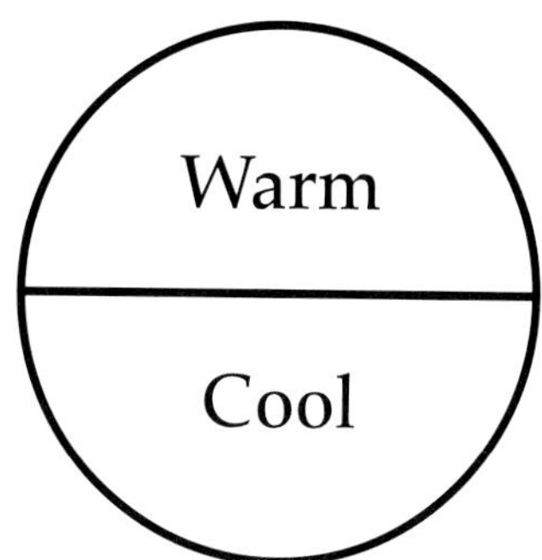


### Cool Contracts: Unites

Heavy and slow, Cool pulls in toward one point, seeking the center. Cool causes things of a different kind to join together, blending everything into one mixture. Cool concentrates, sinking to the south.

## Passive Forces: Moist and Dry

### Moist Conforms: Adapts

Moist adapts to form. Moist things are relative and flexible. Moist allows Air and Water to flow and conform to form. Air and Water can both change their shape. Moist accommodates, flexing in the west.

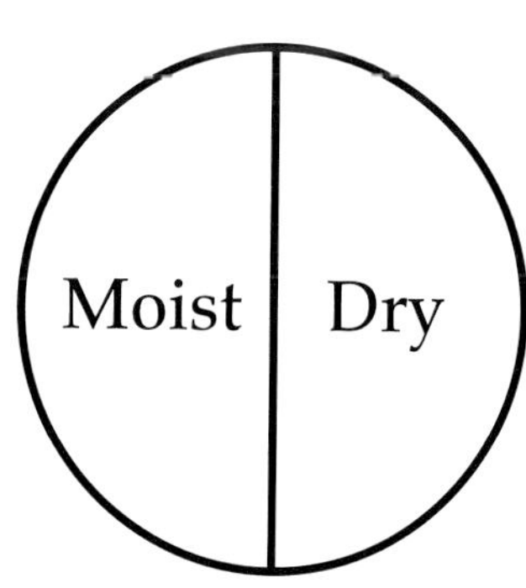


### Dry Forms: Structures

Dry structures form. Dry things are absolute and fixed. Dry gives Earth and Fire their unwavering, inflexible forms. Earth and Fire never change their shape, they always look the same: a fixed sphere and a fixed pyramid. Dry dominates, fixed in the east.

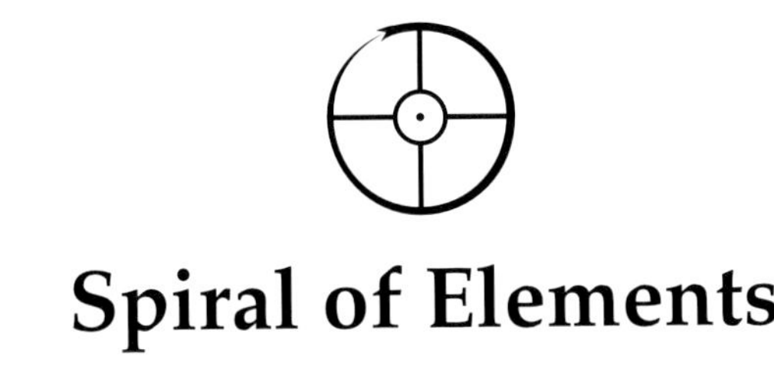

## Spiral of Elements

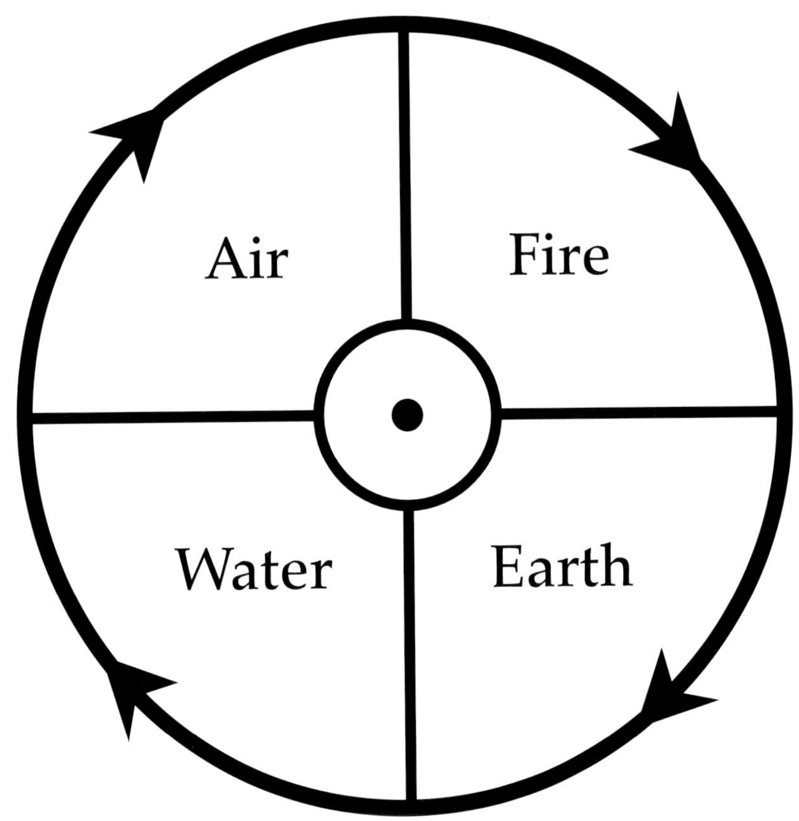


Fire combusts Air
Air evaporates Water
Water dissolves Earth
Earth extinguishes Fire

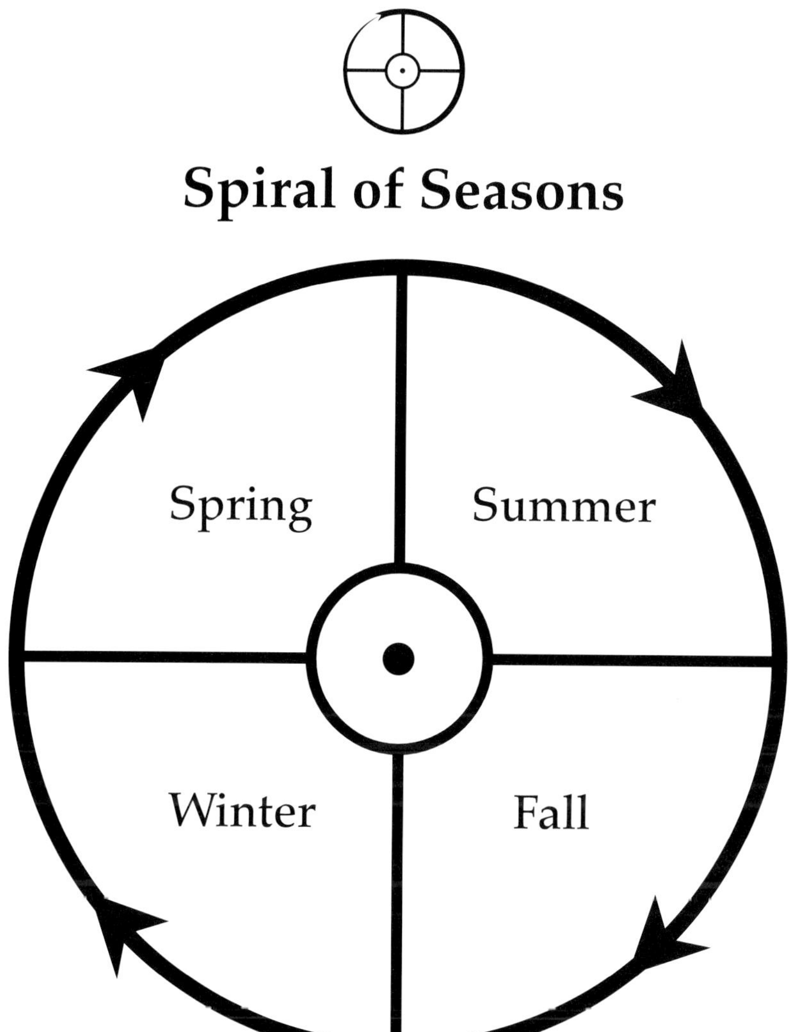
Spiral of Seasons
Spring
Summer
Winter
Fall

# Compass of Forces

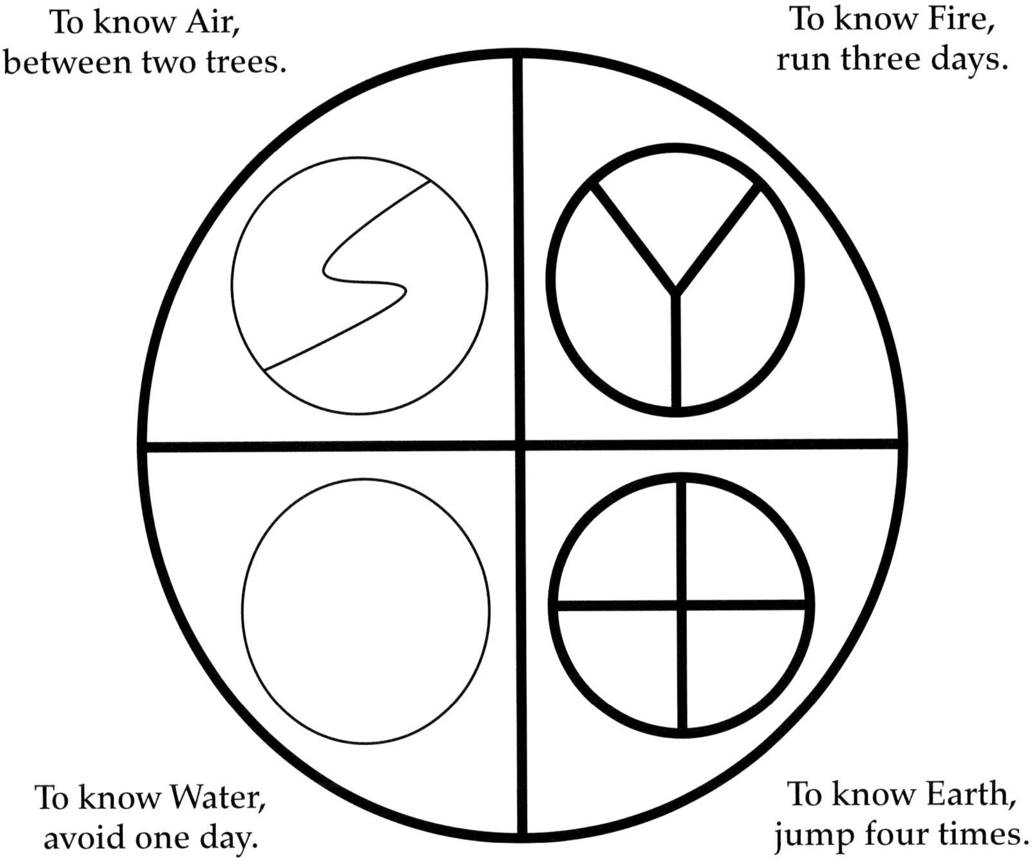

To know Air,
between two trees.

To know Fire,
run three days.

To know Water,
avoid one day.

To know Earth,
jump four times.

## Chapter 3
# The Four Human Natures

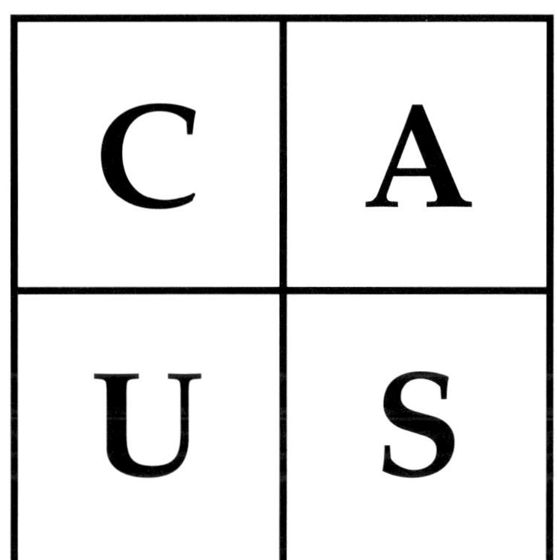


As you see,
you see as me,
and we see as you.

| FAITH<br>Vertical Axis of the Compass of Natures | | | |
|---|---|---|---|
| **Activator** | **Clarifier** | **Stabilizer** | **Unifier** |
| I can do that. | I can do that which I understand | We can trust others in our group. | We can trust others. |
| Boundless | Bounded | Bounded | Boundless |
| **Confidence**<br>Faith in Oneself | | **Trust**<br>Faith in Others | |
| Warm Separates | | Cool Unites | |

| FOCUS<br>Horizontal Axis of the Compass of Natures | | | |
|---|---|---|---|
| **Clarifier** | **Unifier** | **Activator** | **Stabilizer** |
| Distinctions | Similarities | Opportunities | Priorities |
| Adapts Strategically | Adapts Diplomatically | Structures Tactically | Structures Procedurally |
| Conceive and Adapt | | Sense and Structure | |
| **Context**<br>To perceive *outside* the container of the five senses. | | **Content**<br>To perceive *inside* the container of the five senses. | |
| Moist Adapts | | Dry Structures | |

# Compass of Natures

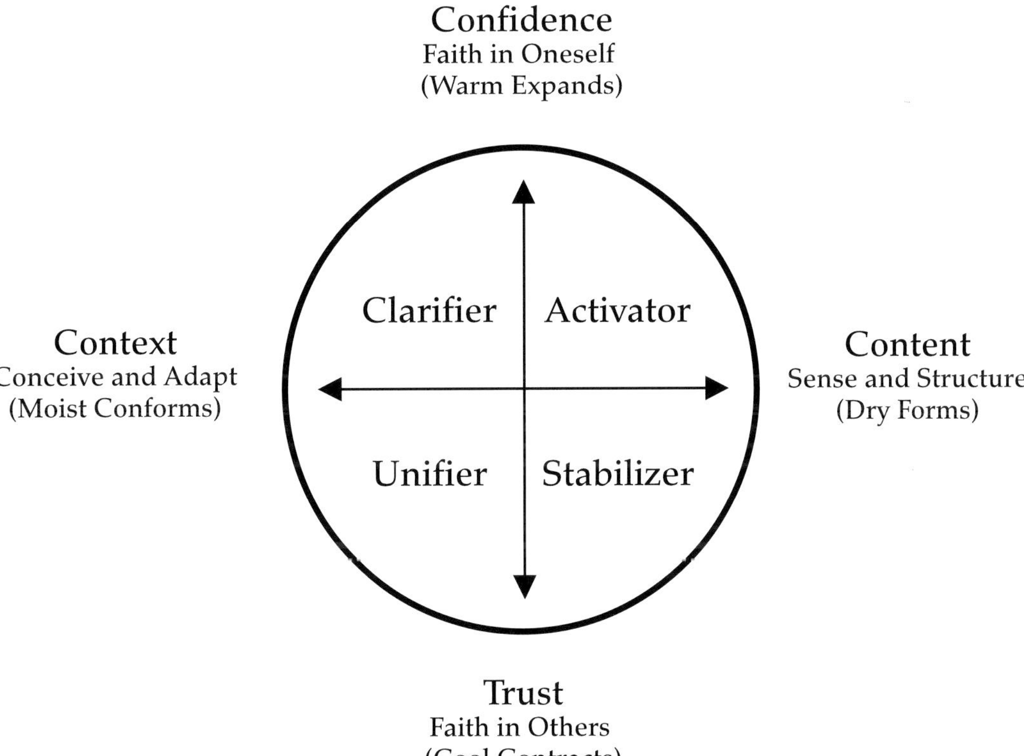

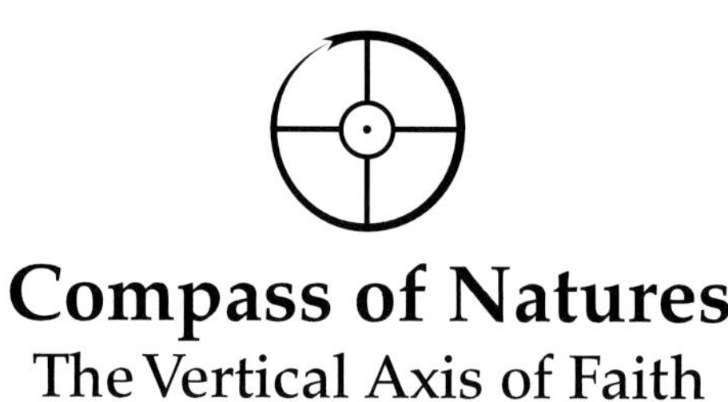

# Compass of Natures

## The Vertical Axis of Faith

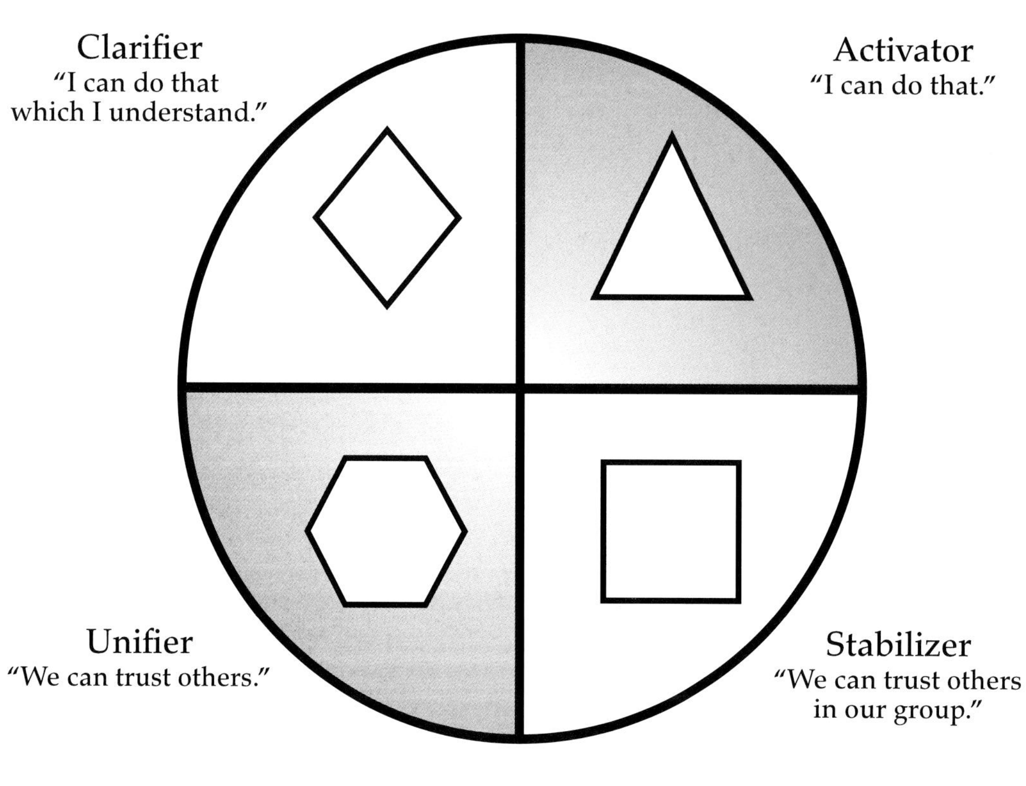

# Faith

## Confidence or Trust

The vertical axis of the Compass of Natures shows the polarity of Faith. The word *faith* comes from the Latin word *fidere* which means to confide and trust. Confidence and trust occupy opposite sides of one coin: faith in ourselves or faith in others. Warm expands and separates, pushing the individual out alone with confidence. Cool contracts and unites, pulling everyone in together in trust. Confidence creates independence, and trust creates interdependence. On the Compass of Natures, confidence rises to the north and trust sinks to the south.

**Boundless Faith** belongs to Activators and Unifiers. Warm is fully expressed in Fire, giving Activators boundless confidence. Cool is fully expressed in Water, giving Unifiers boundless trust.

> **Activators** have boundless confidence, as in: "I can do that." Naturally, Activators want to express their boundless confidence through action. Activators have confidence in their own individual instincts. Independent, they must remain unrestrained.
>
> **Unifiers** have boundless trust, as in: "We can trust others." Naturally, Unifiers want to express their boundless trust by unifying. Unifiers trust universal human affinity. Interdependent, they must attain accord.

**Bounded Faith** belongs to Clarifiers and Stabilizers. Warm is partly expressed in Air, giving Clarifiers bounded confidence. Cool is partly expressed in Earth, giving Stabilizers bounded trust.

> **Clarifiers** have bounded confidence, as in: "I can do that which I understand." Naturally, Clarifiers want to expand the boundaries of their confidence by clarifying. Clarifiers seek confidence through their own individual insights. Independent, they must attain autonomy.
>
> **Stabilizers** have bounded trust, as in: "We can trust others in our group." Naturally, Stabilizers want to solidify the boundaries of their trust by stabilizing. Stabilizers seek trust in group affiliations. Interdependent, they must maintain authority.

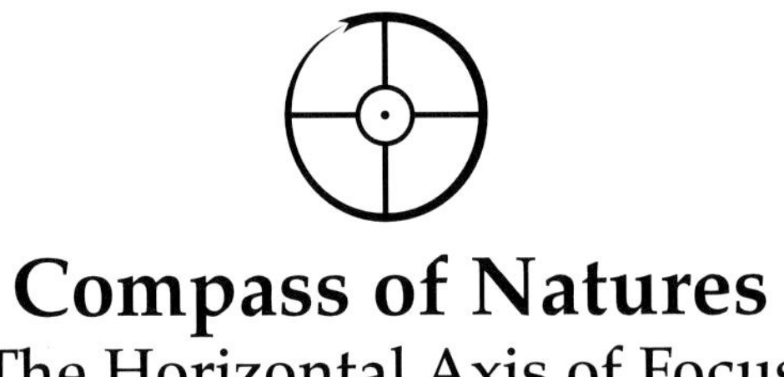

# Compass of Natures

## The Horizontal Axis of Focus

**Clarifier**
Focus on Distinctions
Adapts Strategically

**Activator**
Focus on Opportunities
Structures Tactically

CONTEXT

CONTENT

**Unifier**
Focus on Similarities
Adapts Diplomatically

**Stabilizer**
Focus on Priorities
Structures Procedurally

# Focus

## Context or Content

The horizontal axis of the Compass of Natures shows the polarity of Focus. Unifiers and Clarifiers naturally focus on Context. Activators and Stabilizers naturally focus on Content. Context flexes in the west. Content is fixed in the east.

We conceive Context through a sixth sense. To conceive Context, we focus outside the container of the five senses on what cannot be seen, heard, smelled, touched, or tasted. We conceive both present and future Context. We decipher our world to find novel options in the present. And, we interpret our world to plan in anticipation of our future. Our sixth sense may hit the mark exactly, or may miss by a mile.

We sense Content through our five senses. To sense Content, we focus inside the container of the five senses on what we can see, hear, smell, touch, and taste. We sense both present and past Content. We sense present Content by focusing our attention on the actual experience of the world in the here and now. We sense past Content by focusing on our impressions of what we have sensed at a prior time.

Our Faith steers our Focus because Faith is active and Focus is passive. In the physical world, active things control passive things. For example, the active rudder steers the passive ship. Wind turns the windmill. Likewise, in our mental world, our Faith steers our Focus because the Active Forces power our Faith while the Passive Forces shape our Focus. Boundless Faith steers a boundless Focus, and bounded Faith steers a Focus toward boundaries.

Boundless confidence steers Activators' Focus to boundless opportunities.

Bounded confidence steers Clarifiers' Focus to boundaries: distinctions.

Boundless trust steers Unifiers' Focus to boundless similarities.

Bounded trust steers Stabilizers' Focus to boundaries: priorities.

# Focus

## Context

### Conceive and Adapt

**Clarifiers** focus on distinctions and adapt strategically. Like prepositions, Clarifiers identify positions. They reveal boundaries and catalyze change. Clarifiers want to conceive the most efficient means to an end based on logic.

**Unifiers** focus on similarities and adapt diplomatically. Like conjunctions, Unifiers identify connections. They blend boundaries and nurture change. Unifiers want to conceive the most meaningful means to an end based on value.

## Content

### Sense and Structure

**Activators** focus on opportunities and structure tactically. Like verbs, Activators structure by action. They melt boundaries and cause change. Sensing present Content, they want the most expedient means to an end.

**Stabilizers** focus on priorities and structure procedurally. Like nouns, Stabilizers structure by naming. They establish boundaries and resist change. Sensing past Content, they want the most reliable means to an end.

# Structuring Cupid

## Tactics or Procedures

We focus on Context to conceive, and we focus on Content to structure. Structuring always involves touching with our five senses. Our skin touches what we feel. Likewise, our eyes touch what we see, our ears touch what we hear, our tongue touches what we taste, and our nose touches what we smell. We use our five senses to structure, and we use our sixth sense to conceive.

We structure tactically based on our present experience, and we structure procedurally based on our past impressions. We actively touch to structure tactically with action, and we passively touch to structure procedurally with boundaries. Imagine making an ice sculpture of Cupid. We could proceed in two ways. First, we could chisel Cupid from a block of ice, structuring Cupid tactically by the action of our chisel. With each strike of the hammer, we would observe the changes that we caused in the block of ice and then proceed based on our present experience of what is needed next. Second, we could make our own Cupid mold. Like making ice cubes, we could structure Cupid procedurally by the firm boundaries of our mold to form identical Cupids, all continuing in the tradition of our prototype. The chisel and our mold would both produce fine Cupid sculptures.

In our daily lives, we structure tactically by sensing present Content: the experience of touching the external world with our five senses to exploit present opportunities. We structure procedurally by sensing past Content: our impressions (stamped in memory by the pressure of our prior experiences of touching the external world with our five senses) that establish our priorities. Tactics structure actively with an outward focus on the variables of the present moment. Procedures structure passively with an inward focus on the constant impressions formed in the past. Like verbs, tactics structure by action. Like nouns, procedures structure by naming.

Of course, we all spend much of our waking lives structuring tactically and procedurally. Our physical and social well being depends upon our ability to act appropriately in the moment within procedural boundaries. Everyone must be able to structure in both ways. However, structuring tactically comes most naturally to Activators, and structuring procedurally comes most naturally to Stabilizers.

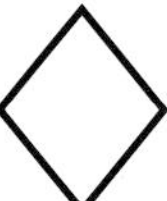

## Clarifier

*Air's Clarity*
10%

Confidence, but.
"I can do that which I understand."

Distinctions
Adapts Strategically

1. Life is a question.
2. Conceives Context: Logic
3. Faith in Individual Insights
4. Must Attain Autonomy
5. Reveals Boundaries and Catalyzes Change
6. Most Efficient Means to an End
7. Identifies Positions (Preposition)
8. Yellow Sky Above

*Clarity Divides Unity*

## Activator

*Fire's Activity*
35%

Confidence
"I can do that."

Opportunities
Structures Tactically

1. Life is to live.
2. Senses Present Content
3. Faith in Individual Instincts
4. Must Remain Unrestrained
5. Melts Boundaries and Causes Change
6. Most Expedient Means to an End
7. Structures by Action (Verb)
8. Red Sun Above

*Activity Blurs Clarity*

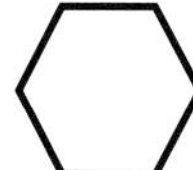

## Unifier

*Water's Unity*
10%

Trust
"We can trust others."

Similarities
Adapts Diplomatically

1. Life is a quest.
2. Conceives Context: Value
3. Faith in Human Affinity
4. Must Attain Accord
5. Blends Boundaries and Nurtures Change
6. Most Meaningful Means to an End
7. Identifies Connections (Conjunction)
8. Blue Sea Below

*Unity Dissolves Stability*

## Stabilizer

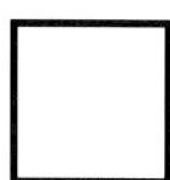

*Earth's Stability*
45%

Trust, but.
"We can trust others in our group."

Priorities
Structures Procedurally

1. Life is to survive.
2. Senses Past Content
3. Faith in Group Affiliations
4. Must Maintain Authority
5. Establishes Boundaries and Resists Change
6. Most Reliable Means to an End
7. Structures by Naming (Noun)
8. Green Earth Below

*Stability Confines Activity*

# World Proportions

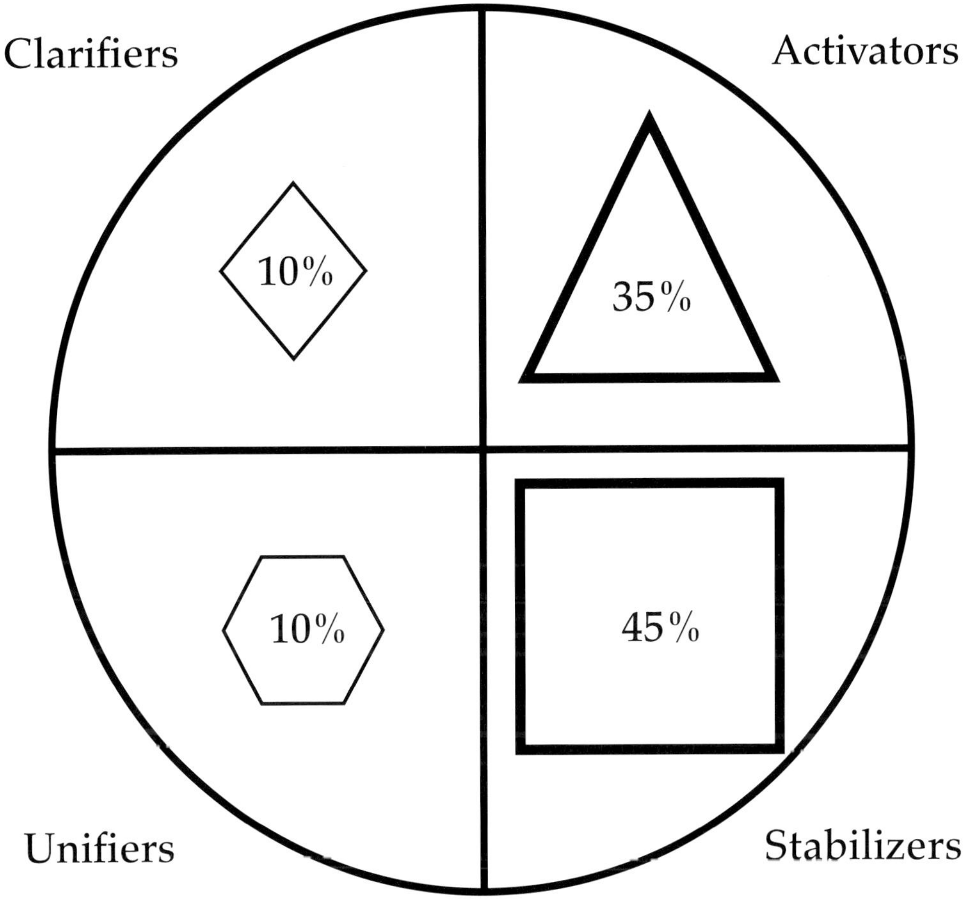

Clarifiers

10%

Activators

35%

Unifiers

10%

Stabilizers

45%

**Because**

Morning's moist saffron sky, born of warm ruby sun,
Up between C and A, my confidence and I.
Deep cooling sapphire seas, old spinning emerald rock,
Down betwixt U and S, our trust in us and we.

*The way up and down are one and the same.*

Heraclitus (535–475 B.C.)

# PART II

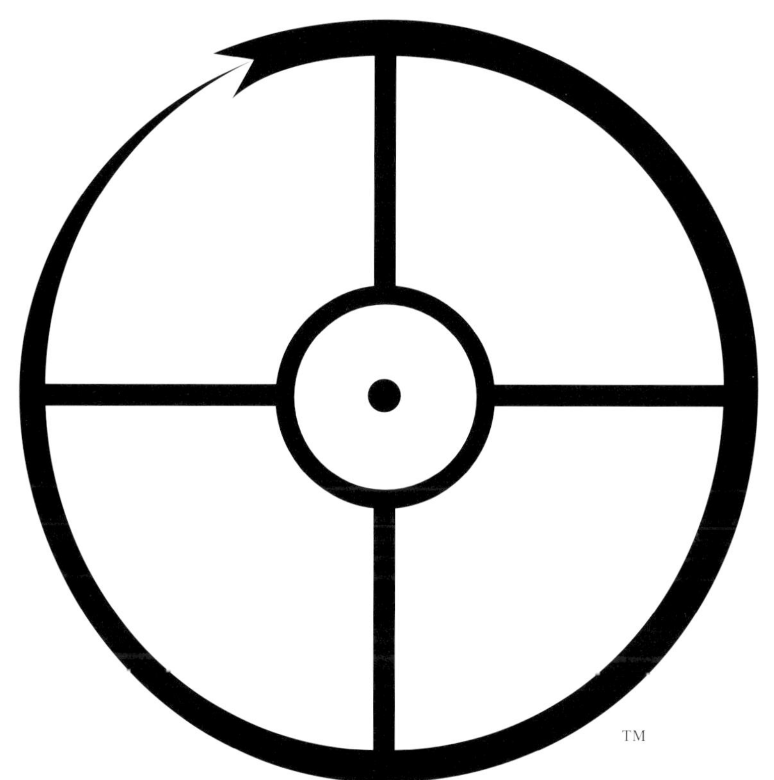


## The Four Styles: Attitude and Role

## The Two Attitudes

### Internal Attitude
*Introversion*

Subject Attraction
Conserves Energy and Contracts
Fascinated by my Subjective World
Inner Directed and Internally Motivated
The external world serves my internal world.

### External Attitude
*Extraversion*

Object Attraction
Expends Energy and Expands
Fascinated by the Objective World
Outer Directed and Externally Motivated
My internal world serves the external world.

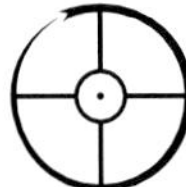

## The Two Roles

### Indirect Role
*Indirection*

Invites Interaction
Informs Others
Implicit Messages
Persuades and Promotes
Relatively Flexible Texture

### Direct Role
*Direction*

Directs Action
Instructs Others
Explicit Messages
Commands and Controls
Absolutely Firm Texture

## Chapter 4

# The Four Social Styles

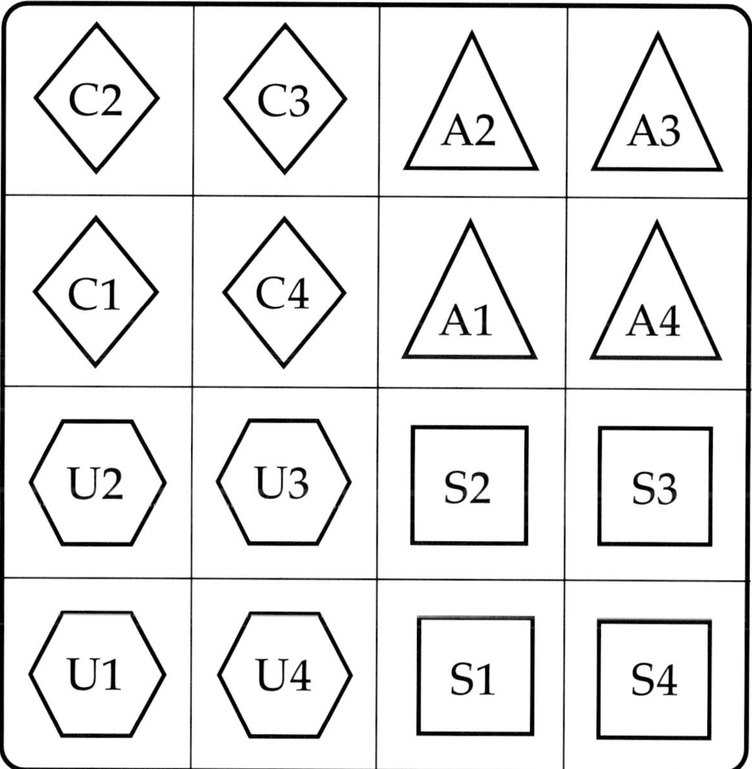

# Compass of Styles

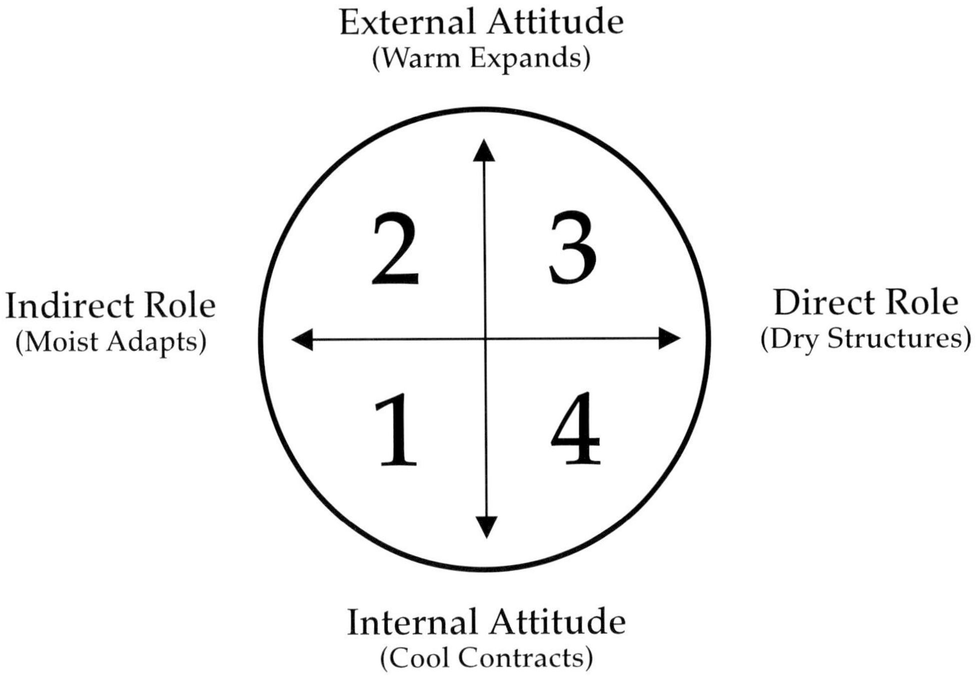

External Attitude
(Warm Expands)

Indirect Role
(Moist Adapts)

2 3

1 4

Direct Role
(Dry Structures)

Internal Attitude
(Cool Contracts)

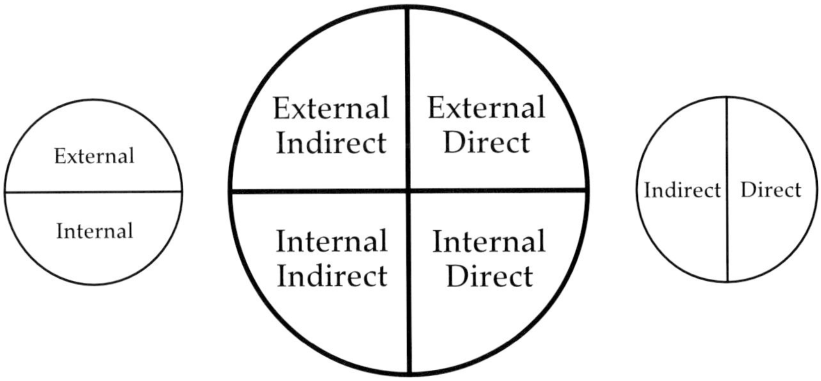

External
Internal

External Indirect | External Direct
Internal Indirect | Internal Direct

Indirect | Direct

External Attitude
*Extraversion*

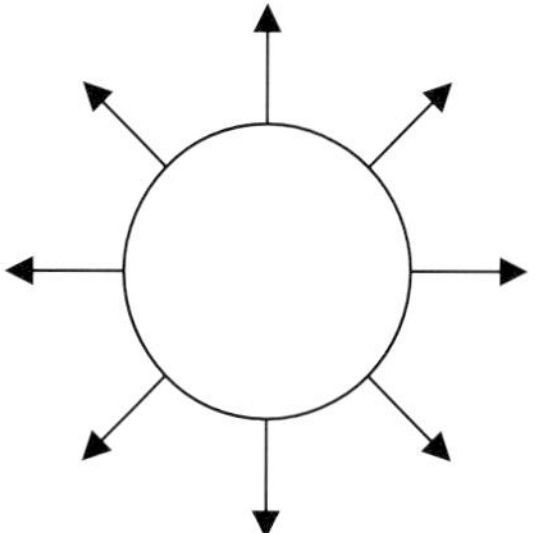

Object Attraction
Expends Energy and Expands
Fascinated by the Objective World
Outer Directed and Externally Motivated
My internal world serves the external world.

Indirect Role
*Indirection*
Invites Interaction
Informs Others
Implicit Messages
Persuades and Promotes
Relatively Flexible Texture

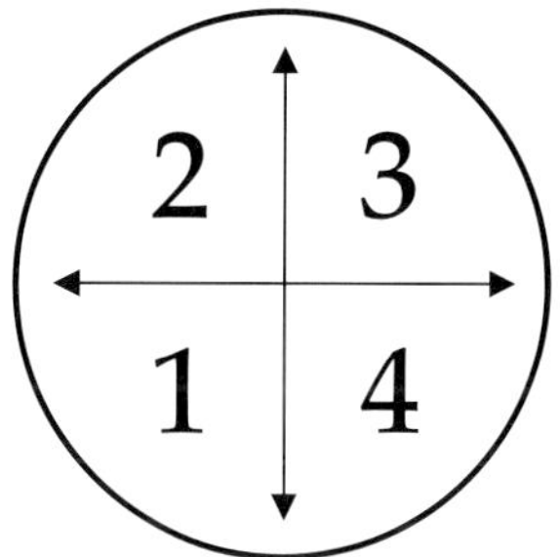


Direct Role
*Direction*
Directs Action
Instructs Others
Explicit Messages
Commands and Controls
Absolutely Firm Texture

Subject Attraction
Conserves Energy and Contracts
Fascinated by my Subjective World
Inner Directed and Internally Motivated
The external world serves my internal world.

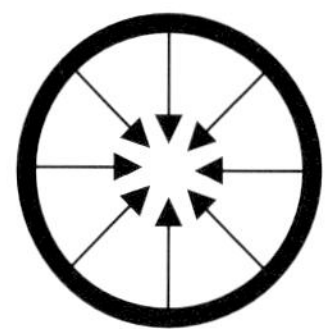

*Introversion*
Internal Attitude

# The Two Attitudes

The vertical axis of the Compass of Styles shows the External Attitude of Extraverts and the Internal Attitude of Introverts. Extraverts rise to the north. Introverts sink to the south. Therefore, the Map of the Four Natures shows the Extraverts (Styles 2 and 3) in the north of each quadrant, and the Introverts (Styles 1 and 4) in the south of each quadrant.

Like a magnet, one world attracts our conscious energy more than the other world. Our fascination with our favorite world fastens us to that world. The word *attitude* comes from the Latin word *apere* which means to attach or fasten. The External Attitude attaches us to the external world, and the Internal Attitude attaches us to our internal world. Extraverts are fascinated by objects in the external world, and Introverts are fascinated by their *subjective reaction* to objects in the external world. Accordingly, Extraverts are motivated by external objects, and Introverts are motivated by their *subjective reaction* to external objects. This subtle but profound distinction can be easily perceived after it has risen into our awareness.

As we incline toward one world, we incline away from the other world. The more conscious we become of one world, the more unconscious our other world remains. Thus, our conscious Attitude is balanced by the opposite unconscious Attitude. While Extraverts are busy shining their Light of Consciousness out toward the external world, an uncivilized Introvert hides in the Dark. And while Introverts concentrate on shining their Light of Consciousness in toward their internal world, an uncivilized Extravert hides in the Dark. When Extraverts push out too far, their introverted Dark Side pulls them in. And when Introverts pull in too far, their extraverted Dark Side pushes them out. The opposite Attitudes of our Light Side and our Dark Side balance each other like a seesaw. Our Dark Side provides the necessary counterweight to our Light Side, compensating for all extremes and excesses of our Light Side.

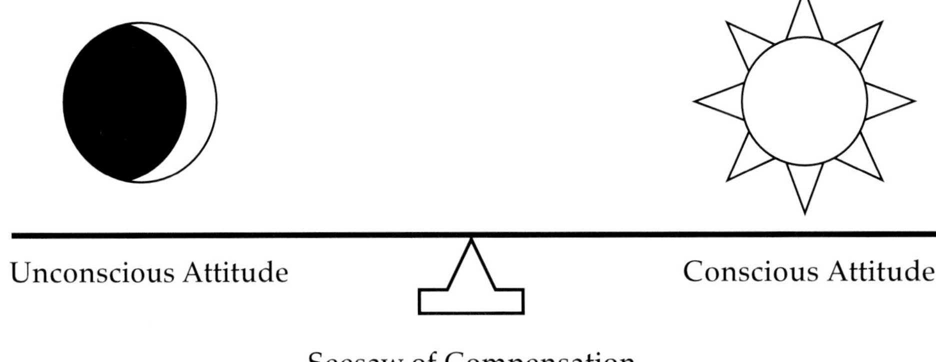


Seesaw of Compensation

## The External Attitude of Extraverts

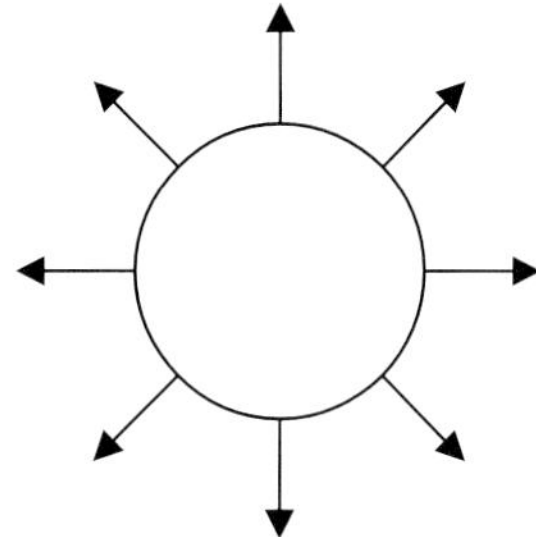

### Styles 2 and 3

I am more attracted to the external world than to my internal world, so I expend energy out toward the external world. I expand and push out, fleeing my center. I am fascinated by objects in the external world. I am outer directed and externally motivated. Most of the time, my internal world serves the external world. As an Extravert, I shine most of my Light of Consciousness out toward the external world. I disown and deny the Introvert that I hide in the Dark, and I deny that I do.

## The Internal Attitude of Introverts

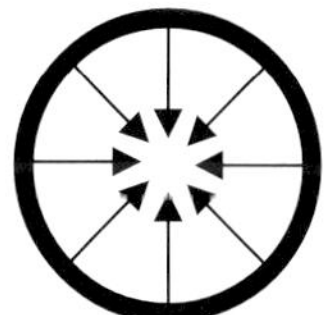

### Styles 1 and 4

I am more attracted to my internal world than to the external world, so I conserve energy for my internal world. I contract and pull in, seeking my center. I am fascinated by my subjective reaction to objects in the external world. I am inner directed and internally motivated. Most of the time, the external world serves my internal world. As an Introvert, I shine most of my Light of Consciousness in toward my internal world. I disown and deny the Extravert that I hide in the Dark, and I deny that I do.

## The Two Roles

The horizontal axis of the Compass of Styles shows the two Roles. Indirectors flex softly in the west, *infolded*. Directors are fixed firmly in the east, *unfolded*. Accordingly, the Map of the Four Natures shows the Indirectors (Styles 1 and 2) in the west of each quadrant, and the Directors (Styles 3 and 4) in the east of each quadrant.

As social beings, our survival depends upon our ability to obtain the cooperation of others in satisfying our needs. We weave in an out of our social interactions as we try to influence others. The texture of our weave provides the key to perceiving the two Roles. Directors have an absolutely firm texture, and Indirectors have a relatively flexible texture. Our words, tone of voice, silence, gestures, actions, and inaction all intertwine to stitch the distinctive texture of our Role.

Everyone plays both Roles: one major and one minor. Directors play a major Direct Role and a minor Indirect Role. Indirectors play a major Indirect Role and a minor Direct Role. Our major Role always remains more natural than our minor Role. We sometimes shift into our minor Role in matters of minor importance. However, for major matters, we usually play our major Role. We rarely shift into our minor Role in matters of major importance, even when our minor Role might be more effective. We can develop and balance our personality by purposefully letting our minor player have a few more lines. With a little patience, we may even find a new star born.

## The Indirect Role of Indirectors

### Style 2
### Style 1

Indirectors invite interaction with others by informing more than instructing. Indirection *folds in* with implicit messages intended to persuade and promote. The texture of Indirectors seems relatively flexible compared to the texture of Directors. In summary, Indirection is implicit: infolded.

## The Direct Role of Directors

### Style 3
### Style 4

Directors direct the actions of others by instructing more than informing. Direction *folds out* with explicit messages intended to command and control. The texture of Directors seems absolutely firm compared to the texture of Indirectors. In summary, Direction is explicit: unfolded.

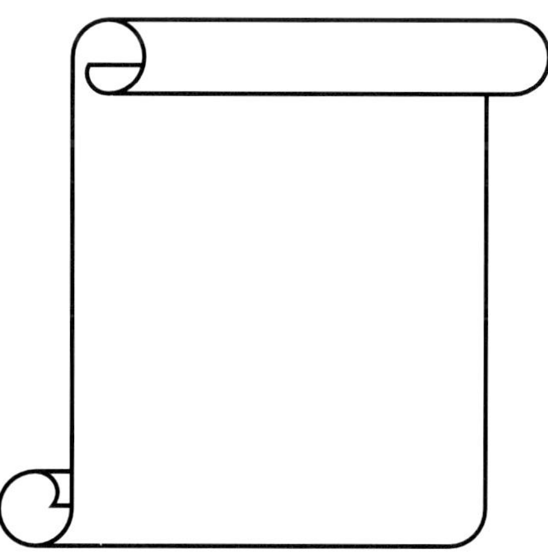

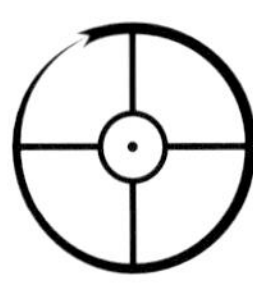

## Nature and Style
## Compass within Compass

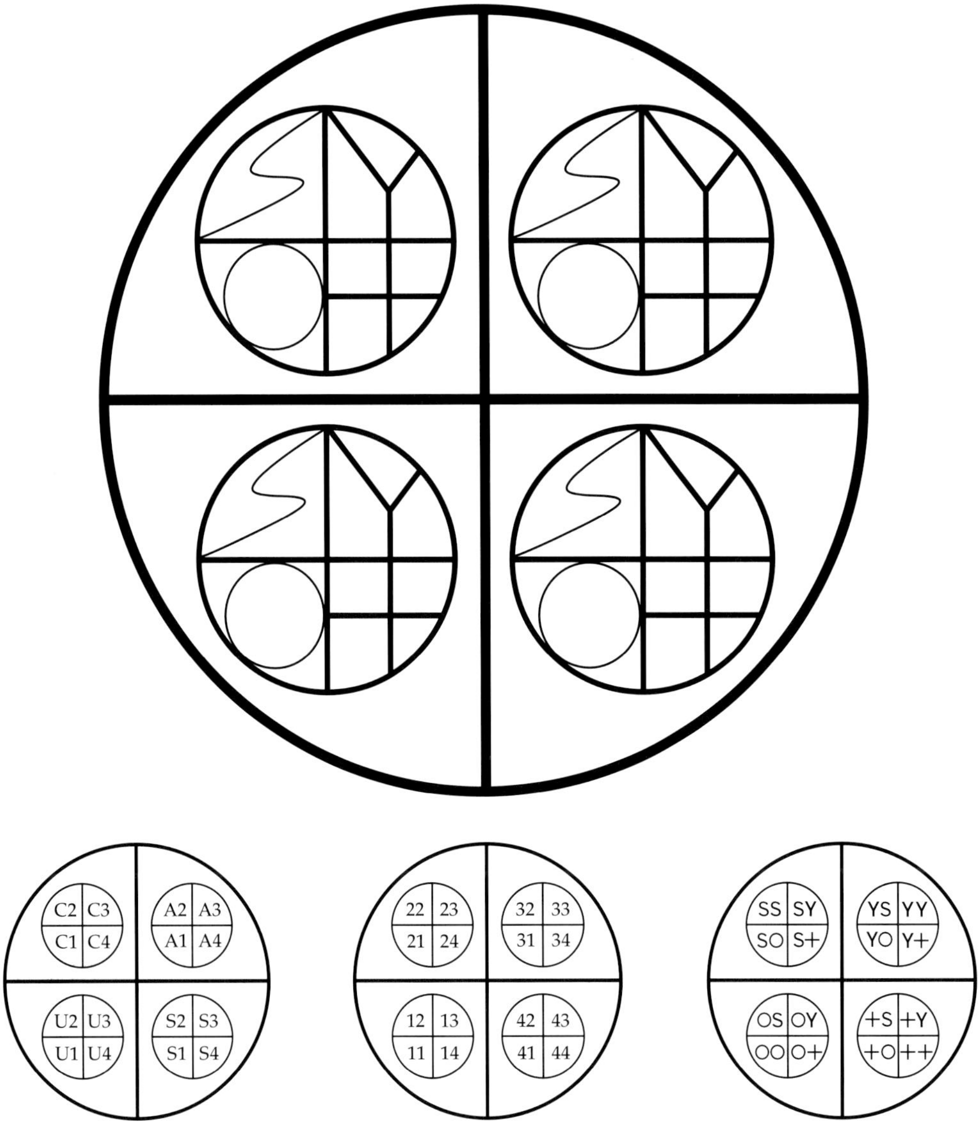

C2 C3
C1 C4

A2 A3
A1 A4

U2 U3
U1 U4

S2 S3
S1 S4

22 23
21 24

32 33
31 34

12 13
11 14

42 43
41 44

SS SY
SO S+

YS YY
YO Y+

OS OY
OO O+

+S +Y
+O ++

# Nature and Style
# Compass within Compass

The Compass of Forces creates both the Compass of Natures and the Compass of Styles. Thus, the Compass of Forces locates the Natures and Styles of the Sixteen Personality Types on the Map of the Four Natures. In total, we use the Compass of Forces five times: once to orient the Four Natures and then four times to orient the Four Styles within each of the Four Natures. Accordingly, each of the Sixteen Personality Types has two homes: one home in the Compass of Natures and one home in the Compass of Styles.

The Outside Corners: Types U1, C2, A3, and S4 each have the *same* home in the Compass of Natures and the Compass of Styles.

The Inside Corners: Types U3, C4, A1, and S2 each have *opposite* homes in the Compass of Natures and the Compass of Styles.

| | | | |
|---|---|---|---|
| C2: 22 = SS | C3: 23 = SY | A2: 32 = YS | A3: 33 = YY |
| C1: 21 = SO | C4: 24 = S+ | A1: 31 = YO | A4: 34 = Y+ |
| U2: 12 = OS | U3: 13 = OY | S2: 42 = +S | S3: 43 = +Y |
| U1: 11 = OO | U4: 14 = O+ | S1: 41 = +O | S4: 44 = ++ |

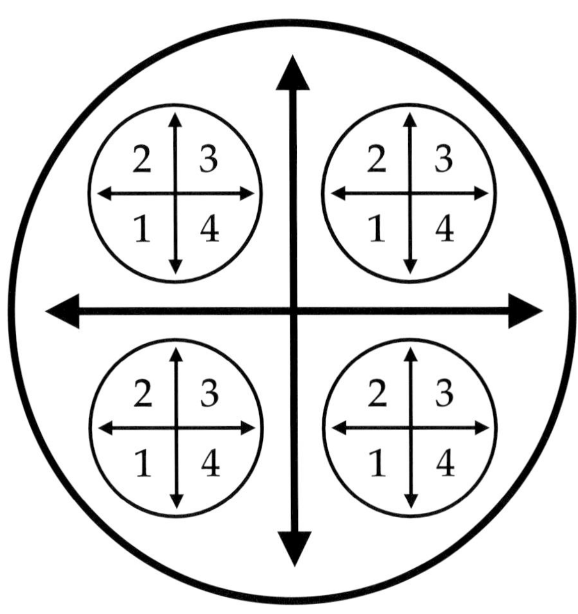


**Nature and Style**
**Compass within Compass**

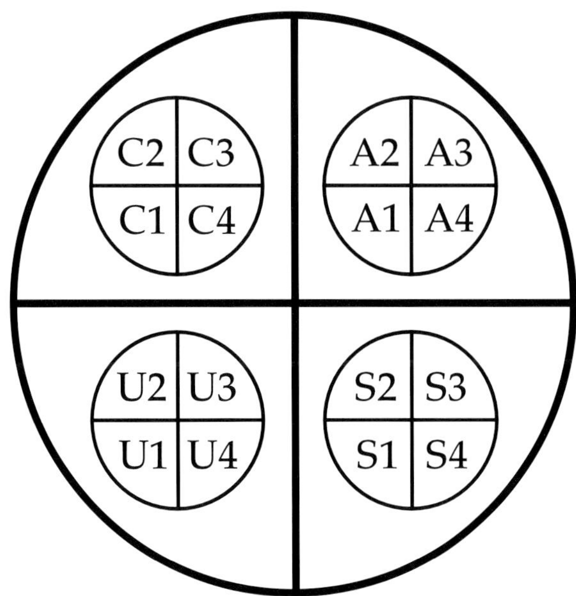

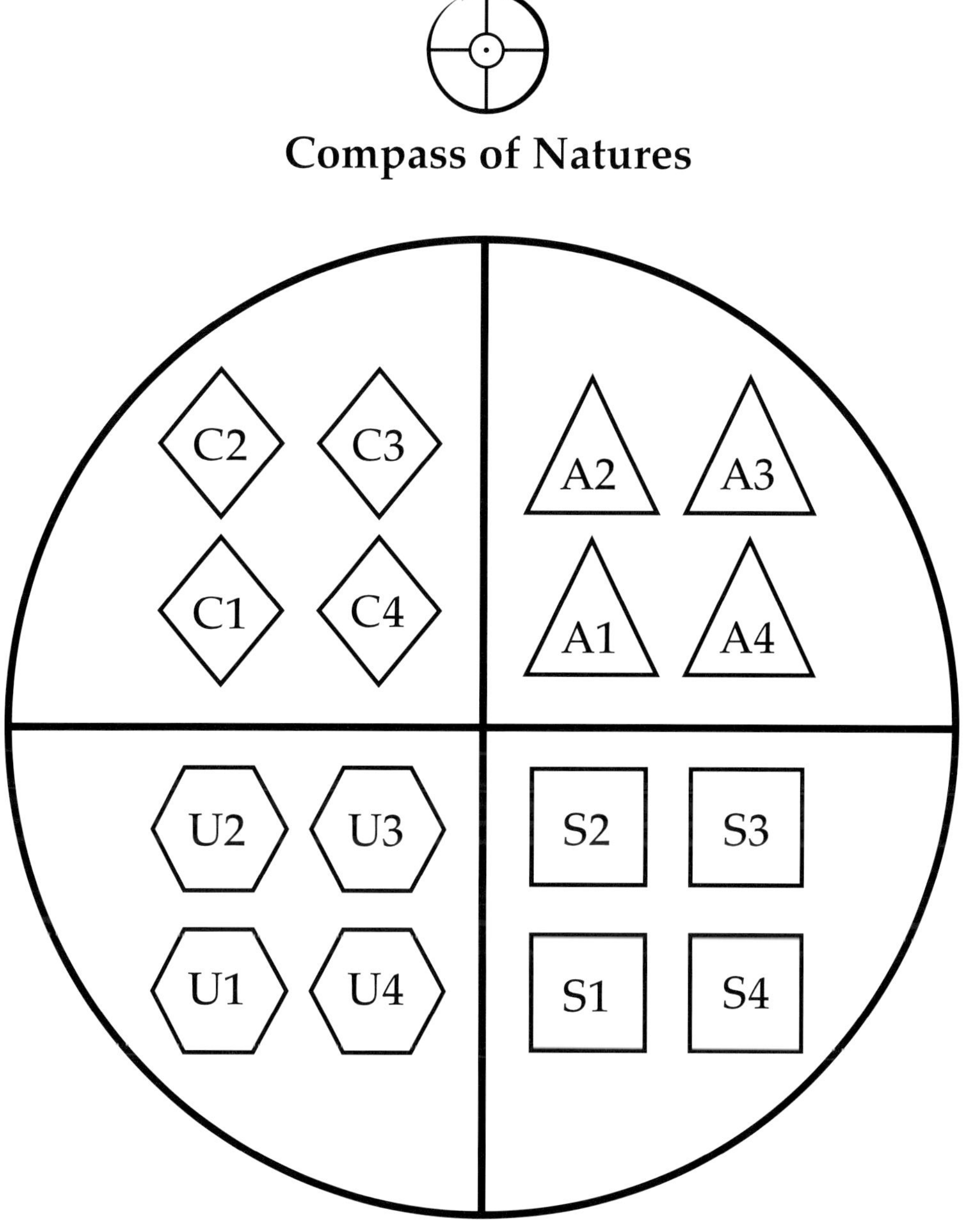


**The Sixteen Personality Types**

The Pictures of Personality™

# Map of the Four Natures

| | | Context | | Content | |
|---|---|---|---|---|---|
| | | Indirect | Direct | Indirect | Direct |
| Confidence | External | C2 | C3 | A2 | A3 |
| | | Clarifiers | | Activators | |
| | Internal | C1 | C4 | A1 | A4 |
| Trust | External | U2 | U3 | S2 | S3 |
| | | Unifiers | | Stabilizers | |
| | Internal | U1 | U4 | S1 | S4 |

# PART III

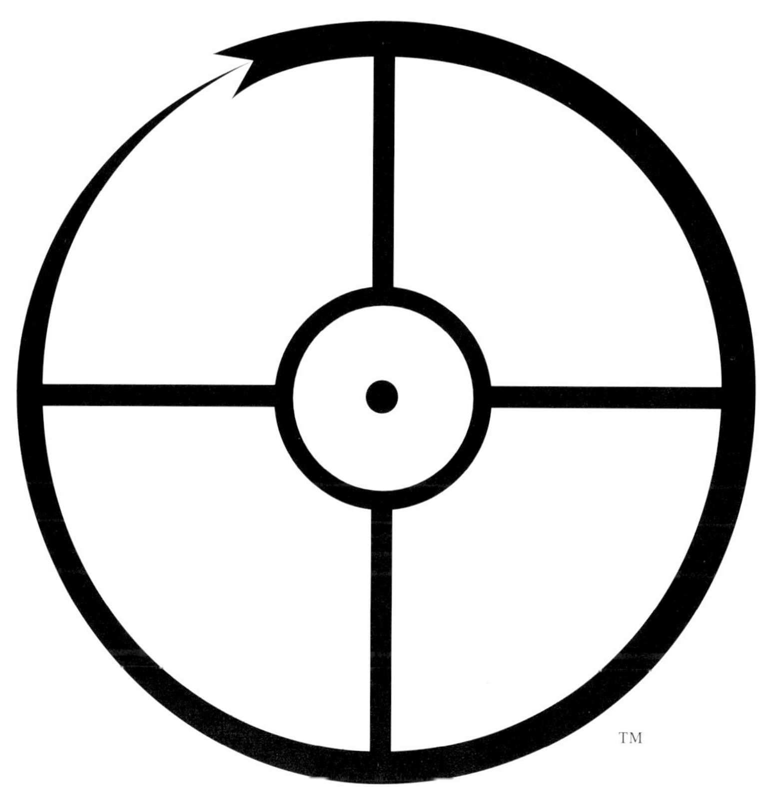


## The Four Realms: Freedom and Focus

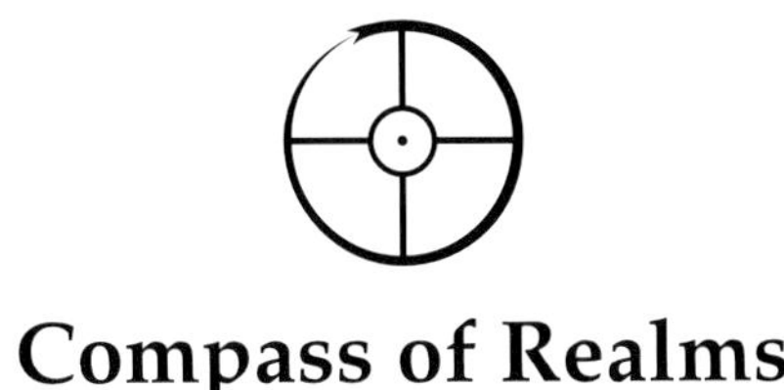

## Compass of Realms

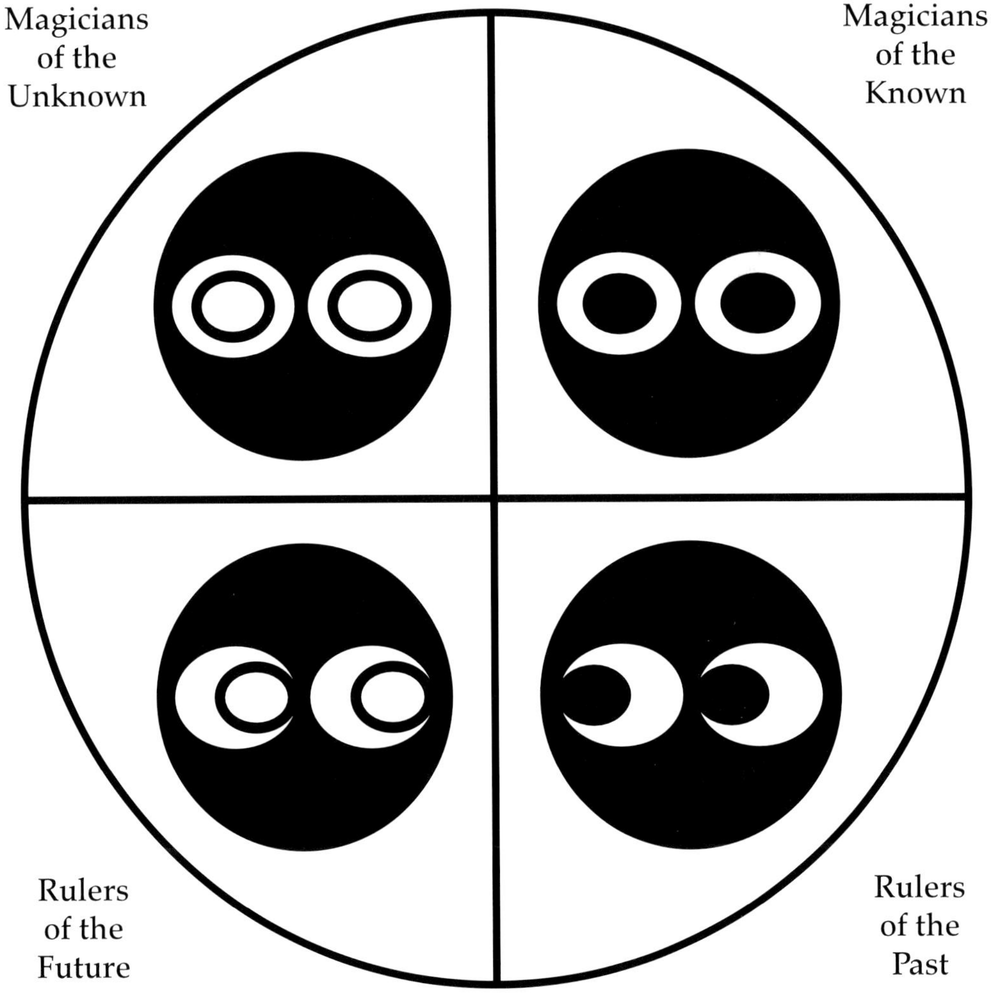

Magicians of the Unknown

Magicians of the Known

Rulers of the Future

Rulers of the Past

# Chapter 5
# Magicians and Rulers

Magicians naturally open perception and refine decisions. Magicians process the whole simultaneously and experientially, from the general to the specific, from the whole to the parts. Magicians focus on variables: what cannot be described nor prescribed. Magicians respond all at once to the whole changing present situation. The Four Global Talents come most naturally to Magicians: External Content and External Context, Internal Harmonizing and Internal Organizing. Magicians perceive objectively (The Actual and The Novel) and decide subjectively (My Ideals and My Ideas). Magicians want *freedom of choice* so that they can explore life's abundant variation.

### Magicians Globalize

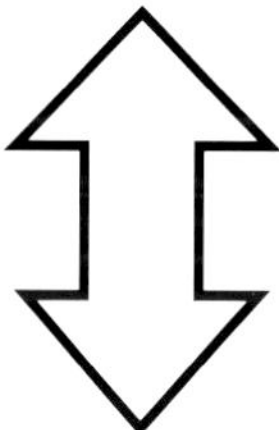

### Rulers Localize

Rulers naturally close perception and confine decisions. Rulers process the parts sequentially and systematically, from the specific to the general, from the parts to the whole. Rulers focus on constants: what can be described and prescribed. Rulers advance step by step, part by part, from the past to the future. The Four Local Talents come most naturally to Rulers: Internal Content and Internal Context, External Harmonizing and External Organizing. Rulers perceive subjectively (My Priorities and My Plans) and decide objectively (The Customs and The Methods). Rulers want *freedom from choice* so that they can pursue a few chosen themes.

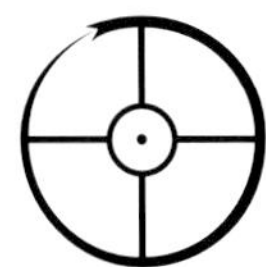

## Compass of Realms

# Magicians

### The Four Global Talents

Open Perception: The Actual and The Novel
Refine Decisions: My Ideals and My Ideas

# Rulers

### The Four Local Talents

Close Perception: My Priorities and My Plans
Confine Decisions: The Customs and The Methods

# Freedom

## Global or Local

The vertical axis of the Compass of Realms shows the polarity of Freedom. Free means at liberty; not constrained. The word *free* arises from the ancient root *pri: to love.* This root also gave birth to the words friend, peace, precious, and Friday. The word *liberty* arises from the ancient root *leudh: to grow.* Accordingly, Freedom is the condition of loving and growing.

But Freedom has two sides: Global and Local. The twin Active Forces of Warm and Cool power the two opposite sides of Freedom: Warm Globalizes and Cool Localizes. Warm expands choices, while Cool contracts choices. Warm separates to create variation (variables), while Cool unites to create themes (constants). Therefore, on the Map of the Four Realms, Magicians rise to the north and Rulers sink to the south. Magicians want freedom of choice (variation), while Rulers want freedom from choice (theme). The word *choice* arises from the ancient root *geus: to taste.* Magicians want the freedom to taste, while Rulers want the freedom not to taste.

Magicians want the freedom to explore life's abundant variation. They are not shackled to a few themes in life. Strict themes imprison Magicians by limiting their choices. Magicians want to experience all of life as it develops and respond spontaneously to the whole changing present situation. Magicians agree with Charles Dickens: "I ask only to be free. The butterflies are free."

Rulers want the freedom to pursue a few chosen themes. They are not shackled to an endless search for life's variety. Unbridled variation imprisons Rulers by compelling unending choices. Rulers want to advance step by step, part by part, from the past to the future in a sequential and systematic progression. Rulers agree with Edmund Burke: "Liberty must be limited in order to be possessed."

In summary, T. S. Eliot describes the polarity of Freedom this way: "Liberty is a different kind of pain from prison."

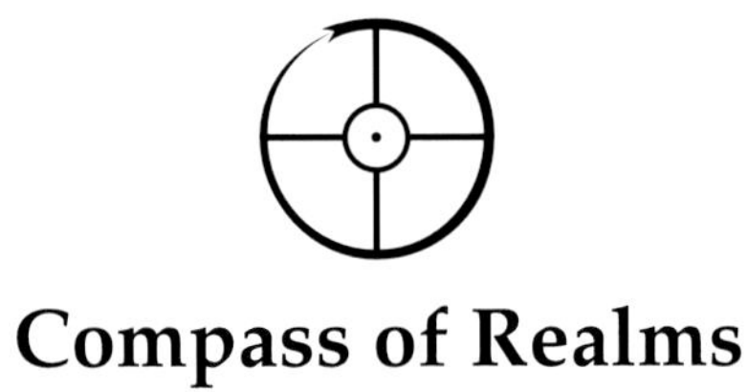

## Compass of Realms

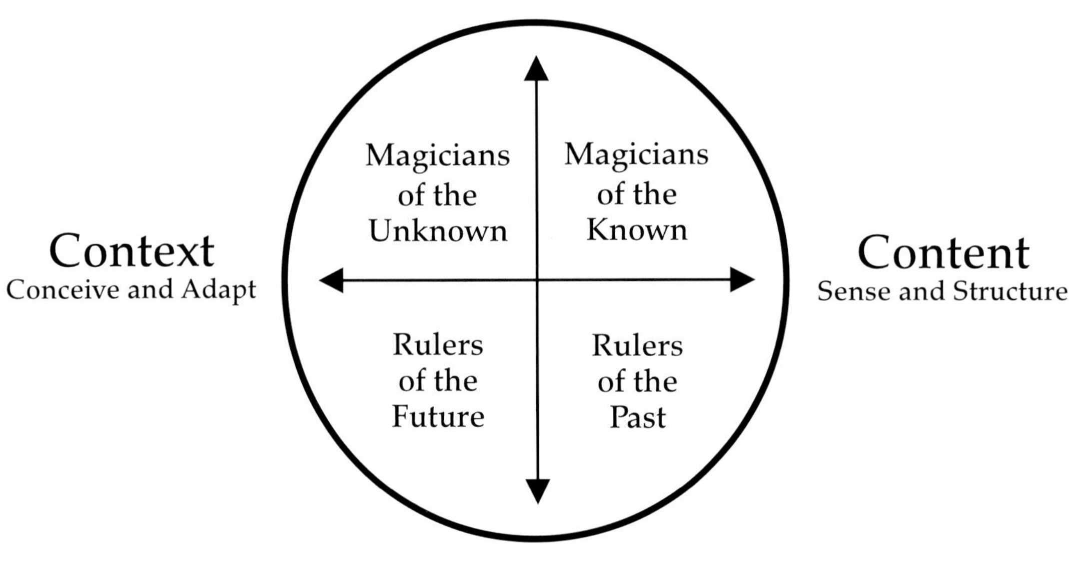

## Perceiving

**Content.** To perceive *inside* the container of the five senses.

**Context.** To perceive *outside* the container of the five senses.

**Harmonize.** To decide based on *value*: more or less.

**Organize.** To decide based on *logic*: true or false.

## Deciding

## Content Eyes

**The Actual: Attention**
**Experience the Object: External Content**
I sense the actual *Content* of the present, experiencing everything with attention open to the known variables and emerging opportunities.

**My Priorities: Continuation**
**My Subjective Impressions: Internal Content**
I sense past *Content*, my impressions of what was, closing out all that does not support the continuation of my priorities.

## Context Eyes

**The Novel: Options**
**Decipher the Object: External Context**
I conceive the novel *Context* of the present, deciphering everything with awareness open to the unknown variables and evolving options.

**My Plans: Anticipation**
**My Subjective Interpretations: Internal Context**
I conceive future *Context*, my interpretations of what will be, closing out all that does not comport with the anticipation of my plans.

# Icon Eyes

## The Four Perceiving Talents

The Icon Eyes show the Four Perceiving Talents. Clocks and timelines proceed left to right, past to future. Likewise, the Icon Eyes point in the direction of perception: left into the past, straight out to the present, and right into the future. Magician Eyes look straight out to the present to experience and decipher the external world. In contrast, Ruler Eyes look in to their internal world: left to their impressions from the past, and right to their interpretations for the future.

**Content Eyes.** Content means to perceive *inside* the container of the five senses, so Content Eyes are filled with Content.

**Present Content: Experience the Object**
To experience means to apprehend an object through the senses; to actively participate with objects leading to the accumulation of knowledge and skill.

**Past Content: Subjective Impressions**
An impression is a memory impressed by the five senses in the past; an imprint stamped in memory by the pressure of prior sensing.

**Context Eyes.** Context means to perceive *outside* the container of the five senses, so Context Eyes are empty of Content.

**Present Context: Decipher the Object**
To decipher means to find the meaning of; to convert into intelligible form; decode; detect; discover.

**Future Context: Subjective Interpretations**
To interpret means to assign meaning to; to explain the future relevance; construe; translate.

## Harmonizing Arms

**My Ideals: Perfection**
**My Subjective Evaluation: Internal Harmonizing**
I *Harmonize* experientially, refining my ideals by my evaluation of natural human values and their perfect expression.

**The Customs: Relations**
**The Objective Conventions: External Harmonizing**
I *Harmonize* systematically, confined to the customs and conventions prescribed by the general rules of human relations.

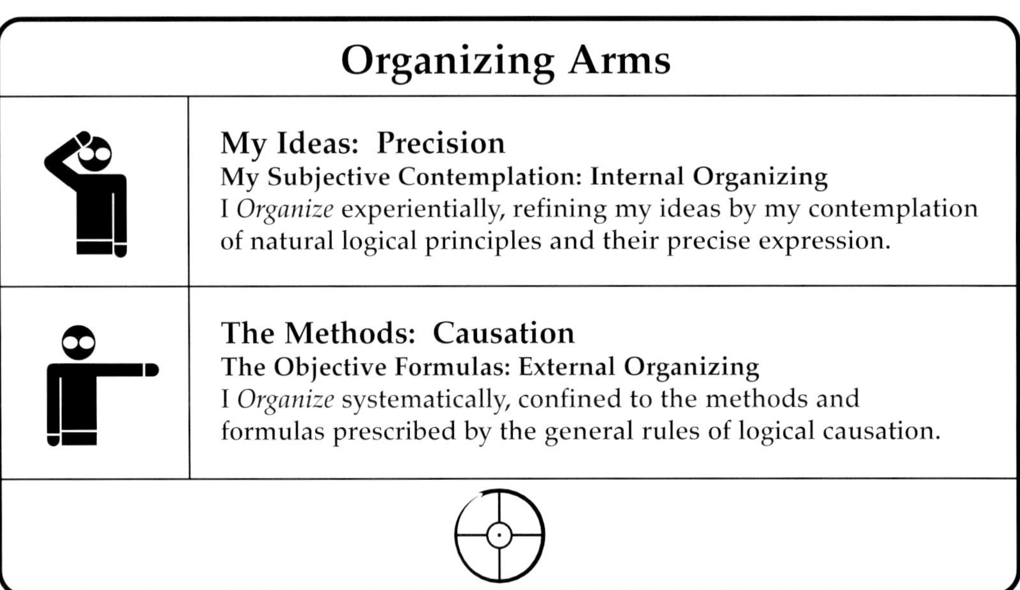

## Organizing Arms

**My Ideas: Precision**
**My Subjective Contemplation: Internal Organizing**
I *Organize* experientially, refining my ideas by my contemplation of natural logical principles and their precise expression.

**The Methods: Causation**
**The Objective Formulas: External Organizing**
I *Organize* systematically, confined to the methods and formulas prescribed by the general rules of logical causation.

# Icon Arms

## The Four Deciding Talents

The Icon Arms show the Four Deciding Talents. Magicians naturally refine decisions by their own internal rules. Rulers naturally confine decisions to the external rules. Accordingly, the Icon Arms always point toward the source of the rules. Magician Arms point in to show Internal Harmonizing and Internal Organizing. Ruler Arms point out to show External Harmonizing and External Organizing.

**Harmonizing** means to decide based on value: more or less. The words *harmonize* and *joint* share the same root. Literally, Harmonizing means to move all of the joints together in agreement. We Harmonize in two opposite ways:

**Internal Harmonizing: Subjective Evaluation**
To evaluate means to personally consider; appraise; estimate worth; to form an opinion based on value.

**External Harmonizing: Objective Conventions**
Conventions are the prescribed rules for ordering and evaluating human relationships; the generally agreed upon cultural customs.

**Organizing** means to decide based on logic: true or false. The words *organize* and *organ* share the same root. Literally, Organizing means to assemble a set of organs logically to make a functioning body. We Organize in two opposite ways:

**Internal Organizing: Subjective Contemplation**
To contemplate means to personally consider; ponder both sides of an issue; to form an opinion based on logic.

**External Organizing: Objective Formulas**
Formulas are the prescribed rules for ordering and analyzing causal relationships (the rules of causation); the generally agreed upon logical methods.

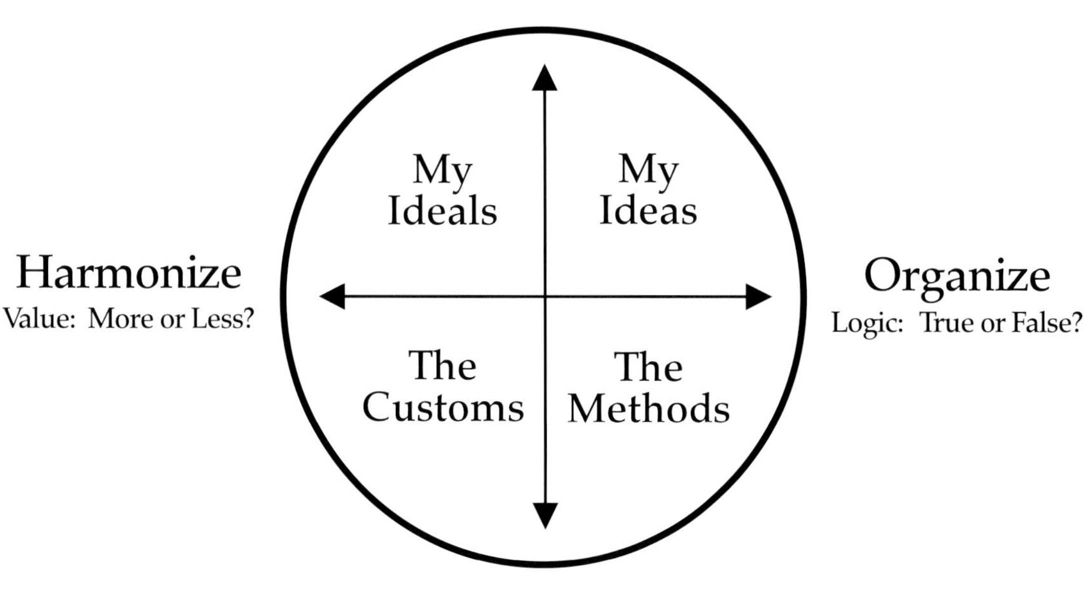
Magicians Globalize
Refine Decisions by My Rules
My Ideals
My Ideas
Harmonize
Value: More or Less?
Organize
Logic: True or False?
The Customs
The Methods
Rulers Localize
Confine Decisions to The Rules

# Compass of Realms

## Magicians Globalize

Refine Decisions by My Rules

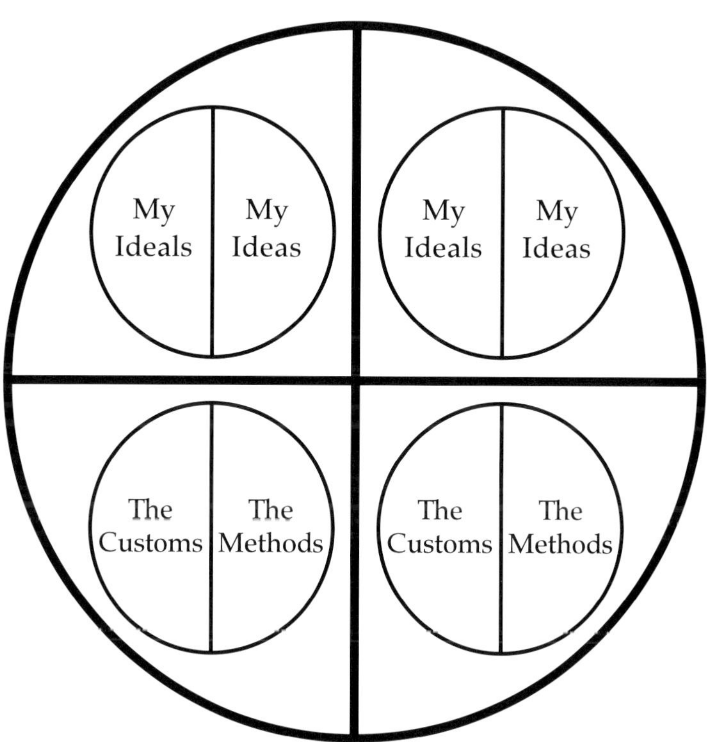


## Rulers Localize

Confine Decisions to The Rules

## The Icon Eyes

| My Perception | | The Perception | |
|---|---|---|---|
| My Past | My Future | The Present | |
|  | 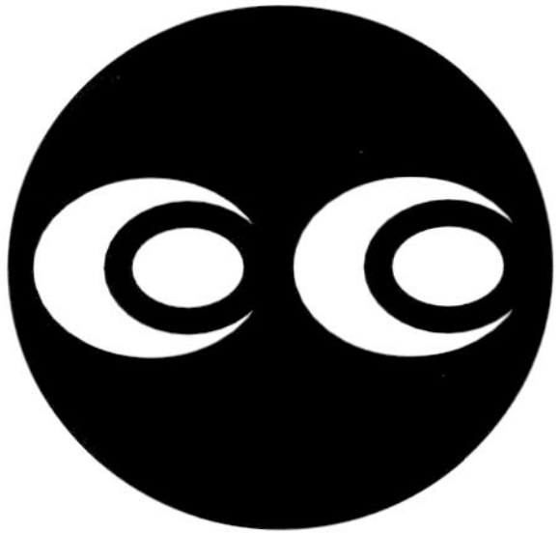 |  |  |
| Internal | | External | |
| Content | Context | Content | Context |
| My Priorities: Continuation | My Plans: Anticipation | The Actual: Attention | The Novel: Options |
| Subjective Impressions | Subjective Interpretations | Experience the Object | Decipher the Object |
| Rulers Localize: Close Perception | | Magicians Globalize: Open Perception | |

**The Four Perceiving Talents**

## The Icon Arms

| The Decision | | My Decision | |
|---|---|---|---|
| The Rules | | My Rules | |
|  |  |  |  |
| External | | Internal | |
| Organize | Harmonize | Organize | Harmonize |
| The Methods: Causation | The Customs: Relations | My Ideas: Precision | My Ideals: Perfection |
| Objective Formulas | Objective Conventions | Subjective Contemplation | Subjective Evaluation |
| Rulers Localize: Confine Decisions | | Magicians Globalize: Refine Decisions | |

**The Four Deciding Talents**

## The Eight Talents

| My Past | The Present | | My Future | My Rules | The Rules | | My Rules |
|---|---|---|---|---|---|---|---|
| Internal | External | | Internal | Internal | External | | Internal |
| Content | | Context | | Organize | | Harmonize | |
| Subjective Impressions | Experience the Object | Decipher the Object | Subjective Interpretations | Subjective Contemplation | Objective Formulas | Objective Conventions | Subjective Evaluation |
| My Priorities: Continuation | The Actual: Attention | The Novel: Options | My Plans: Anticipation | My Ideas: Precision | The Methods: Causation | The Customs: Relations | My Ideals: Perfection |
| Close Perception | Open Perception | | Close Perception | Refine Decisions | Confine Decisions | | Refine Decisions |
| **Perceive** | | | | **Decide** | | | |

## The Eight Talents

| My Perception | | The Decision | | My Decision | | The Perception | |
|---|---|---|---|---|---|---|---|
| My Past | My Future | The Rules | | My Rules | | The Present | |
| Internal | | External | | Internal | | External | |
| Content | Context | Organize | Harmonize | Organize | Harmonize | Content | Context |
| My Priorities: Continuation | My Plans: Anticipation | The Methods: Causation | The Customs: Relations | My Ideas: Precision | My Ideals: Perfection | The Actual: Attention | The Novel: Options |
| Subjective Impressions | Subjective Interpretations | Objective Formulas | Objective Conventions | Subjective Contemplation | Subjective Evaluation | Experience the Object | Decipher the Object |
| Close Perception | | Confine Decisions | | Refine Decisions | | Open Perception | |
| **Localize** | | | | **Globalize** | | | |
| Theme<br>Local: The Parts<br>Sequential • Systematic<br>Specific to General • Parts to Whole<br>Close Perception and Confine Decisions<br>My Specific Perception and The General Rules<br>What Can Be Described and Prescribed: The Constants<br>Advance Step by Step, Part by Part, from My Past to My Future<br>World Population 55% | | | | Variation<br>Global: The Whole<br>Simultaneous • Experiential<br>General to Specific • Whole to Parts<br>Open Perception and Refine Decisions<br>The General Perception and My Specific Rules<br>What Cannot Be Described nor Prescribed: The Variables<br>Respond All at Once to the Whole Changing Present Situation<br>World Population 45% | | | |
| **Rulers** | | | | **Magicians** | | | |

# From Nature to Realm

## Fire and Earth Stay Right There, Water and Air Play Musical Chairs.

**Flow Around.** True to their flowing Natures, Unifiers and Clarifiers flow around once in pairs from their positions on the Map of the Four Natures to find their homes on the Map of the Four Realms. As expected, the Indirect Unifiers and Indirect Clarifiers (Styles 1 and 2) are Magicians of the Unknown, and the Direct Unifiers and Direct Clarifiers (Styles 3 and 4) are Rulers of the Future.

**Stay Fixed.** True to their fixed Natures, Activators and Stabilizers stay fixed in the same position whether mapped by Nature or Realm. All Activators are Magicians of the Known, and all Stabilizers are Rulers of the Past.

**Attitudes.** Whether mapped by Nature or Realm, Extraverts (Styles 2 and 3) always rise to the north of each quadrant, and Introverts (Styles 1 and 4) always sink to the south of each quadrant.

Extraverts Rise North

Introverts Sink South

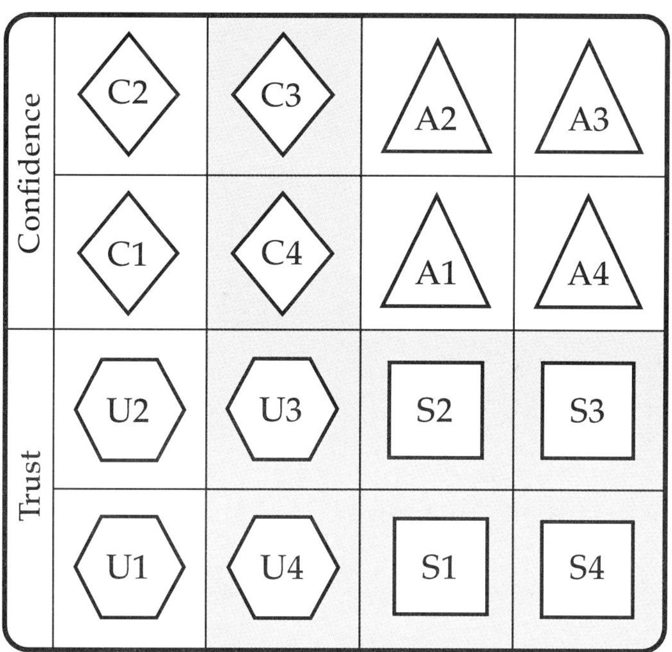


Before Musical Chairs: **Map of the Four Natures**
After Musical Chairs: **Map of the Four Realms**

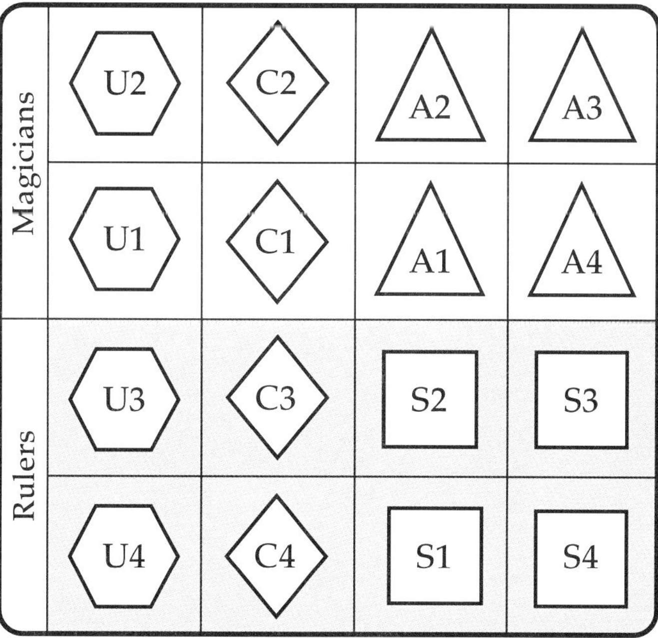

The Pictures of Personality™

# Map of the Four Natures

| | | Context | | Content | |
|---|---|---|---|---|---|
| | | Indirect | Direct | Indirect | Direct |
| Confidence | External | C2 | C3 | A2 | A3 |
| | | *Clarifiers* | | *Activators* | |
| | Internal | C1 | C4 | A1 | A4 |
| Trust | External | U2 | U3 | S2 | S3 |
| | | *Unifiers* | | *Stabilizers* | |
| | Internal | U1 | U4 | S1 | S4 |

The Pictures of Personality™

# Map of the Four Realms

| | | Context | | Content | |
|---|---|---|---|---|---|
| | | Harmonize | Organize | Harmonize | Organize |
| Globalize | External | U2 | C2 | A2 | A3 |
| | | *Magicians of the Unknown* | | *Magicians of the Known* | |
| | Internal | U1 | C1 | A1 | A4 |
| Localize | External | U3 | C3 | S2 | S3 |
| | | *Rulers of the Future* | | *Rulers of the Past* | |
| | Internal | U4 | C4 | S1 | S4 |

## How does the Map of the Four Natures become the Map of the Four Realms?

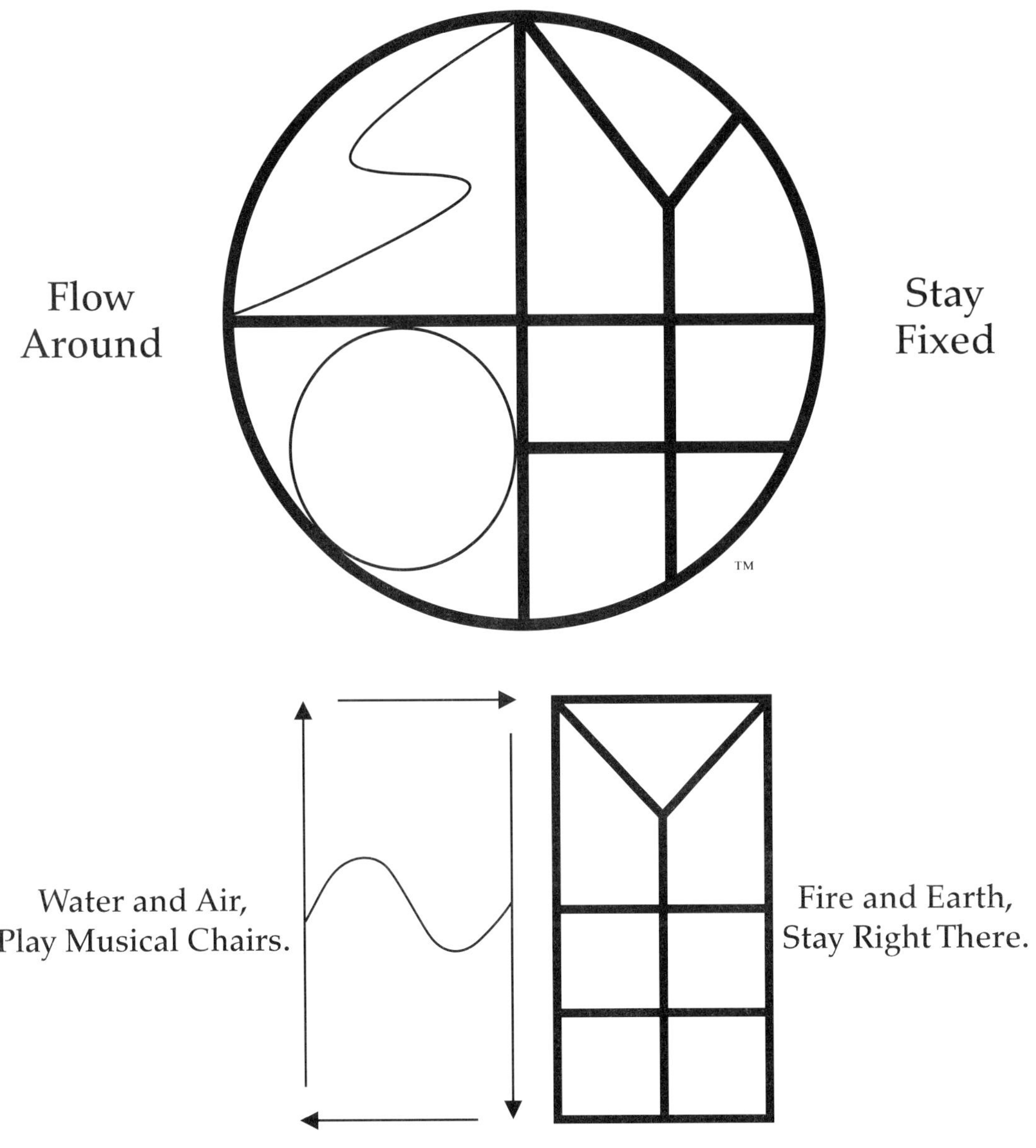

# Chapter 6
# Patterns of Attraction

*Magicians and Rulers*
*sixteen in all,*
*live in castles*
*one inch tall.*

We may be made of matter, but we live our lives in space. We live between chaos and cosmos, in the midst of disorder and order. Constantly changing, our universe is infinite, but ordered. Space is the Original Force.

The Four Attractors reveal how cosmos arises from chaos. The Attractors reveal "basins of attraction" that predict the preferred position of things and events. For example, a marble rolling around inside a bowl will finally settle in one spot. That spot (not the bowl) is the final basin of attraction for the marble. An infinite number of basins compete to become the final basin for everything that happens in our universe, including all of the perceptions and decisions of every person. The Attractors simply predict behavior, they do not control behavior.

All of our perceptions and decisions – both individual and collective – fall under the spell of the Four Attractors. The Point Attractor, Cycle Attractor, Torus Attractor, and Strange Attractor create the Four Patterns of Attraction that show how we use our Eight Talents to balance the chaos of our internal and external worlds. Each Attractor relates to one of the four dimensions. Again, all dimensions are equally valid and valuable, just as all Eight Talents and all Sixteen Personality Types are equally valid and valuable.

### Four Patterns of Attraction

| Waves | Rows | Cycles | Points |
|---|---|---|---|
| 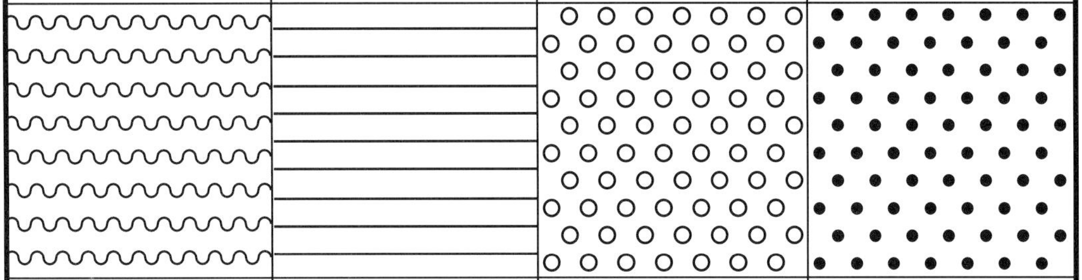 | | | |
| Context | Content | Organize | Harmonize |
| 4th Dimension | 3rd Dimension | 2nd Dimension | 1st Dimension |
| Perceive | | Decide | |

*Confusion is a word we have invented for an order which is not understood.*
Henry Miller (1891–1980)

## • • • • Harmonizing Point and Organizing Cycle ○ ○ ○ ○

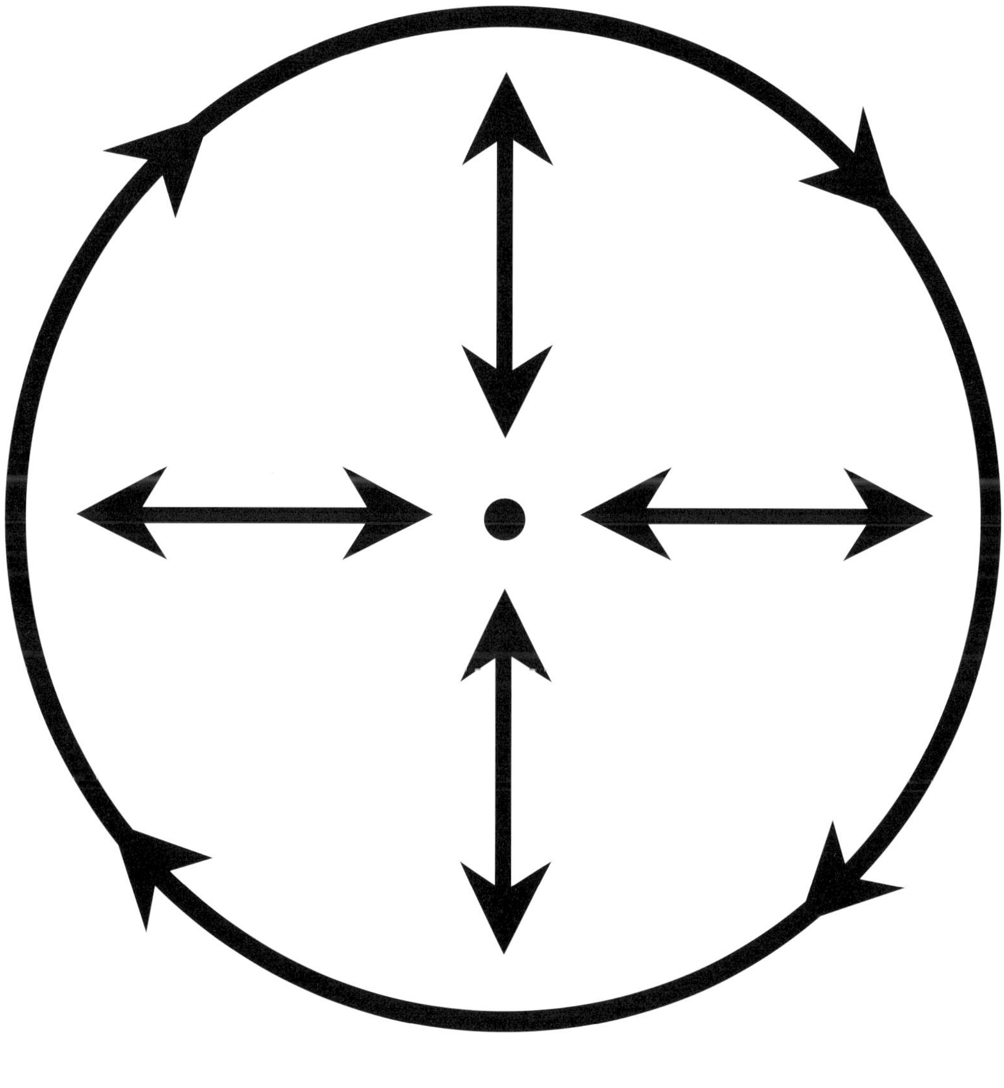

# Harmonizing Points

## First Dimension

Harmonizing means to decide based on value: more or less. When we Harmonize, internally or externally, we fall under the spell of the Point Attractor. Imagine hearing a sound in a dark tunnel. If the sounds attracts us, we move closer. If the sound repels us, we move away. We harmonize our position based on our positive or negative evaluation of the sound. We eventually settle into a Harmonizing Point somewhere along an imaginary line leading to and from the source of the sound.

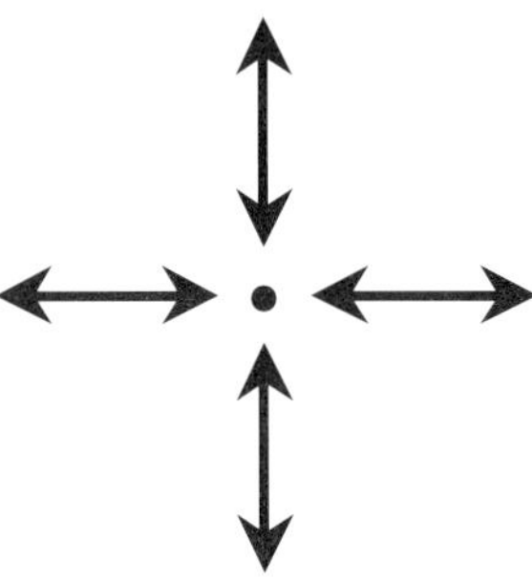

Harmonizing Points and the Point Attractor belong to the first dimension of the line. A line is an infinite collection of points. Harmonizing decides among the many continuous points along a line between two opposites. Harmonizing reasons with value judgments, based upon either internal or external rules, to decide the worth of something along a range of values. Harmonizing decides among all the shades between black and white.

**Magicians build castles with Internal Harmonizing Points**

| Harmonizing Points | |
|---|---|
| **My Ideals: Perfection**<br>**My Subjective Evaluation: Internal Harmonizing**<br>I *Harmonize* experientially, refining my ideals by my evaluation of natural human values and their perfect expression. | |
| **The Customs: Relations**<br>**The Objective Conventions: External Harmonizing**<br>I *Harmonize* systematically, confined to the customs and conventions prescribed by the general rules of human relations. | |

**Rulers build castles with External Harmonizing Points**

# Organizing Cycles

## Second Dimension

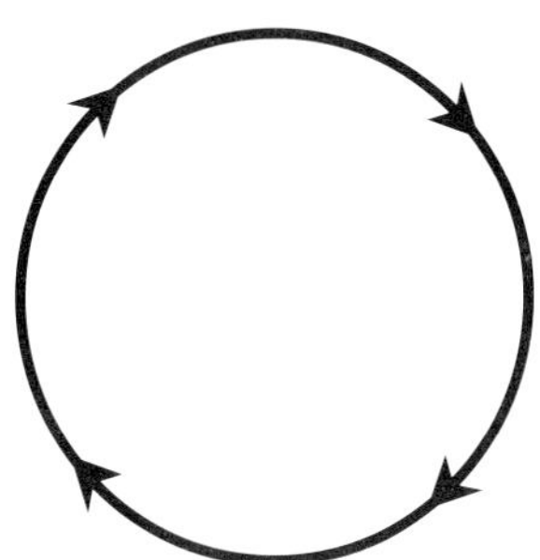

Organizing means to decide based on logic: true or false. When we Organize, internally or externally, we fall under the spell of the Cycle Attractor. Imagine a merry-go-round, or the Earth orbiting the sun. As we Organize, we cycle around something until finally we settle on one side or the other of the Organizing Cycle. Or, we may settle on a third option that arises from a synthesis of the two sides.

Organizing Cycles and the Cycle Attractor belong to the second dimension of the plane. A plane is an infinite collection of lines. Organizing decides between two opposite sides of an Organizing Cycle. Organizing reasons with logical judgments, based upon either internal or external rules, to decide between two opposites: true or false, yes or no, on or off, one or zero. Organizing decides only between black and white, but Harmonizing decides among all the shades in between.

**Magicians build castles with Internal Organizing Cycles**

## Organizing Cycles

**My Ideas: Precision**
**My Subjective Contemplation: Internal Organizing**
I *Organize* experientially, refining my ideas by my contemplation of natural logical principles and their precise expression.

**The Methods: Causation**
**The Objective Formulas: External Organizing**
I *Organize* systematically, confined to the methods and formulas prescribed by the general rules of logical causation.

**Rulers build castles with External Organizing Cycles**

# Content Rows

## Third Dimension

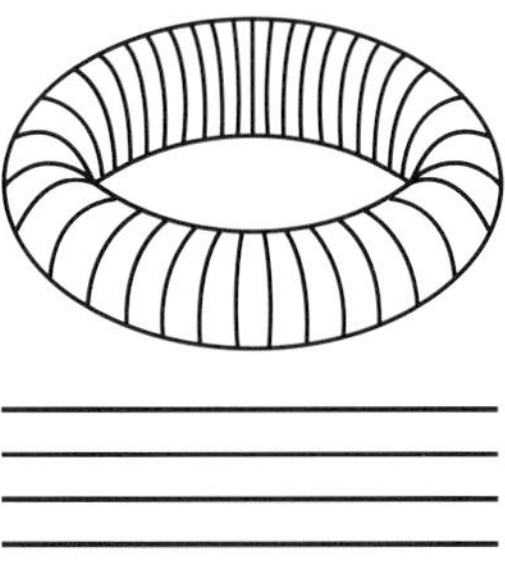

Content means to perceive inside the container of the five senses. When we perceive Content, internal or external, we fall under the spell of the Torus Attractor. Imagine slicing a bagel or a donut into many thin disks. With each slice, we twist the position of our knife slightly. Likewise, Content perception senses and structures straight around the container of the five senses, repeatedly referring back to itself, journey after journey.

Content Rows and the Torus Attractor belong to the third dimension of the solid. A solid is an infinite collection of planes. Content perception spirals forward in a fixed and finite path that is complex but predictable and predetermined. Content Rows are straight like our line of sight, the horizon, walls and fences, the path of falling objects, crop rows, crows flying, sliced bread, and dry spaghetti.

**Magicians of the Known build castles with External Content Rows.**

## Content Rows

### The Actual: Attention

**Experience the Object: External Content**

I sense the actual *Content* of the present, experiencing everything with attention open to the known variables and emerging opportunities.

### My Priorities: Continuation

**My Subjective Impressions: Internal Content**

I sense past *Content*, my impressions of what was, closing out all that does not support the continuation of my priorities.

**Rulers of the Past build castles with Internal Content Rows.**

# Context Waves

## Fourth Dimension

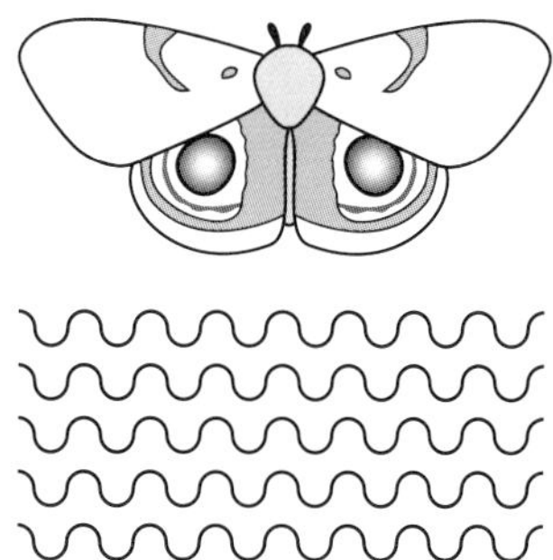

Context means to perceive outside the container of the five senses. When we perceive Context, internal or external, we fall under the spell of the Strange Attractor. The Io moth, with eyespots on the back of its wings, represents the Strange Attractor which orders chaos in strange ways that we can recognize only in hindsight. Context perception conceives and adapts, deciphering and interpreting fractions of reality with our sixth sense.

Context Waves and the Strange Attractor belong to the fourth dimension of time and space. Context perception is flowing and infinite, complex and erratic, wandering and wavy. Context Waves curve like ocean waves, flags waving, the path of wings in flight, the path of fish swimming, drifting clouds, and moist spaghetti.

**Magicians of the Unknown build castles with External Context Waves.**

| Context Waves | |
|---|---|
| **The Novel: Options**<br>**Decipher the Object: External Context**<br>I conceive the novel *Context* of the present, deciphering everything with awareness open to the unknown variables and evolving options. | |
| **My Plans: Anticipation**<br>**My Subjective Interpretations: Internal Context**<br>I conceive future *Context*, my interpretations of what will be, closing out all that does not comport with the anticipation of my plans. | |

**Rulers of the Future build castles with Internal Context Waves.**

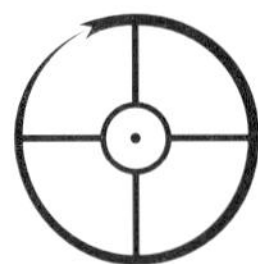

## Compass of Realms

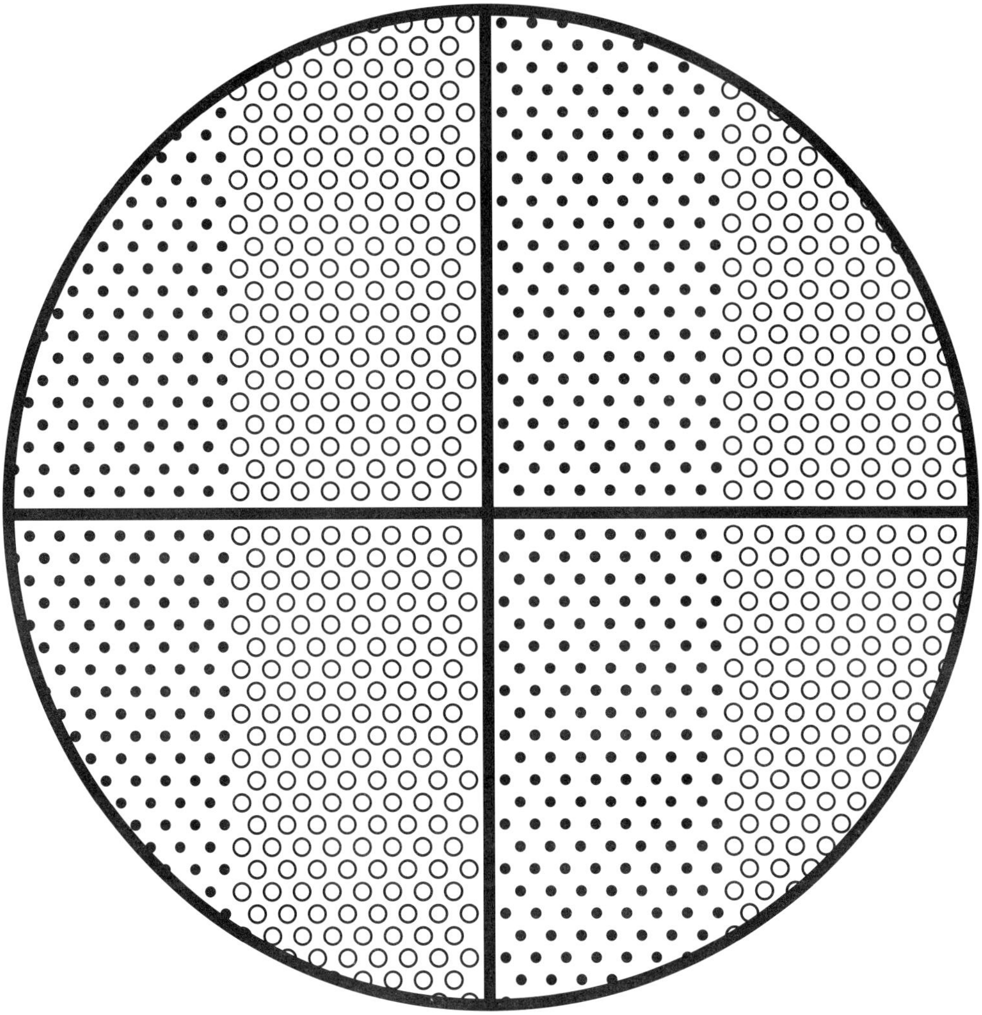

• • • • • • • Harmonizing Points • • • • • • •

○○○○○○○ Organizing Cycles ○○○○○○○

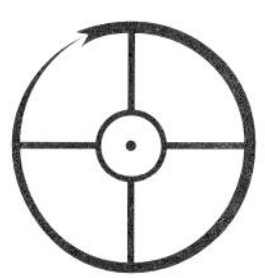

## Compass of Realms

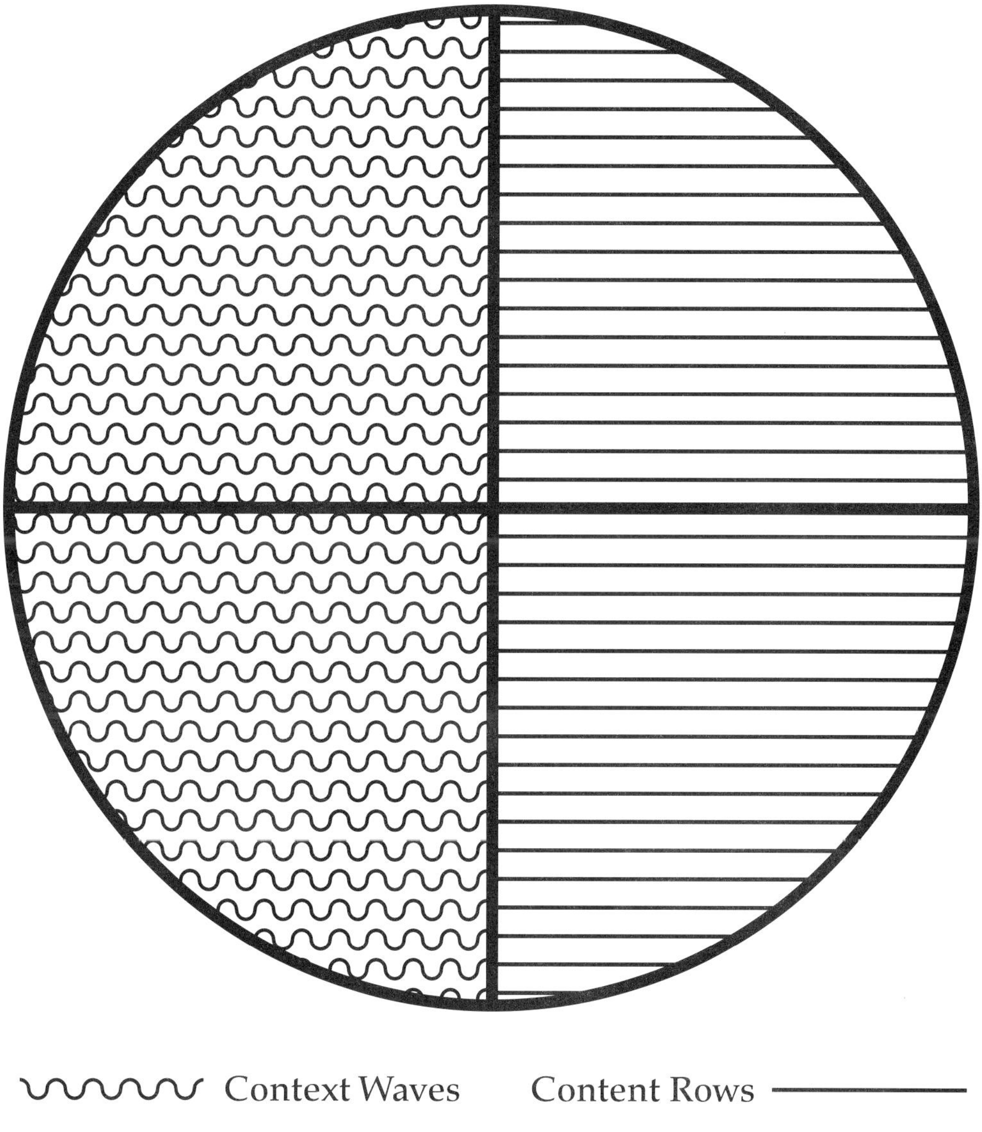

Context Waves Content Rows

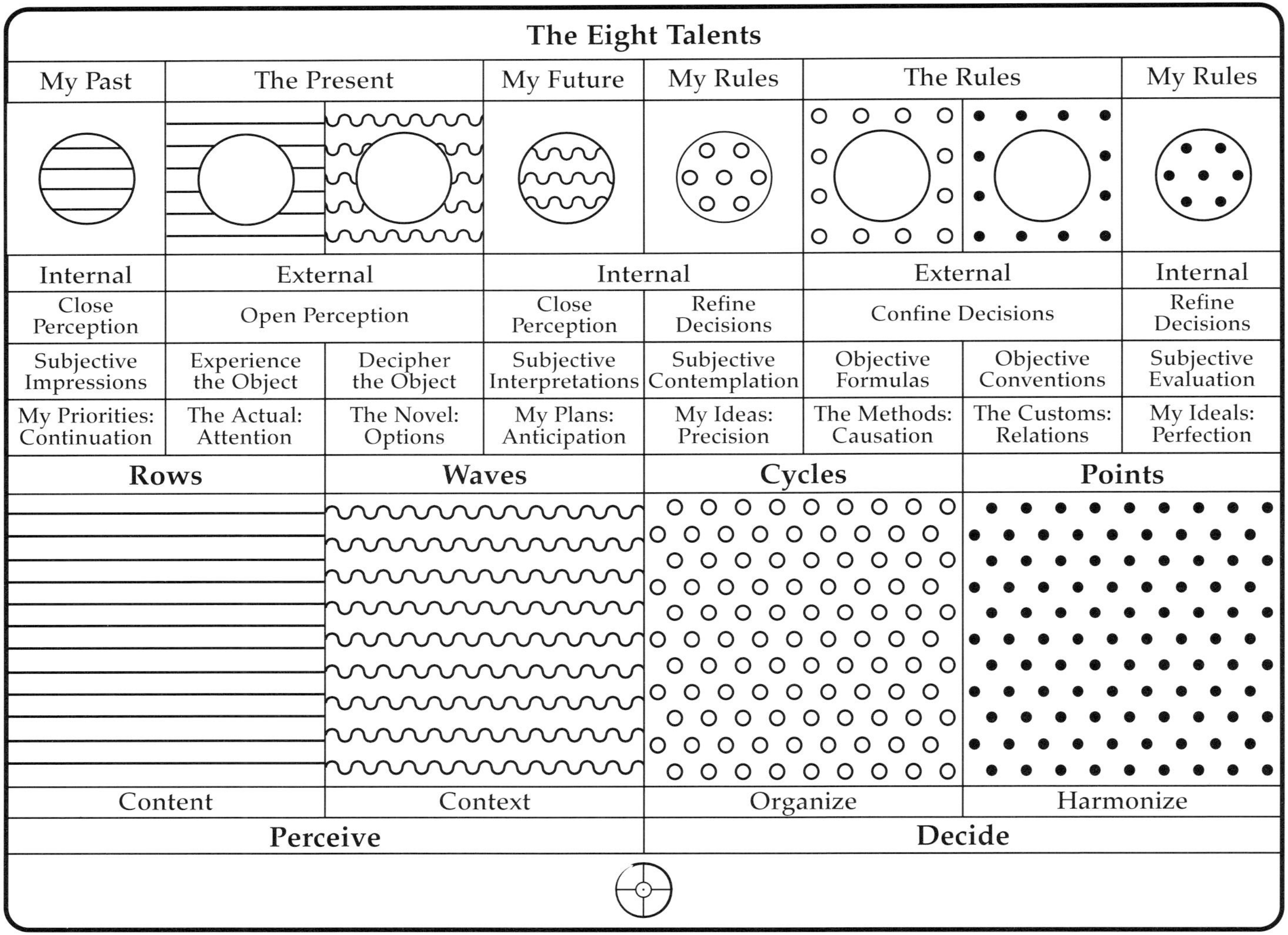

## The Eight Talents

| My Past | The Present | | My Future | My Rules | The Rules | | My Rules |
|---|---|---|---|---|---|---|---|
| Internal | External | | Internal | | External | | Internal |
| Close Perception | Open Perception | | Close Perception | Refine Decisions | Confine Decisions | | Refine Decisions |
| Subjective Impressions | Experience the Object | Decipher the Object | Subjective Interpretations | Subjective Contemplation | Objective Formulas | Objective Conventions | Subjective Evaluation |
| My Priorities: Continuation | The Actual: Attention | The Novel: Options | My Plans: Anticipation | My Ideas: Precision | The Methods: Causation | The Customs: Relations | My Ideals: Perfection |
| **Rows** | | **Waves** | | **Cycles** | | **Points** | |
| Content | | Context | | Organize | | Harmonize | |
| **Perceive** | | | | **Decide** | | | |

## The Eight Talents

| My Perception | | The Decision | | My Decision | | The Perception | |
|---|---|---|---|---|---|---|---|
| My Past | My Future | The Rules | | My Rules | | The Present | |
| Internal | | External | | Internal | | External | |
| Content | Context | Organize | Harmonize | Organize | Harmonize | Content | Context |
| My Priorities: Continuation | My Plans: Anticipation | The Methods: Causation | The Customs: Relations | My Ideas: Precision | My Ideals: Perfection | The Actual: Attention | The Novel: Options |
| Subjective Impressions | Subjective Interpretations | Objective Formulas | Objective Conventions | Subjective Contemplation | Subjective Evaluation | Experience the Object | Decipher the Object |
| Close Perception | | Confine Decisions | | Refine Decisions | | Open Perception | |

| Localize | Globalize |
|---|---|
| Theme<br>Local: The Parts<br>Sequential • Systematic<br>Specific to General • Parts to Whole<br>Close Perception and Confine Decisions<br>My Specific Perception and The General Rules<br>What Can Be Described and Prescribed: The Constants<br>Advance Step by Step, Part by Part, from My Past to My Future<br>World Population 55% | Variation<br>Global: The Whole<br>Simultaneous • Experiential<br>General to Specific • Whole to Parts<br>Open Perception and Refine Decisions<br>The General Perception and My Specific Rules<br>What Cannot Be Described nor Prescribed: The Variables<br>Respond All at Once to the Whole Changing Present Situation<br>World Population 45% |
| **Rulers** | **Magicians** |

*Four per shoulder*
*two will fall,*
*growing wings*
*one mile small.*

*In the middle*
*little me,*
*out of nothing*
*flying free.*

*One side dark*
*one side light,*
*together lift*
*my life in flight.*

# Chapter 7
# Our Light Side and *Our Dark Side!*

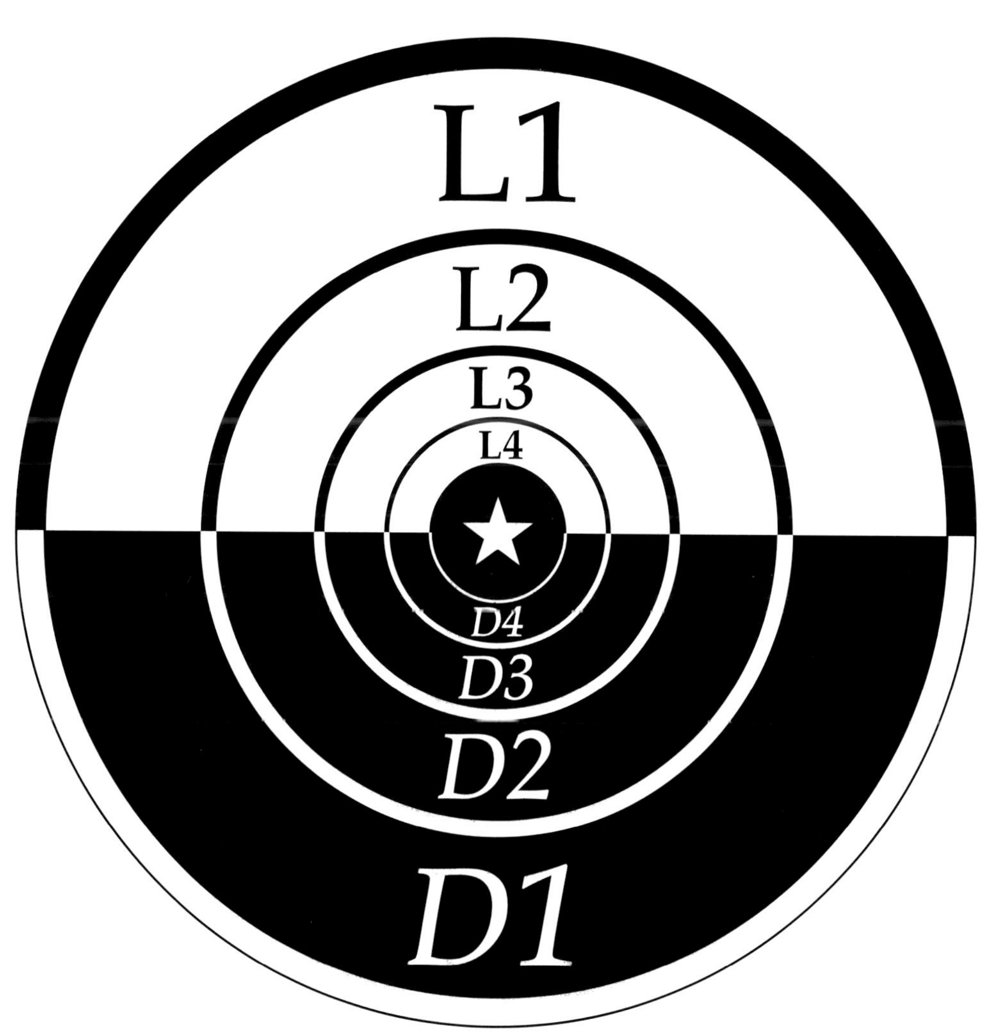

**Conscious**
**Civilized but Fragile**
**The Person I Own and Operate.**

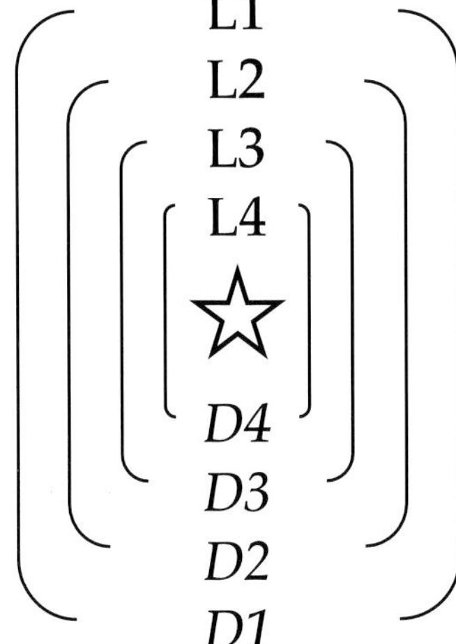


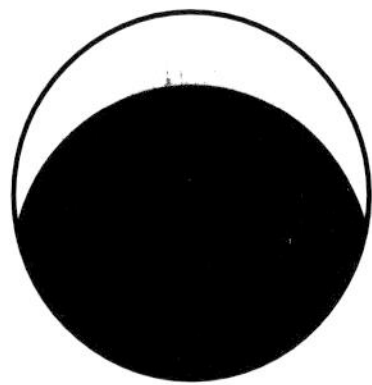

***The Person I Disown and Deny!***
***Uncivilized and Powerful***
***Unconscious***

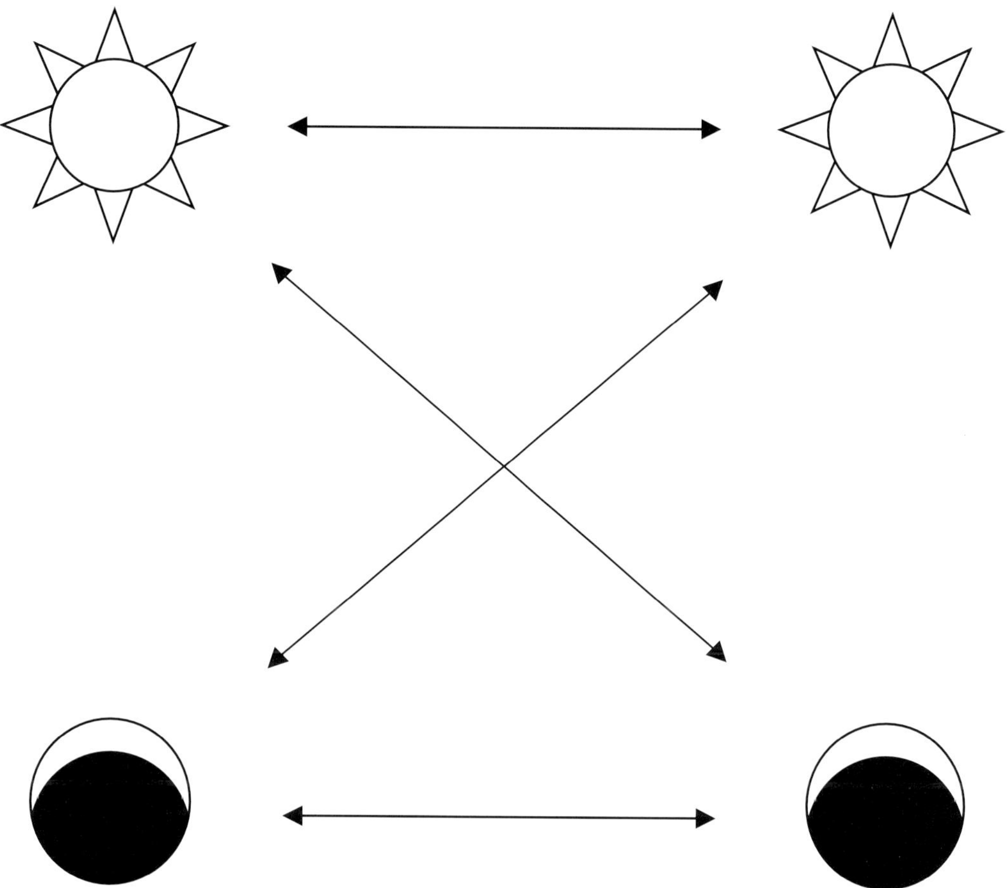

When two persons meet, four personalities greet.

# One Pebble in a Pond

## Global or Local

**The Four Global Talents and the Four Local Talents always ride opposite sides of the Four Ripples.**

## Four Ripple Pairs

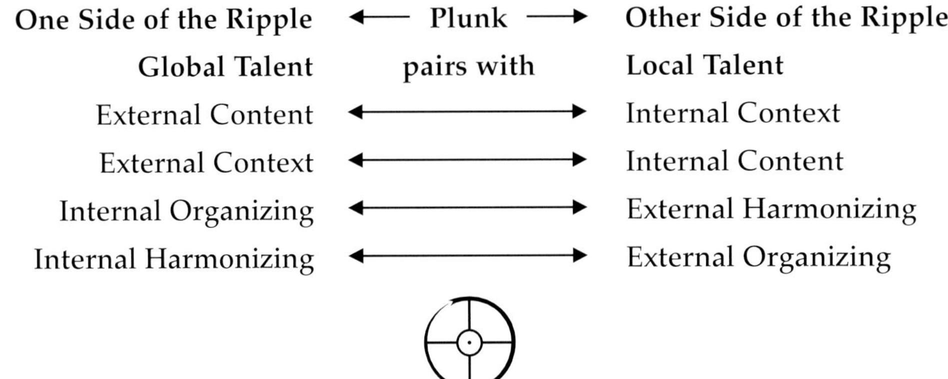

| One Side of the Ripple | ← Plunk → | Other Side of the Ripple |
|---|---|---|
| **Global Talent** | **pairs with** | **Local Talent** |
| External Content | ↔ | Internal Context |
| External Context | ↔ | Internal Content |
| Internal Organizing | ↔ | External Harmonizing |
| Internal Harmonizing | ↔ | External Organizing |

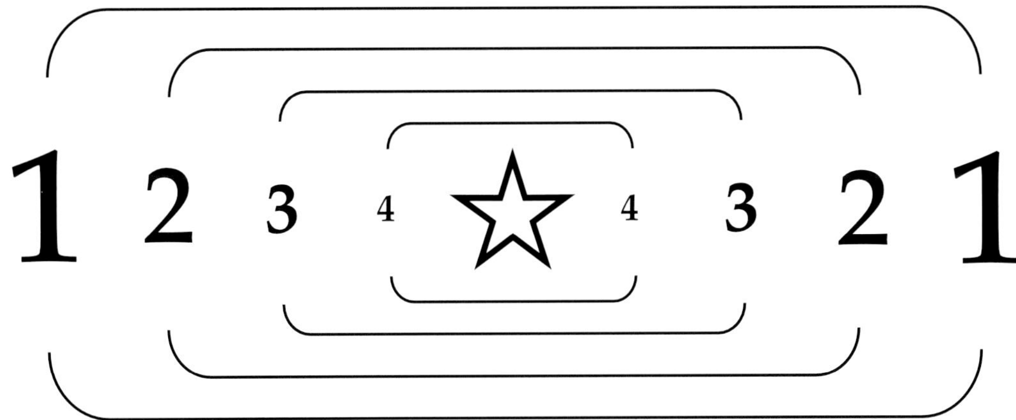

## Global or Local

Global Talents expand and Local Talents contract. Global Talents open perception and refine decisions. Local Talents close perception and confine decisions. It is impossible to Globalize and Localize at the same time. Nothing in nature expands while contracting, opens while closing, rises while falling, warms while cooling, or hardens while softening. Nature always alternates between opposites, like day and night. We know this just by listening to our heart, taking a breath, and opening our eyes.

The more we own and operate our Light Side, the more we disown and deny our Dark Side. We develop our Four Light Talents and neglect our Four Dark Talents for the same reason that we develop one hand and neglect the other. Magicians naturally develop the Four Global Talents and neglect the Four Local Talents. Rulers naturally develop the Four Local Talents and neglect the Four Global Talents. In summary, Magicians naturally Globalize and Rulers naturally Localize.

Every Magician hides a Ruler in the Dark, and every Ruler hides a Magician in the Dark. Together, our Light Side and Dark Side counterbalance each other like day and night. One side cannot exist without the other side any more than we can have day without night. It takes two to ride a seesaw. Coins have two sides. Ripples have two sides. And humans have two sides.

# One Pebble in a Pond

## External or Internal

| Styles 2 & 3 | | Styles 1 & 4 |
|---|---|---|
| External Attitude | Light Side | Internal Attitude |
| External | **L1** | Internal |
| Internal | L2 | External |
| Internal | L3 | External |
| External | L4 | Internal |
| ↑ **Plunk** ↓ | Mirror<br>One neglects to reflect clearly, and one merely reflects neglect.<br>*Mirror!* | ↑ **Plunk** ↓ |
| *Internal!* | *D4* | *External!* |
| *External!* | *D3* | *Internal!* |
| *External!* | *D2* | *Internal!* |
| *Internal!* | ***D1*** | *External!* |
| *Internal Attitude* | *Dark Side* | *External Attitude* |

## External or Internal

On both our Light Side and our Dark Side, two Talents of the same Attitude are always sandwiched between two Talents of the opposite Attitude. Our Light Side takes the Attitude of Talent L1, and our Dark Side takes the Attitude of Talent D1.

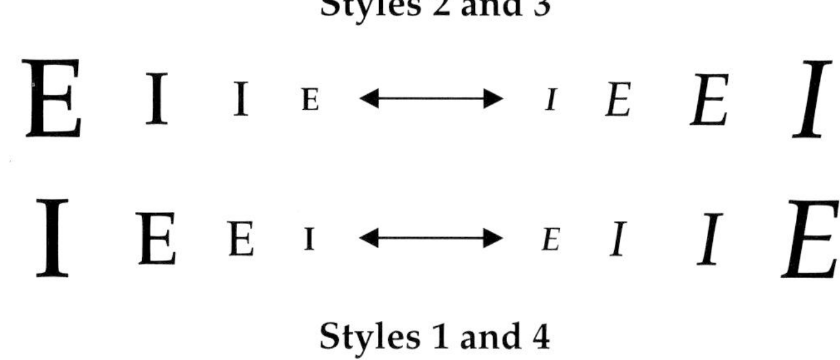


On the Ripples ride the opposite Attitudes
of our Light Side and our Dark Side.
In. Out.
*Out! In!*
Gratitudes to Jekyll
and the person I Hyde.

# One Pebble in a Pond

## Perceiving or Deciding

| Style 2 & 3 Magicians<br>Style 1 & 4 Rulers | | Style 2 & 3 Rulers<br>Style 1 & 4 Magicians |
|---|---|---|
| Most Natural Talents | | Most Natural Talents |
| Perceive | L1 | Decide |
| Decide | L2 | Perceive |
| Decide | L3 | Perceive |
| Perceive | L4 | Decide |
| ↑ **Plunk** ↓ | | ↑ **Plunk** ↓ |
| *Perceive!* | *D4* | *Decide!* |
| *Decide!* | *D3* | *Perceive!* |
| *Decide!* | *D2* | *Perceive!* |
| *Perceive!* | *D1* | *Decide!* |
| *Least Natural Talents* | | *Least Natural Talents* |

## Perceiving or Deciding

P D D P ⟷ *P D D P*

**or**

D P P D ⟷ *D P P D*

We have two kinds of Talents: Perceiving and Deciding. On both our Light Side and our Dark Side, two Talents of the same kind are always sandwiched between two Talents of the opposite kind. Specifically, Ripples 1 and 4 carry the same kind of Talents, and Ripples 2 and 3 carry the same kind of Talents.

Our Global Side points two Perceiving Talents *out* and two Deciding Talents *in*. Our Local Side points two Perceiving Talents *in* and two Deciding Talents *out*. To switch from our Light Talents to our Dark Talents, we must reverse our direction 180 degrees because our Dark Talents go in the opposite direction of our Light Talents. We resist using our Dark Talents just as we resist using our opposite hand because both seem to go against our natural direction.

L1 L2 L3 L4 ⟷ *D4 D3 D2 D1*

On the Ripples ride our most and our least,
what we pride and what we hide,
our boast and our beast.
Mirror.
*Mirror!*
Closer and Closer.
Clearer and Clearer.

## The Tyrant Above in the Boat

Talent L1 captains our Boat on the Sea as our most powerful Talent. However, as power corrupts, Talent L1 soon becomes Tyrant L1. Fortunately, our Light Side has a system of checks and balances to avoid the absolute tyranny of Tyrant L1. In short, Talents L1 and L4 steer the boat as Captain and Co-Captain, while Talents L2 and L3 manage the boat as Co-Navigators. Our Four Light Talents keep us afloat upon the Sea without mutiny and usually heading on a safe course around the rocks and through the storms toward our destinations.

**The Co-Captain Checks the Tyrant.** L4 can check (restrain) the power of L1 because both Talents are always of the same kind and Attitude. L1 and L4 both grip the boat's steering wheel. When L1 steers excessively one way, L4 steers the other way.

L1–External Perceiving is checked by an External Perceiving Talent at L4.

L1–Internal Deciding is checked by an Internal Deciding Talent at L4.

L1–Internal Perceiving is checked by an Internal Perceiving Talent at L4.

L1–External Deciding is checked by an External Deciding Talent at L4.

**The Co-Navigators Balance the Tyrant.** As Co-Navigators, L2 and L3 can balance the power of L1 because both oppose L1 in kind and Attitude.

L1–External Perceiving is balanced by Internal Deciding Talents at L2 and L3.

L1–Internal Deciding is balanced by External Perceiving Talents at L2 and L3.

L1–Internal Perceiving is balanced by External Deciding Talents at L2 and L3.

L1–External Deciding is balanced by Internal Perceiving Talents at L2 and L3.

## The Rebel Below in the Sea

While Talent L1 develops into a powerful but intolerant Tyrant above, Talent D1 swells into a massive and mysterious Rebel below. The Sea is the natural home of the Rebel and all Four Dark Talents. The Dark Talents remain forever loyal to the Sea because they draw their power from the Sea. While the Rebel always remains too large to be lifted from the Sea, Talents D2, D3, and D4 can be lifted from the Sea because they live closer to the surface. However, our Four Dark Talents always retain their affinity with the Dark, just as our Four Light Talents always retain their affinity with the Light.

Tyrants and rebels are neither good nor bad. The first tyrants sowed the seeds of democracy, and many of the world's greatest accomplishments have been the work of rebels. Our Tyrant and our Rebel both have great potential as our two most powerful Talents, but only if we learn to give them equal respect.

The Rebel surfaces from the depths of the Sea with vital messages. To our Tyrant, the Rebel appears as an enemy. Our Tyrant fears that the Rebel will sink the Boat. In truth, the Rebel has no desire to sink the Boat. Rather, the Rebel just needs to be heard. The Rebel will deliver its messages gently if the Tyrant will hold still and listen carefully. If not, then the Rebel has no choice but to explode through the surface of the water like a wounded whale and demand to be heard.

The Rebel appears to be a troublemaker because it is so disruptive and its goal so well hidden. However, our Tyrant, with its thirst for absolute power, creates the most problems. The more our Tyrant struggles to control the rebellion brewing below, the more tension builds between our Light Side and Dark Side. Rather than listening to the Rebel, we usually try to press it back down into the Sea. When repression fails, we project our Dark Side onto the external world. We project everything that we are afraid to own. We worship heroes and other objects because owning our positive qualities is even harder than owning our negative qualities. However, projection only delays the conflicts between our Tyrant and our Rebel that are necessary to revitalize and balance our personality.

Note: A small image of the Rebel (Talent D1) for each of the Sixteen Personality Types appears on the Symbol Cards and Icon Cards shown in Part IV.

Above, in the Boat, lives the person that I know, the person I own and operate. Mostly a product of my culture, my Light Side is civilized but fragile. The Light illuminates my social purpose and identity, and provides the mask that I wear to survive in the external world.

*Below, in the Dark Sea, lives the person that I do not know, the person I disown and deny! The Dark Sea hides everything that I have no wish to be. Uncivilized, the Dark Sea is fluid, deep, and powerful. Everything blends together in a mysterious, but purposeful swirl. I have no conscious knowledge or control over anything in the Dark Sea because I cannot distinguish one thing from another. I share the Dark Sea – the Original Source – with all humanity.*

**Magicians naturally develop the Four Global Talents and neglect the Four Local Talents. Magicians have two sides: a Light Side Magician and a Dark Side Ruler.**

| **Conscious** | **Civilized Magician** | **Light** |
|---|---|---|
| L1 | Global Talent | |
| L2 | Global Talent | |
| L3 | Global Talent | |
| L4 | Global Talent | |
| **Middle** | **Center** | **Balance** |
| *D4* | *Local Talent!* | |
| *D3* | *Local Talent!* | |
| *D2* | *Local Talent!* | |
| *D1* | *Local Talent!* | |
| ***Unconscious*** | ***Uncivilized Ruler*** | ***Dark*** |

| **Conscious** | **Civilized Ruler** | **Light** |
|---|---|---|
| L1 | Local Talent | |
| L2 | Local Talent | |
| L3 | Local Talent | |
| L4 | Local Talent | |
| **Middle** | **Center** | **Balance** |
| *D4* | *Global Talent!* | |
| *D3* | *Global Talent!* | |
| *D2* | *Global Talent!* | |
| *D1* | *Global Talent!* | |
| ***Unconscious*** | ***Uncivilized Magician*** | ***Dark*** |

**Rulers have two sides: a Light Side Ruler and a Dark Side Magician. Rulers naturally develop the Four Local Talents and neglect the Four Global Talents.**

The Pictures of Personality™

# Map of the Four Natures

| | | Context | | Content | |
|---|---|---|---|---|---|
| | | **Indirect** | **Direct** | **Indirect** | **Direct** |
| **Confidence** | **External** | **CLARIFIER 2**<br>**Magician of the Unknown**<br>External Context<br>Internal Organizing<br>Internal Harmonizing<br>External Content<br>*Internal Context*<br>*External Organizing*<br>*External Harmonizing*<br>*Internal Content* | **CLARIFIER 3**<br>**Ruler of the Future**<br>External Organizing<br>Internal Context<br>Internal Content<br>External Harmonizing<br>*Internal Organizing*<br>*External Context*<br>*External Content*<br>*Internal Harmonizing* | **ACTIVATOR 2**<br>**Magician of the Known**<br>External Content<br>Internal Harmonizing<br>Internal Organizing<br>External Context<br>*Internal Content*<br>*External Harmonizing*<br>*External Organizing*<br>*Internal Context* | **ACTIVATOR 3**<br>**Magician of the Known**<br>External Content<br>Internal Organizing<br>Internal Harmonizing<br>External Context<br>*Internal Content*<br>*External Organizing*<br>*External Harmonizing*<br>*Internal Context* |
| **Confidence** | **Internal** | **CLARIFIER 1**<br>**Magician of the Unknown**<br>Internal Organizing<br>External Context<br>External Content<br>Internal Harmonizing<br>*External Organizing*<br>*Internal Context*<br>*Internal Content*<br>*External Harmonizing* | **CLARIFIER 4**<br>**Ruler of the Future**<br>Internal Context<br>External Organizing<br>External Harmonizing<br>Internal Content<br>*External Context*<br>*Internal Organizing*<br>*Internal Harmonizing*<br>*External Content* | **ACTIVATOR 1**<br>**Magician of the Known**<br>Internal Harmonizing<br>External Content<br>External Context<br>Internal Organizing<br>*External Harmonizing*<br>*Internal Content*<br>*Internal Context*<br>*External Organizing* | **ACTIVATOR 4**<br>**Magician of the Known**<br>Internal Organizing<br>External Content<br>External Context<br>Internal Harmonizing<br>*External Organizing*<br>*Internal Content*<br>*Internal Context*<br>*External Harmonizing* |
| **Trust** | **External** | **UNIFIER 2**<br>**Magician of the Unknown**<br>External Context<br>Internal Harmonizing<br>Internal Organizing<br>External Content<br>*Internal Context*<br>*External Harmonizing*<br>*External Organizing*<br>*Internal Content* | **UNIFIER 3**<br>**Ruler of the Future**<br>External Harmonizing<br>Internal Context<br>Internal Content<br>External Organizing<br>*Internal Harmonizing*<br>*External Context*<br>*External Content*<br>*Internal Organizing* | **STABILIZER 2**<br>**Ruler of the Past**<br>External Harmonizing<br>Internal Content<br>Internal Context<br>External Organizing<br>*Internal Harmonizing*<br>*External Content*<br>*External Context*<br>*Internal Organizing* | **STABILIZER 3**<br>**Ruler of the Past**<br>External Organizing<br>Internal Content<br>Internal Context<br>External Harmonizing<br>*Internal Organizing*<br>*External Content*<br>*External Context*<br>*Internal Harmonizing* |
| **Trust** | **Internal** | **UNIFIER 1**<br>**Magician of the Unknown**<br>Internal Harmonizing<br>External Context<br>External Content<br>Internal Organizing<br>*External Harmonizing*<br>*Internal Context*<br>*Internal Content*<br>*External Organizing* | **UNIFIER 4**<br>**Ruler of the Future**<br>Internal Context<br>External Harmonizing<br>External Organizing<br>Internal Content<br>*External Context*<br>*Internal Harmonizing*<br>*Internal Organizing*<br>*External Content* | **STABILIZER 1**<br>**Ruler of the Past**<br>Internal Content<br>External Harmonizing<br>External Organizing<br>Internal Context<br>*External Content*<br>*Internal Harmonizing*<br>*Internal Organizing*<br>*External Context* | **STABILIZER 4**<br>**Ruler of the Past**<br>Internal Content<br>External Organizing<br>External Harmonizing<br>Internal Context<br>*External Content*<br>*Internal Organizing*<br>*Internal Harmonizing*<br>*External Context* |

The Pictures of Personality™

# Map of the Four Natures

| | | Context | | Content | |
|---|---|---|---|---|---|
| | | **Indirect** | **Direct** | **Indirect** | **Direct** |
| **Confidence** | **External** | **CLARIFIER 2**<br>**Magician of the Unknown**<br>The Novel: Options<br>My Ideas: Precision<br>My Ideals: Perfection<br>The Actual: Attention<br>*My Plans: Anticipation*<br>*The Methods: Causation*<br>*The Customs: Relations*<br>*My Priorities: Continuation* | **CLARIFIER 3**<br>**Ruler of the Future**<br>The Methods: Causation<br>My Plans: Anticipation<br>My Priorities: Continuation<br>The Customs: Relations<br>*My Ideas: Precision*<br>*The Novel: Options*<br>*The Actual: Attention*<br>*My Ideals: Perfection* | **ACTIVATOR 2**<br>**Magician of the Known**<br>The Actual: Attention<br>My Ideals: Perfection<br>My Ideas: Precision<br>The Novel: Options<br>*My Priorities: Continuation*<br>*The Customs: Relations*<br>*The Methods: Causation*<br>*My Plans: Anticipation* | **ACTIVATOR 3**<br>**Magician of the Known**<br>The Actual: Attention<br>My Ideas: Precision<br>My Ideals: Perfection<br>The Novel: Options<br>*My Priorities: Continuation*<br>*The Methods: Causation*<br>*The Customs: Relations*<br>*My Plans: Anticipation* |
| **Confidence** | **Internal** | **CLARIFIER 1**<br>**Magician of the Unknown**<br>My Ideas: Precision<br>The Novel: Options<br>The Actual: Attention<br>My Ideals: Perfection<br>*The Methods: Causation*<br>*My Plans: Anticipation*<br>*My Priorities: Continuation*<br>*The Customs: Relations* | **CLARIFIER 4**<br>**Ruler of the Future**<br>My Plans: Anticipation<br>The Methods: Causation<br>The Customs: Relations<br>My Priorities: Continuation<br>*The Novel: Options*<br>*My Ideas: Precision*<br>*My Ideals: Perfection*<br>*The Actual: Attention* | **ACTIVATOR 1**<br>**Magician of the Known**<br>My Ideals: Perfection<br>The Actual: Attention<br>The Novel: Options<br>My Ideas: Precision<br>*The Customs: Relations*<br>*My Priorities: Continuation*<br>*My Plans: Anticipation*<br>*The Methods: Causation* | **ACTIVATOR 4**<br>**Magician of the Known**<br>My Ideas: Precision<br>The Actual: Attention<br>The Novel: Options<br>My Ideals: Perfection<br>*The Methods: Causation*<br>*My Priorities: Continuation*<br>*My Plans: Anticipation*<br>*The Customs: Relations* |
| **Trust** | **External** | **UNIFIER 2**<br>**Magician of the Unknown**<br>The Novel: Options<br>My Ideals: Perfection<br>My Ideas: Precision<br>The Actual: Attention<br>*My Plans: Anticipation*<br>*The Customs: Relations*<br>*The Methods: Causation*<br>*My Priorities: Continuation* | **UNIFIER 3**<br>**Ruler of the Future**<br>The Customs: Relations<br>My Plans: Anticipation<br>My Priorities: Continuation<br>The Methods: Causation<br>*My Ideals: Perfection*<br>*The Novel: Options*<br>*The Actual: Attention*<br>*My Ideas: Precision* | **STABILIZER 2**<br>**Ruler of the Past**<br>The Customs: Relations<br>My Priorities: Continuation<br>My Plans: Anticipation<br>The Methods: Causation<br>*My Ideals: Perfection*<br>*The Actual: Attention*<br>*The Novel: Options*<br>*My Ideas: Precision* | **STABILIZER 3**<br>**Ruler of the Past**<br>The Methods: Causation<br>My Priorities: Continuation<br>My Plans: Anticipation<br>The Customs: Relations<br>*My Ideas: Precision*<br>*The Actual: Attention*<br>*The Novel: Options*<br>*My Ideals: Perfection* |
| **Trust** | **Internal** | **UNIFIER 1**<br>**Magician of the Unknown**<br>My Ideals: Perfection<br>The Novel: Options<br>The Actual: Attention<br>My Ideas: Precision<br>*The Customs: Relations*<br>*My Plans: Anticipation*<br>*My Priorities: Continuation*<br>*The Methods: Causation* | **UNIFIER 4**<br>**Ruler of the Future**<br>My Plans: Anticipation<br>The Customs: Relations<br>The Methods: Causation<br>My Priorities: Continuation<br>*The Novel: Options*<br>*My Ideals: Perfection*<br>*My Ideas: Precision*<br>*The Actual: Attention* | **STABILIZER 1**<br>**Ruler of the Past**<br>My Priorities: Continuation<br>The Customs: Relations<br>The Methods: Causation<br>My Plans: Anticipation<br>*The Actual: Attention*<br>*My Ideals: Perfection*<br>*My Ideas: Precision*<br>*The Novel: Options* | **STABILIZER 4**<br>**Ruler of the Past**<br>My Priorities: Continuation<br>The Methods: Causation<br>The Customs: Relations<br>My Plans: Anticipation<br>*The Actual: Attention*<br>*My Ideas: Precision*<br>*My Ideals: Perfection*<br>*The Novel: Options* |

The Pictures of Personality™

# Map of the Four Realms

| | | Context | | Content | |
|---|---|---|---|---|---|
| | | Harmonize | Organize | Harmonize | Organize |
| Globalize | External | **UNIFIER 2**<br>**Magician of the Unknown**<br>External Context<br>Internal Harmonizing<br>Internal Organizing<br>External Content<br>*Internal Context*<br>*External Harmonizing*<br>*External Organizing*<br>*Internal Content* | **CLARIFIER 2**<br>**Magician of the Unknown**<br>External Context<br>Internal Organizing<br>Internal Harmonizing<br>External Content<br>*Internal Context*<br>*External Organizing*<br>*External Harmonizing*<br>*Internal Content* | **ACTIVATOR 2**<br>**Magician of the Known**<br>External Content<br>Internal Harmonizing<br>Internal Organizing<br>External Context<br>*Internal Content*<br>*External Harmonizing*<br>*External Organizing*<br>*Internal Context* | **ACTIVATOR 3**<br>**Magician of the Known**<br>External Content<br>Internal Organizing<br>Internal Harmonizing<br>External Context<br>*Internal Content*<br>*External Organizing*<br>*External Harmonizing*<br>*Internal Context* |
| Globalize | Internal | **UNIFIER 1**<br>**Magician of the Unknown**<br>Internal Harmonizing<br>External Context<br>External Content<br>Internal Organizing<br>*External Harmonizing*<br>*Internal Context*<br>*Internal Content*<br>*External Organizing* | **CLARIFIER 1**<br>**Magician of the Unknown**<br>Internal Organizing<br>External Context<br>External Content<br>Internal Harmonizing<br>*External Organizing*<br>*Internal Context*<br>*Internal Content*<br>*External Harmonizing* | **ACTIVATOR 1**<br>**Magician of the Known**<br>Internal Harmonizing<br>External Content<br>External Context<br>Internal Organizing<br>*External Harmonizing*<br>*Internal Content*<br>*Internal Context*<br>*External Organizing* | **ACTIVATOR 4**<br>**Magician of the Known**<br>Internal Organizing<br>External Content<br>External Context<br>Internal Harmonizing<br>*External Organizing*<br>*Internal Content*<br>*Internal Context*<br>*External Harmonizing* |
| Localize | External | **UNIFIER 3**<br>**Ruler of the Future**<br>External Harmonizing<br>Internal Context<br>Internal Content<br>External Organizing<br>*Internal Harmonizing*<br>*External Context*<br>*External Content*<br>*Internal Organizing* | **CLARIFIER 3**<br>**Ruler of the Future**<br>External Organizing<br>Internal Context<br>Internal Content<br>External Harmonizing<br>*Internal Organizing*<br>*External Context*<br>*External Content*<br>*Internal Harmonizing* | **STABILIZER 2**<br>**Ruler of the Past**<br>External Harmonizing<br>Internal Content<br>Internal Context<br>External Organizing<br>*Internal Harmonizing*<br>*External Content*<br>*External Context*<br>*Internal Organizing* | **STABILIZER 3**<br>**Ruler of the Past**<br>External Organizing<br>Internal Content<br>Internal Context<br>External Harmonizing<br>*Internal Organizing*<br>*External Content*<br>*External Context*<br>*Internal Harmonizing* |
| Localize | Internal | **UNIFIER 4**<br>**Ruler of the Future**<br>Internal Context<br>External Harmonizing<br>External Organizing<br>Internal Content<br>*External Context*<br>*Internal Harmonizing*<br>*Internal Organizing*<br>*External Content* | **CLARIFIER 4**<br>**Ruler of the Future**<br>Internal Context<br>External Organizing<br>External Harmonizing<br>Internal Content<br>*External Context*<br>*Internal Organizing*<br>*Internal Harmonizing*<br>*External Content* | **STABILIZER 1**<br>**Ruler of the Past**<br>Internal Content<br>External Harmonizing<br>External Organizing<br>Internal Context<br>*External Content*<br>*Internal Harmonizing*<br>*Internal Organizing*<br>*External Context* | **STABILIZER 4**<br>**Ruler of the Past**<br>Internal Content<br>External Organizing<br>External Harmonizing<br>Internal Context<br>*External Content*<br>*Internal Organizing*<br>*Internal Harmonizing*<br>*External Context* |

The Pictures of Personality™

# Map of the Four Realms

| | | Context | | Content | |
|---|---|---|---|---|---|
| | | **Harmonize** | **Organize** | **Harmonize** | **Organize** |
| **Globalize** | **External** | **UNIFIER 2**<br>**Magician of the Unknown**<br>The Novel: Options<br>My Ideals: Perfection<br>My Ideas: Precision<br>The Actual: Attention<br>*My Plans: Anticipation*<br>*The Customs: Relations*<br>*The Methods: Causation*<br>*My Priorities: Continuation* | **CLARIFIER 2**<br>**Magician of the Unknown**<br>The Novel: Options<br>My Ideas: Precision<br>My Ideals: Perfection<br>The Actual: Attention<br>*My Plans: Anticipation*<br>*The Methods: Causation*<br>*The Customs: Relations*<br>*My Priorities: Continuation* | **ACTIVATOR 2**<br>**Magician of the Known**<br>The Actual: Attention<br>My Ideals: Perfection<br>My Ideas: Precision<br>The Novel: Options<br>*My Priorities: Continuation*<br>*The Customs: Relations*<br>*The Methods: Causation*<br>*My Plans: Anticipation* | **ACTIVATOR 3**<br>**Magician of the Known**<br>The Actual: Attention<br>My Ideas: Precision<br>My Ideals: Perfection<br>The Novel: Options<br>*My Priorities: Continuation*<br>*The Methods: Causation*<br>*The Customs: Relations*<br>*My Plans: Anticipation* |
| | **Internal** | **UNIFIER 1**<br>**Magician of the Unknown**<br>My Ideals: Perfection<br>The Novel: Options<br>The Actual: Attention<br>My Ideas: Precision<br>*The Customs: Relations*<br>*My Plans: Anticipation*<br>*My Priorities: Continuation*<br>*The Methods: Causation* | **CLARIFIER 1**<br>**Magician of the Unknown**<br>My Ideas: Precision<br>The Novel: Options<br>The Actual: Attention<br>My Ideals: Perfection<br>*The Methods: Causation*<br>*My Plans: Anticipation*<br>*My Priorities: Continuation*<br>*The Customs: Relations* | **ACTIVATOR 1**<br>**Magician of the Known**<br>My Ideals: Perfection<br>The Actual: Attention<br>The Novel: Options<br>My Ideas: Precision<br>*The Customs: Relations*<br>*My Priorities: Continuation*<br>*My Plans: Anticipation*<br>*The Methods: Causation* | **ACTIVATOR 4**<br>**Magician of the Known**<br>My Ideas: Precision<br>The Actual: Attention<br>The Novel: Options<br>My Ideals: Perfection<br>*The Methods: Causation*<br>*My Priorities: Continuation*<br>*My Plans: Anticipation*<br>*The Customs: Relations* |
| **Localize** | **External** | **UNIFIER 3**<br>**Ruler of the Future**<br>The Customs: Relations<br>My Plans: Anticipation<br>My Priorities: Continuation<br>The Methods: Causation<br>*My Ideals: Perfection*<br>*The Novel: Options*<br>*The Actual: Attention*<br>*My Ideas: Precision* | **CLARIFIER 3**<br>**Ruler of the Future**<br>The Methods: Causation<br>My Plans: Anticipation<br>My Priorities: Continuation<br>The Customs: Relations<br>*My Ideas: Precision*<br>*The Novel: Options*<br>*The Actual: Attention*<br>*My Ideals: Perfection* | **STABILIZER 2**<br>**Ruler of the Past**<br>The Customs: Relations<br>My Priorities: Continuation<br>My Plans: Anticipation<br>The Methods: Causation<br>*My Ideals: Perfection*<br>*The Actual: Attention*<br>*The Novel: Options*<br>*My Ideas: Precision* | **STABILIZER 3**<br>**Ruler of the Past**<br>The Methods: Causation<br>My Priorities: Continuation<br>My Plans: Anticipation<br>The Customs: Relations<br>*My Ideas: Precision*<br>*The Actual: Attention*<br>*The Novel: Options*<br>*My Ideals: Perfection* |
| | **Internal** | **UNIFIER 4**<br>**Ruler of the Future**<br>My Plans: Anticipation<br>The Customs: Relations<br>The Methods: Causation<br>My Priorities: Continuation<br>*The Novel: Options*<br>*My Ideals: Perfection*<br>*My Ideas: Precision*<br>*The Actual: Attention* | **CLARIFIER 4**<br>**Ruler of the Future**<br>My Plans: Anticipation<br>The Methods: Causation<br>The Customs: Relations<br>My Priorities: Continuation<br>*The Novel: Options*<br>*My Ideas: Precision*<br>*My Ideals: Perfection*<br>*The Actual: Attention* | **STABILIZER 1**<br>**Ruler of the Past**<br>My Priorities: Continuation<br>The Customs: Relations<br>The Methods: Causation<br>My Plans: Anticipation<br>*The Actual: Attention*<br>*My Ideals: Perfection*<br>*My Ideas: Precision*<br>*The Novel: Options* | **STABILIZER 4**<br>**Ruler of the Past**<br>My Priorities: Continuation<br>The Methods: Causation<br>The Customs: Relations<br>My Plans: Anticipation<br>*The Actual: Attention*<br>*My Ideas: Precision*<br>*My Ideals: Perfection*<br>*The Novel: Options* |

## Magicians Globalize: Open Perception and Refine Decisions

| | | |
|---|---|---|
|  | **The Actual: Attention**<br>Experience the Object: External Content<br>I sense the actual *Content* of the present, experiencing everything with attention open to the known variables and emerging opportunities. | 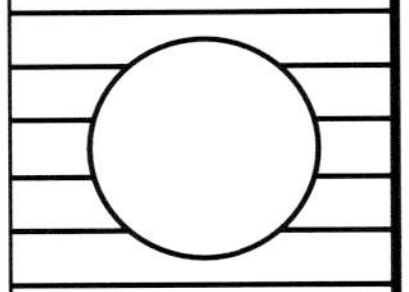 |
|  | **The Novel: Options**<br>Decipher the Object: External Context<br>I conceive the novel *Context* of the present, deciphering everything with awareness open to the unknown variables and evolving options. | 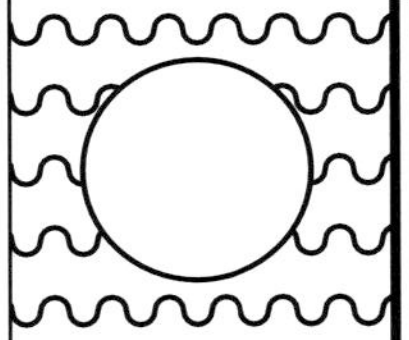 |
|  | **My Ideas: Precision**<br>My Subjective Contemplation: Internal Organizing<br>I *Organize* experientially, refining my ideas by my contemplation of natural logical principles and their precise expression. | 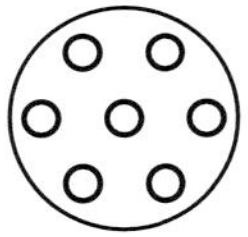 |
|  | **My Ideals: Perfection**<br>My Subjective Evaluation: Internal Harmonizing<br>I *Harmonize* experientially, refining my ideals by my evaluation of natural human values and their perfect expression. | 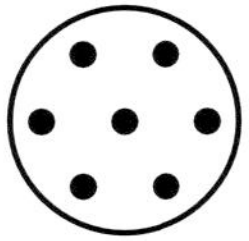 |

## The Four Global Talents

## Rulers Localize: Close Perception and Confine Decisions

| | | |
|---|---|---|
|  | **My Priorities: Continuation**<br>My Subjective Impressions: Internal Content<br>I sense past *Content*, my impressions of what was,<br>closing out all that does not support the continuation of my priorities. | 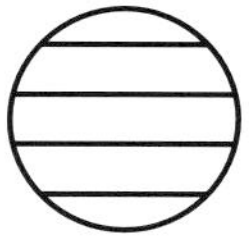 |
|  | **My Plans: Anticipation**<br>My Subjective Interpretations: Internal Context<br>I conceive future *Context*, my interpretations of what will be,<br>closing out all that does not comport with the anticipation of my plans. |  |
|  | **The Methods: Causation**<br>The Objective Formulas: External Organizing<br>I *Organize* systematically, confined to the methods and formulas<br>prescribed by the general rules of logical causation. | 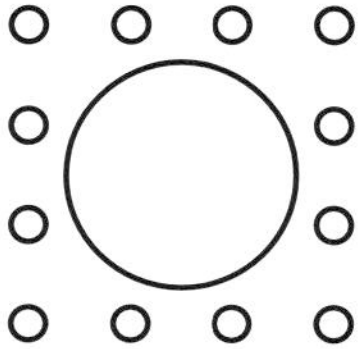 |
|  | **The Customs: Relations**<br>The Objective Conventions: External Harmonizing<br>I *Harmonize* systematically, confined to the customs and conventions<br>prescribed by the general rules of human relations. | 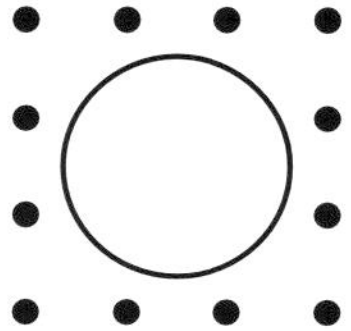 |

## The Four Local Talents

Our Light Side

Conscious • Civilized • Fragile

*Our Dark Side*

*Unconscious • Uncivilized • Powerful*

# PART IV

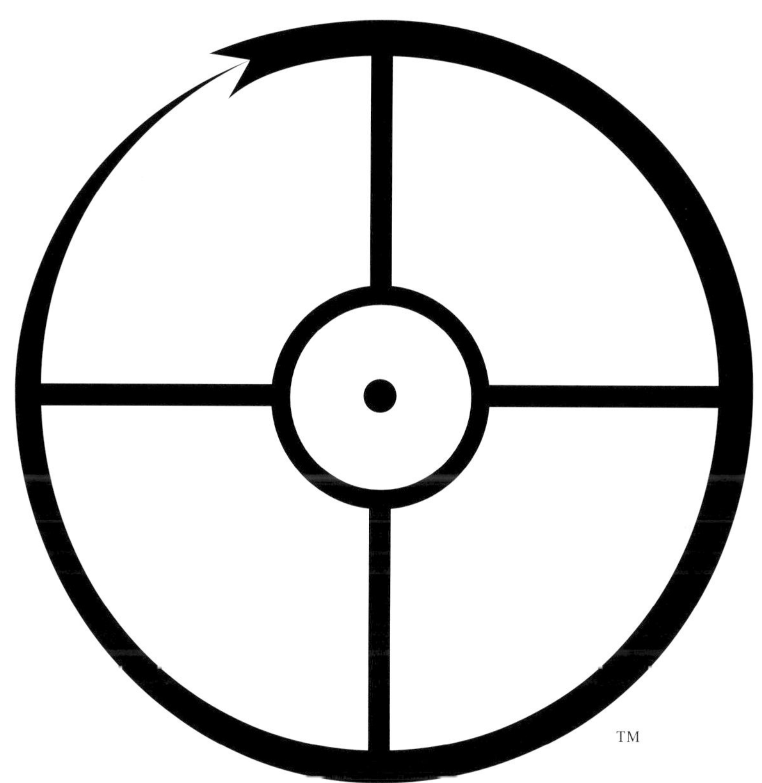


## The Sixteen Personality Types: Symbols and Icons

Nature

# Unifier

Water's Unity

Trust
"We can trust others."

Focus on Similarities
Adapts Diplomatically

Style

## Style 1

### Internal Attitude

Introversion

Subject Attraction
Conserves Energy and Contracts
Fascinated by Subjective World
Inner Directed and Internally Motivated
"The external world serves my internal world."

### Indirect Role

Indirection

Invites Interaction
Informs Others
Implicit Messages
Persuades and Promotes
Relatively Flexible Texture

Realm

## Magician of the Unknown

Variation
Global: The Whole
Simultaneous • Experiential
General to Specific • Whole to Parts
Opens Perception and Refines Decisions
The General Perception and My Specific Rules
What Cannot Be Described nor Prescribed: The Variables
Responds All at Once to the Whole Changing Present Situation

| **Global** | **Most Natural Talents** | **Light** |
|---|---|---|
| L1 | My Ideals: Perfection | |
| L2 | The Novel: Options | |
| L3 | The Actual: Attention | |
| L4 | My Ideas: Precision | |
| *D4* | *The Customs: Relations!* | |
| *D3* | *My Plans: Anticipation!* | |
| *D2* | *My Priorities: Continuation!* | |
| *D1* | *The Methods: Causation!* | |
| ***Local*** | ***Least Natural Talents*** | ***Dark*** |

Compass of Natures

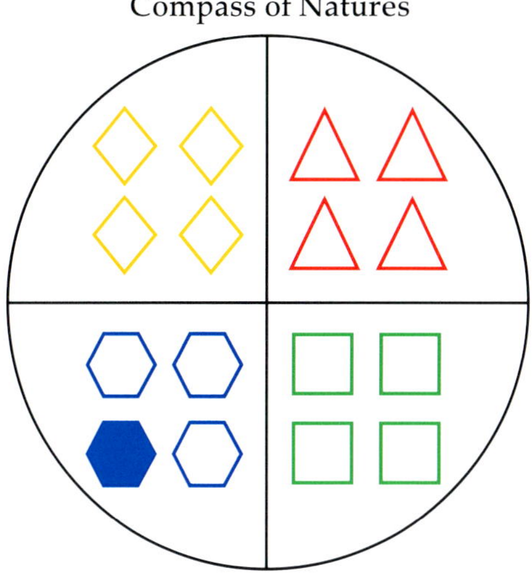

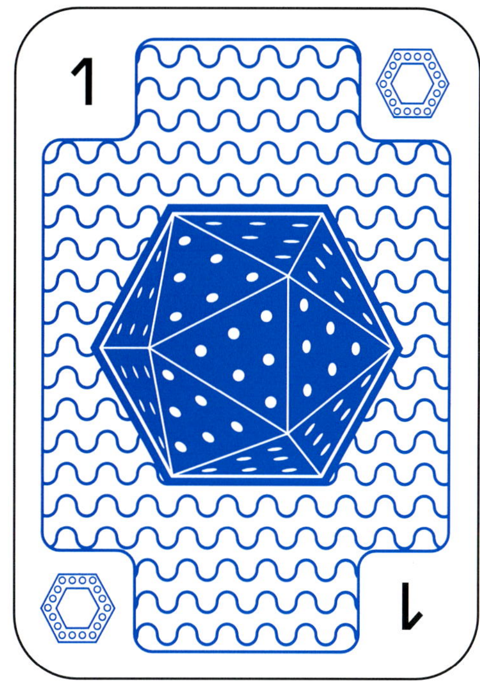


# Unifier 1
# Magician of the Unknown

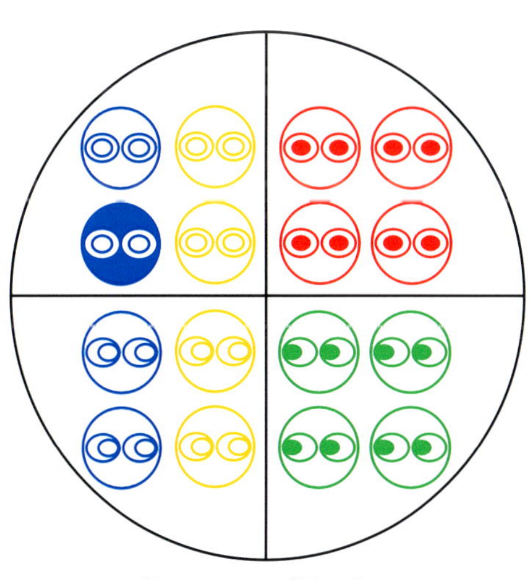

Compass of Realms

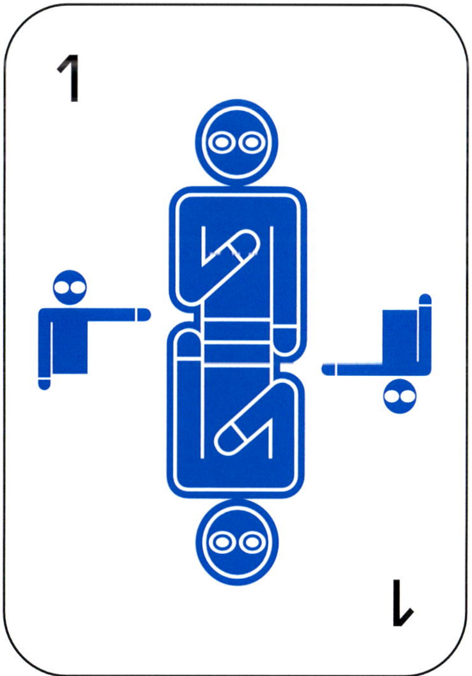

Nature

# Unifier

Water's Unity

Trust
"We can trust others."

Focus on Similarities
Adapts Diplomatically

Style

## Style 2

**External Attitude**
Extraversion

Object Attraction
Expends Energy and Expands
Fascinated by Objective World
Outer Directed and Externally Motivated
"My internal world serves the external world."

**Indirect Role**
Indirection

Invites Interaction
Informs Others
Implicit Messages
Persuades and Promotes
Relatively Flexible Texture

Realm

## Magician of the Unknown

Variation
Global: The Whole
Simultaneous • Experiential
General to Specific • Whole to Parts
Opens Perception and Refines Decisions
The General Perception and My Specific Rules
What Cannot Be Described nor Prescribed: The Variables
Responds All at Once to the Whole Changing Present Situation

| **Global** | **Most Natural Talents** | **Light** |
|---|---|---|
| L1 | The Novel: Options | |
| L2 | My Ideals: Perfection | |
| L3 | My Ideas: Precision | |
| L4 | The Actual: Attention | |
| *D4* | *My Plans: Anticipation!* | |
| *D3* | *The Customs: Relations!* | |
| *D2* | *The Methods: Causation!* | |
| *D1* | *My Priorities: Continuation!* | |
| ***Local*** | ***Least Natural Talents*** | ***Dark*** |

Compass of Natures

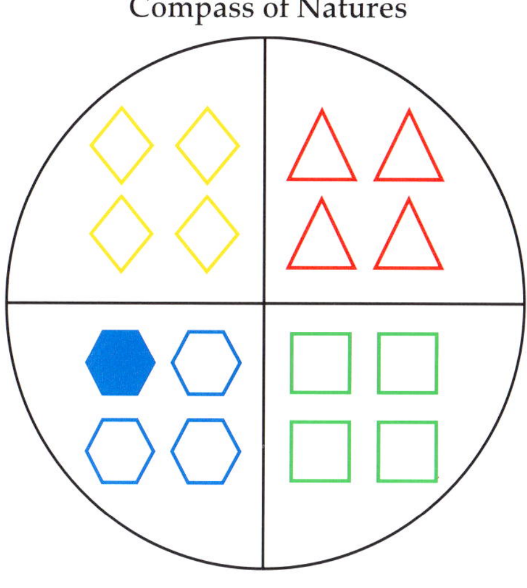

# Unifier 2
# Magician of the Unknown

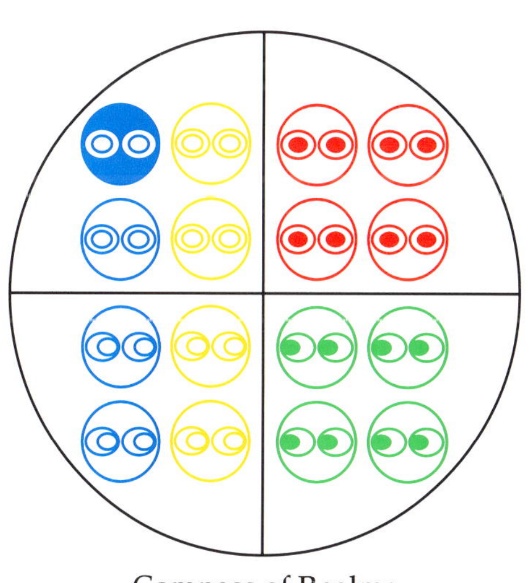

Compass of Realms

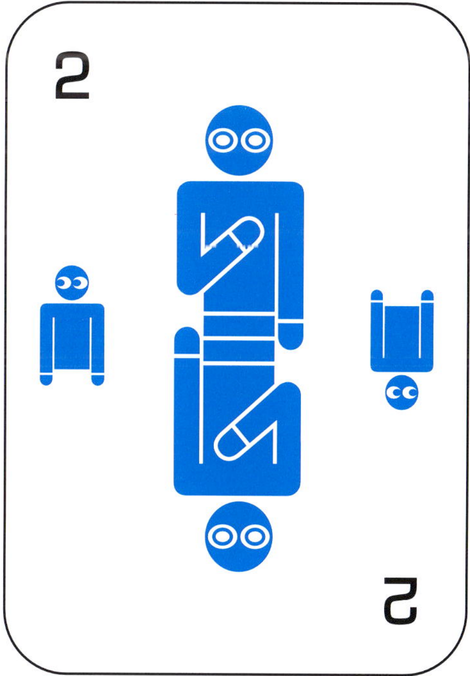

Nature

# Unifier

Water's Unity

Trust
"We can trust others."

Focus on Similarities
Adapts Diplomatically

Style

## Style 3

### External Attitude

Extraversion

Object Attraction
Expends Energy and Expands
Fascinated by Objective World
Outer Directed and Externally Motivated
"My internal world serves the external world."

### Direct Role

Direction

Directs Action
Instructs Others
Explicit Messages
Commands and Controls
Absolutely Firm Texture

Realm

## Ruler of the Future

Theme
Local: The Parts
Sequential • Systematic
Specific to General • Parts to Whole
Closes Perception and Confines Decisions
My Specific Perception and The General Rule
What Can Be Described and Prescribed: The Constants
Advances Step by Step, Part by Part, from My Past to My Future

| **Local** | **Most Natural Talents** | **Light** |
|---|---|---|
| L1 | The Customs: Relations | |
| L2 | My Plans: Anticipation | |
| L3 | My Priorities: Continuation | |
| L4 | The Methods: Causation | |
| *D4* | *My Ideals: Perfection!* | |
| *D3* | *The Novel: Options!* | |
| *D2* | *The Actual: Attention!* | |
| *D1* | *My Ideas: Precision!* | |
| ***Global*** | ***Least Natural Talents*** | ***Dark*** |

Compass of Natures

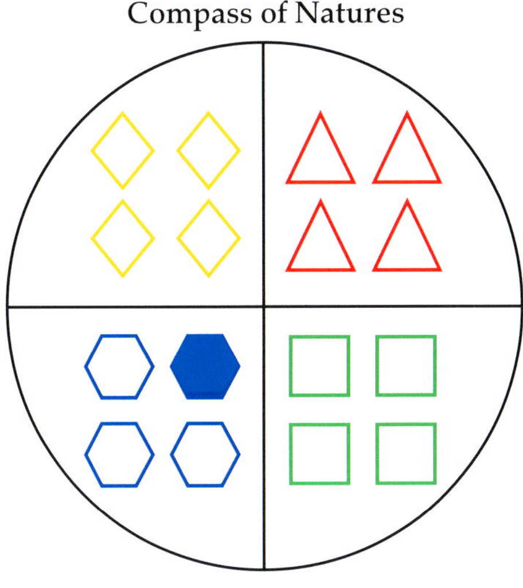

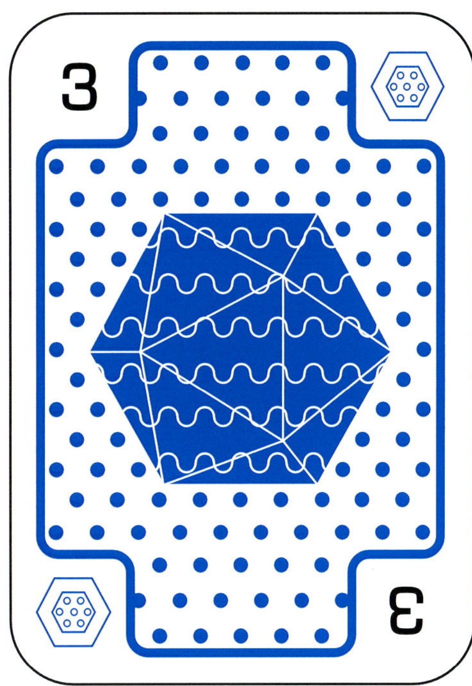


# Unifier 3
# Ruler of the Future

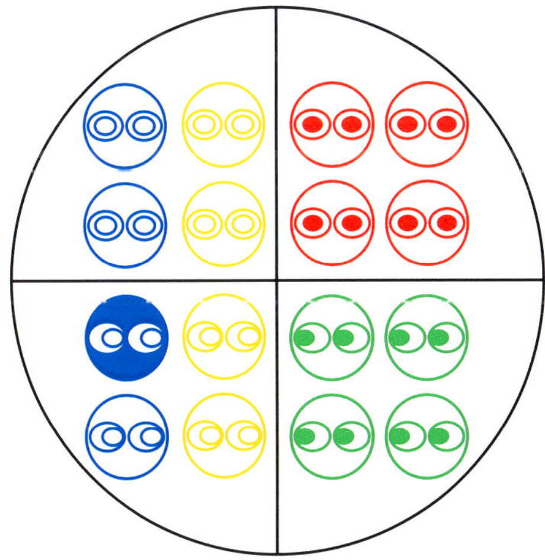

Compass of Realms

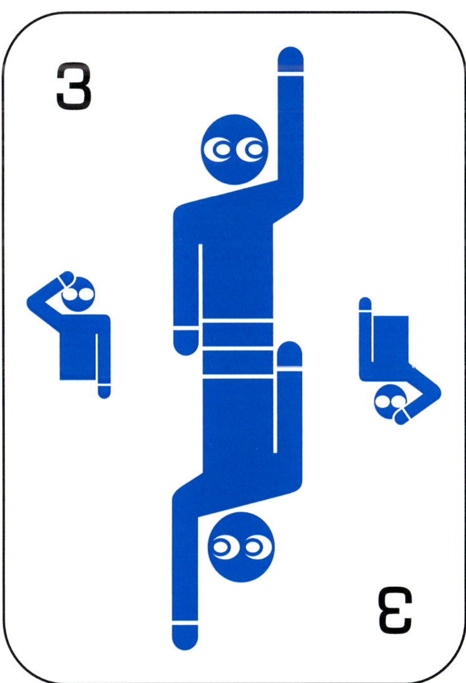

Nature

# Unifier

Water's Unity

Trust
"We can trust others."

Focus on Similarities
Adapts Diplomatically

Style

## Style 4

**Internal Attitude**
Introversion

Subject Attraction
Conserves Energy and Contracts
Fascinated by Subjective World
Inner Directed and Internally Motivated
"The external world serves my internal world."

**Direct Role**
Direction

Directs Action
Instructs Others
Explicit Messages
Commands and Controls
Absolutely Firm Texture

Realm

## Ruler of the Future

Theme
Local: The Parts
Sequential • Systematic
Specific to General • Parts to Whole
Closes Perception and Confines Decisions
My Specific Perception and The General Rule
What Can Be Described and Prescribed: The Constants
Advances Step by Step, Part by Part, from My Past to My Future

| **Local** | **Most Natural Talents** | **Light** |
|---|---|---|
| L1 | My Plans: Anticipation |  |
| L2 | The Customs: Relations | |
| L3 | The Methods: Causation | |
| L4 | My Priorities: Continuation | |
| *D4* | *The Novel: Options!* |  |
| *D3* | *My Ideals: Perfection!* | |
| *D2* | *My Ideas: Precision!* | |
| *D1* | *The Actual: Attention!* | |
| ***Global*** | ***Least Natural Talents*** | ***Dark*** |

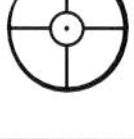

Compass of Natures

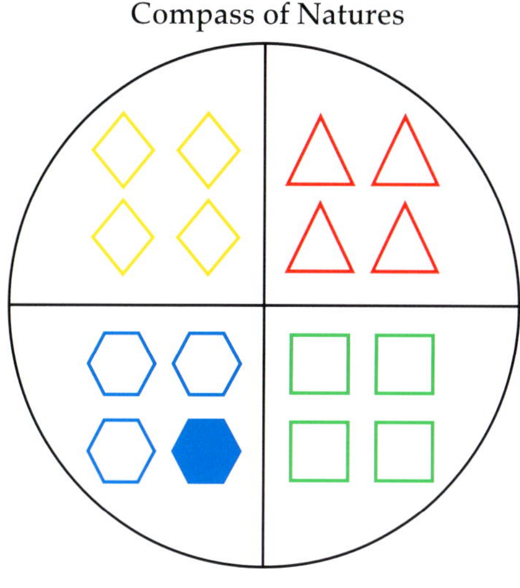

# Unifier 4
# Ruler of the Future

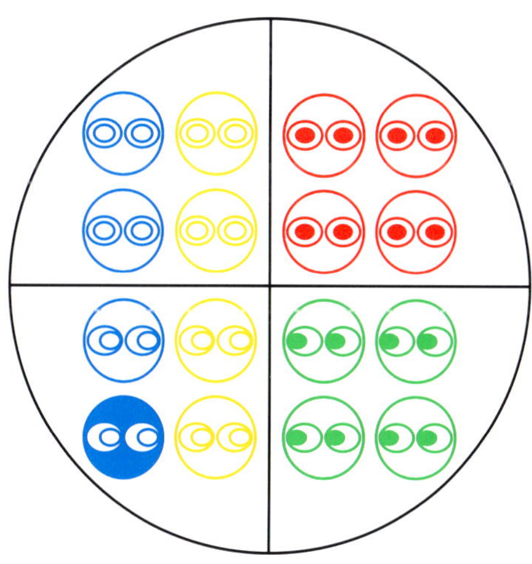

Compass of Realms

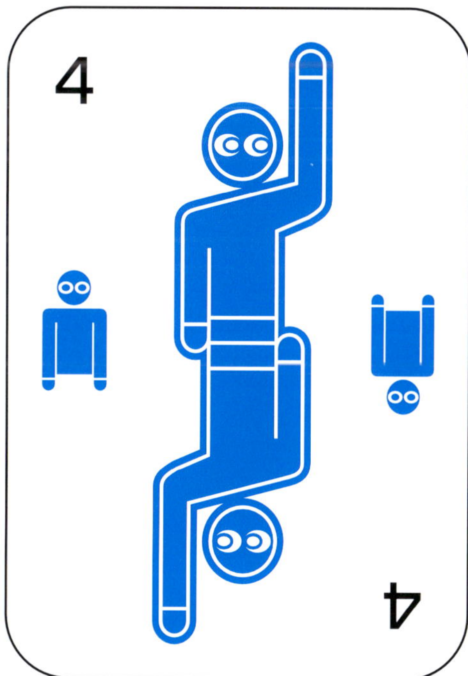

Nature

# Clarifier

Air's Clarity

Confidence, but.
"I can do that which I understand."

Focus on Distinctions
Adapts Strategically

Style

# Style 1

**Internal Attitude**
Introversion

Subject Attraction
Conserves Energy and Contracts
Fascinated by Subjective World
Inner Directed and Internally Motivated
"The external world serves my internal world."

**Indirect Role**
Indirection

Invites Interaction
Informs Others
Implicit Messages
Persuades and Promotes
Relatively Flexible Texture

Realm

# Magician of the Unknown

Variation
Global: The Whole
Simultaneous • Experiential
General to Specific • Whole to Parts
Opens Perception and Refines Decisions
The General Perception and My Specific Rules
What Cannot Be Described nor Prescribed: The Variables
Responds All at Once to the Whole Changing Present Situation

| **Global** | **Most Natural Talents** | **Light** |
|---|---|---|
| L1 | My Ideas: Precision | |
| L2 | The Novel: Options | |
| L3 | The Actual: Attention | |
| L4 | My Ideals: Perfection | |
| *D4* | *The Methods: Causation!* | |
| *D3* | *My Plans: Anticipation!* | |
| *D2* | *My Priorities: Continuation!* | |
| *D1* | *The Customs: Relations!* | |
| ***Local*** | ***Least Natural Talents*** | ***Dark*** |

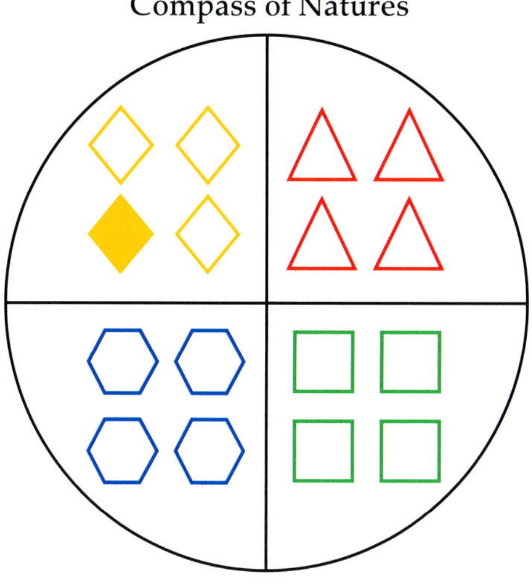

# Clarifier 1
# Magician of the Unknown

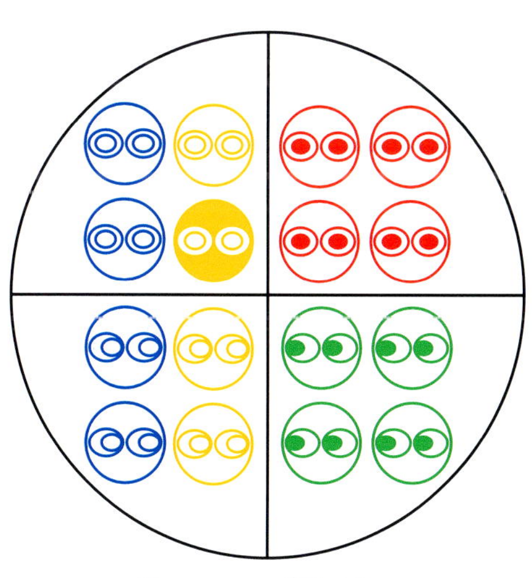

Nature

# Clarifier

Air's Clarity

Confidence, but.
"I can do that which I understand."

Focus on Distinctions
Adapts Strategically

Style

## Style 2

**External Attitude**
Extraversion

Object Attraction
Expends Energy and Expands
Fascinated by Objective World
Outer Directed and Externally Motivated
"My internal world serves the external world."

**Indirect Role**
Indirection

Invites Interaction
Informs Others
Implicit Messages
Persuades and Promotes
Relatively Flexible Texture

Realm

## Magician of the Unknown

Variation
Global: The Whole
Simultaneous • Experiential
General to Specific • Whole to Parts
Opens Perception and Refines Decisions
The General Perception and My Specific Rules
What Cannot Be Described nor Prescribed: The Variables
Responds All at Once to the Whole Changing Present Situation

| **Global** | **Most Natural Talents** | **Light** |
|---|---|---|
| L1 | The Novel: Options | |
| L2 | My Ideas: Precision | |
| L3 | My Ideals: Perfection | |
| L4 | The Actual: Attention | |
| *D4* | *My Plans: Anticipation!* | |
| *D3* | *The Methods: Causation!* | |
| *D2* | *The Customs: Relations!* | |
| *D1* | *My Priorities: Continuation!* | |
| ***Local*** | ***Least Natural Talents*** | ***Dark*** |

Compass of Natures

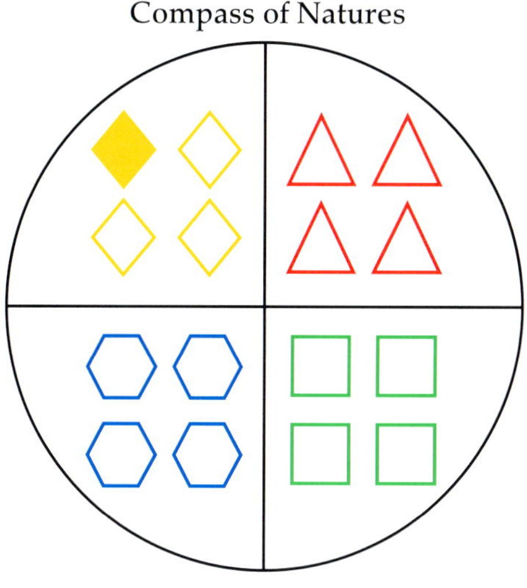

# Clarifier 2
# Magician of the Unknown

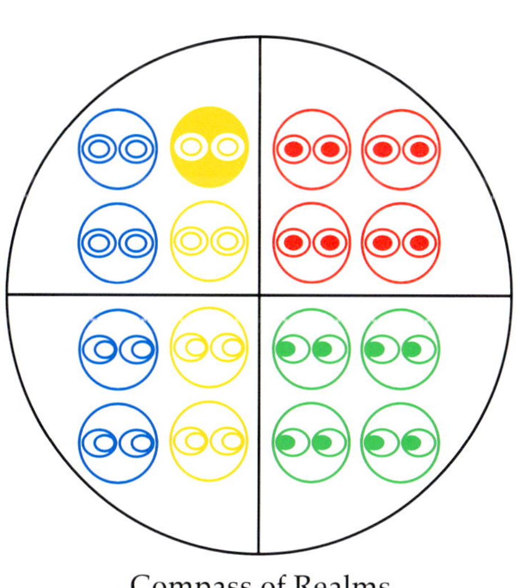

Compass of Realms

Nature

# Clarifier

Air's Clarity

Confidence, but.
"I can do that which I understand."

Focus on Distinctions
Adapts Strategically

Style

# Style 3

**External Attitude**
Extraversion

Object Attraction
Expends Energy and Expands
Fascinated by Objective World
Outer Directed and Externally Motivated
"My internal world serves the external world."

**Direct Role**
Direction

Directs Action
Instructs Others
Explicit Messages
Commands and Controls
Absolutely Firm Texture

Realm

# Ruler of the Future

Theme
Local: The Parts
Sequential • Systematic
Specific to General • Parts to Whole
Closes Perception and Confines Decisions
My Specific Perception and The General Rule
What Can Be Described and Prescribed: The Constants
Advances Step by Step, Part by Part, from My Past to My Future

| **Local** | **Most Natural Talents** | **Light** |
|---|---|---|
| L1 | The Methods: Causation | |
| L2 | My Plans: Anticipation | |
| L3 | My Priorities: Continuation | |
| L4 | The Customs: Relations | |
| *D4* | *My Ideas: Precision!* | |
| *D3* | *The Novel: Options!* | |
| *D2* | *The Actual: Attention!* | |
| *D1* | *My Ideals: Perfection!* | |
| ***Global*** | ***Least Natural Talents*** | ***Dark*** |

Compass of Natures

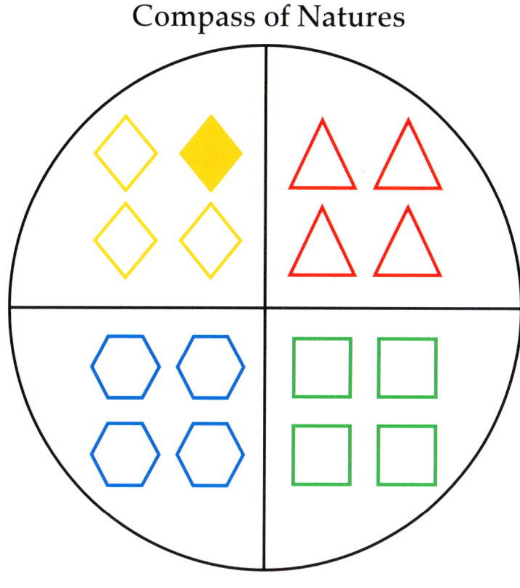

## Clarifier 3
## Ruler of the Future

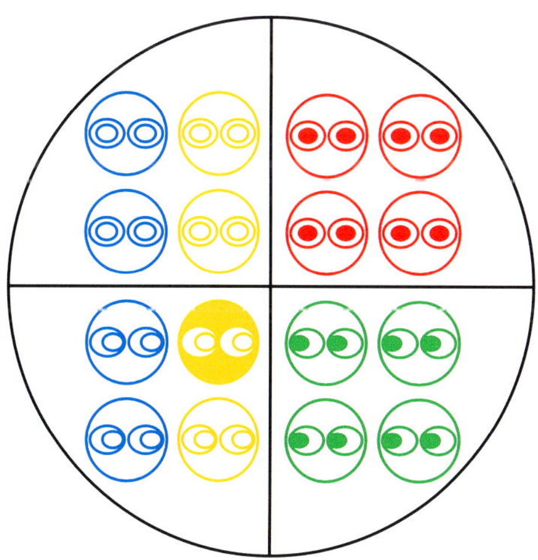

Compass of Realms

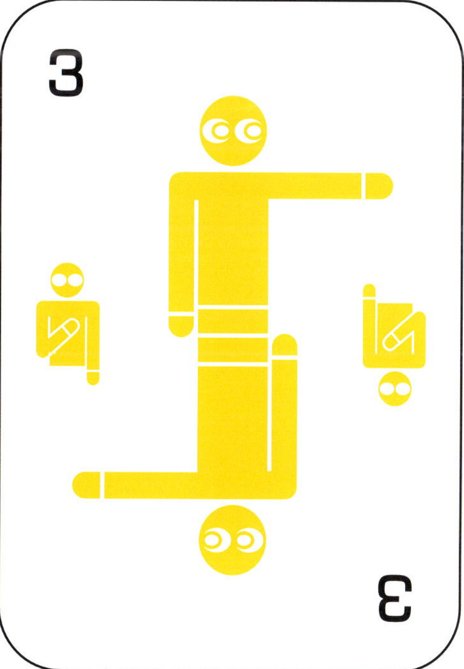

Nature

# Clarifier

Air's Clarity

Confidence, but.
"I can do that which I understand."

Focus on Distinctions
Adapts Strategically

Style

## Style 4

**Internal Attitude**
Introversion

Subject Attraction
Conserves Energy and Contracts
Fascinated by Subjective World
Inner Directed and Internally Motivated
"The external world serves my internal world."

**Direct Role**
Direction

Directs Action
Instructs Others
Explicit Messages
Commands and Controls
Absolutely Firm Texture

Realm

## Ruler of the Future

Theme
Local: The Parts
Sequential • Systematic
Specific to General • Parts to Whole
Closes Perception and Confines Decisions
My Specific Perception and The General Rule
What Can Be Described and Prescribed: The Constants
Advances Step by Step, Part by Part, from My Past to My Future

| **Local** | **Most Natural Talents** | **Light** |
|---|---|---|
| L1 | My Plans: Anticipation | |
| L2 | The Methods: Causation | |
| L3 | The Customs: Relations | |
| L4 | My Priorities: Continuation | |
| *D4* | *The Novel: Options!* | |
| *D3* | *My Ideas: Precision!* | |
| *D2* | *My Ideals: Perfection!* | |
| *D1* | *The Actual: Attention!* | |
| ***Global*** | ***Least Natural Talents*** | ***Dark*** |

Compass of Natures

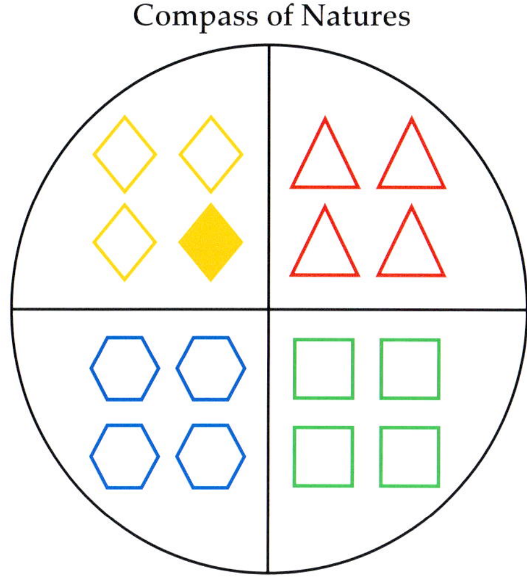

# Clarifier 4
# Ruler of the Future

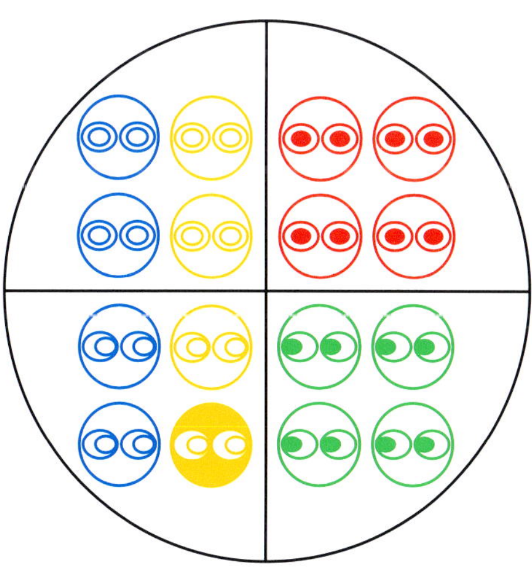

Compass of Realms

Nature

# Activator

Fire's Activity

Confidence
"I can do that."

Focus on Opportunities
Structures Tactically

Style

## Style 1

### Internal Attitude

Introversion

Subject Attraction
Conserves Energy and Contracts
Fascinated by Subjective World
Inner Directed and Internally Motivated
"The external world serves my internal world."

### Indirect Role

Indirection

Invites Interaction
Informs Others
Implicit Messages
Persuades and Promotes
Relatively Flexible Texture

Realm

## Magician of the Known

Variation
Global: The Whole
Simultaneous • Experiential
General to Specific • Whole to Parts
Opens Perception and Refines Decisions
The General Perception and My Specific Rules
What Cannot Be Described nor Prescribed: The Variables
Responds All at Once to the Whole Changing Present Situation

| **Global** | **Most Natural Talents** | **Light** |
|---|---|---|
| L1 | My Ideals: Perfection | |
| L2 | The Actual: Attention | |
| L3 | The Novel: Options | |
| L4 | My Ideas: Precision | |
| *D4* | *The Customs: Relations!* | |
| *D3* | *My Priorities: Continuation!* | |
| *D2* | *My Plans: Anticipation!* | |
| *D1* | *The Methods: Causation!* | |
| ***Local*** | ***Least Natural Talents*** | ***Dark*** |

Compass of Natures

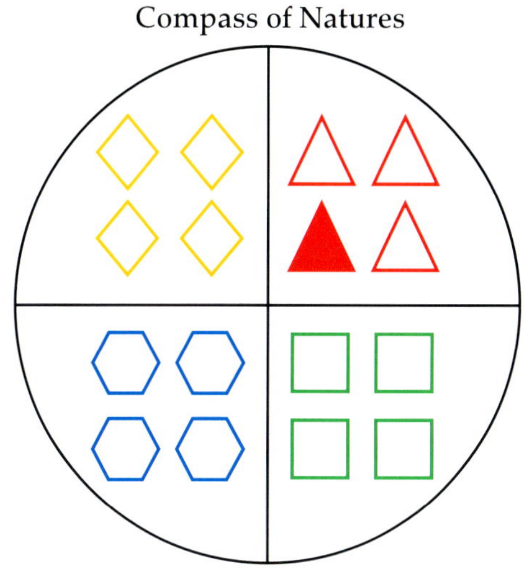

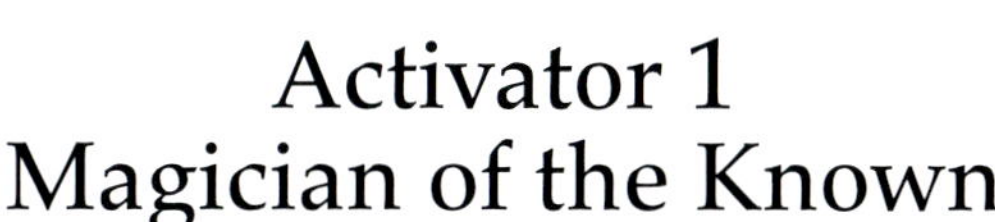

# Activator 1
# Magician of the Known

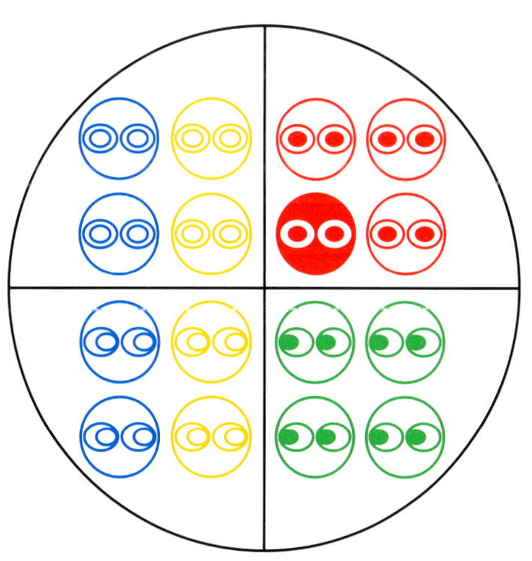

Compass of Realms

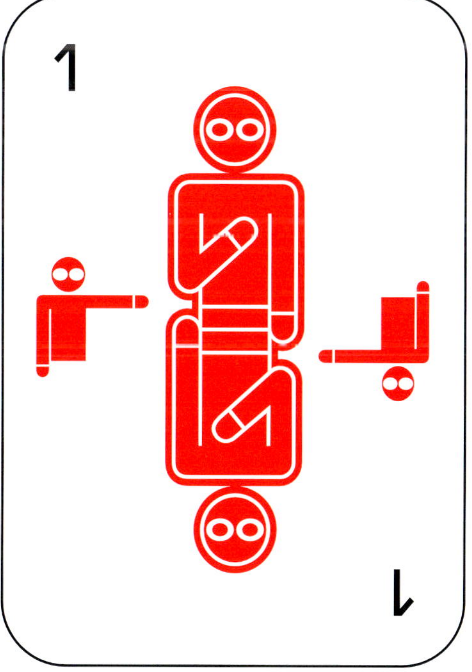

Nature

# Activator

Fire's Activity

Confidence
"I can do that."

Focus on Opportunities
Structures Tactically

Style

## Style 2

### External Attitude

Extraversion

Object Attraction
Expends Energy and Expands
Fascinated by Objective World
Outer Directed and Externally Motivated
"My internal world serves the external world."

### Indirect Role

Indirection

Invites Interaction
Informs Others
Implicit Messages
Persuades and Promotes
Relatively Flexible Texture

Realm

## Magician of the Known

Variation
Global: The Whole
Simultaneous • Experiential
General to Specific • Whole to Parts
Opens Perception and Refines Decisions
The General Perception and My Specific Rules
What Cannot Be Described nor Prescribed: The Variables
Responds All at Once to the Whole Changing Present Situation

| **Global** | **Most Natural Talents** | **Light** |
|---|---|---|
| L1 | The Actual: Attention | |
| L2 | My Ideals: Perfection | |
| L3 | My Ideas: Precision | |
| L4 | The Novel: Options | |
| *D4* | *My Priorities: Continuation!* | |
| *D3* | *The Customs: Relations!* | |
| *D2* | *The Methods: Causation!* | |
| *D1* | *My Plans: Anticipation!* | |
| ***Local*** | ***Least Natural Talents*** | ***Dark*** |

Compass of Natures

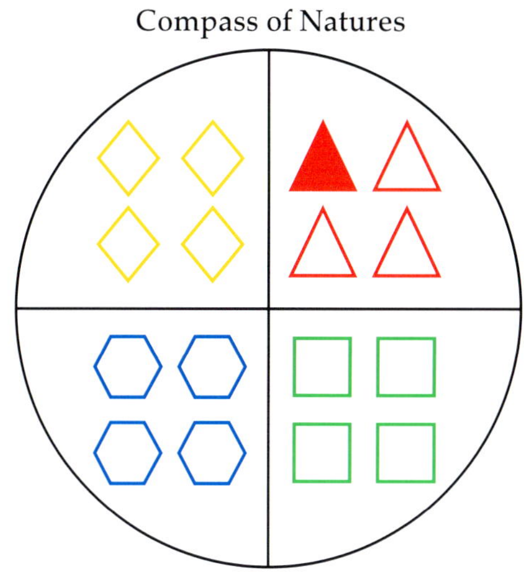

## Activator 2
## Magician of the Known

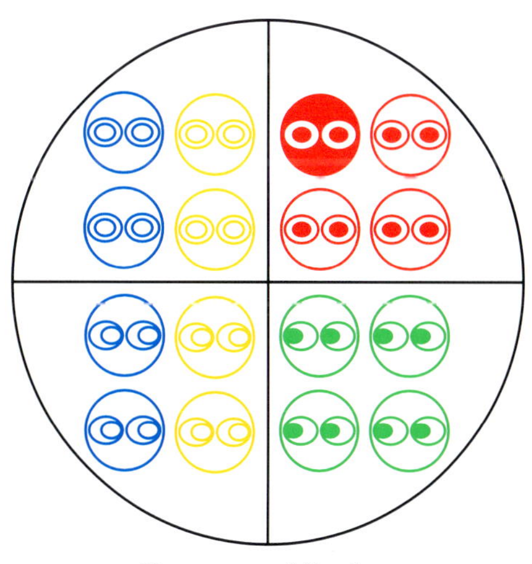

Compass of Realms

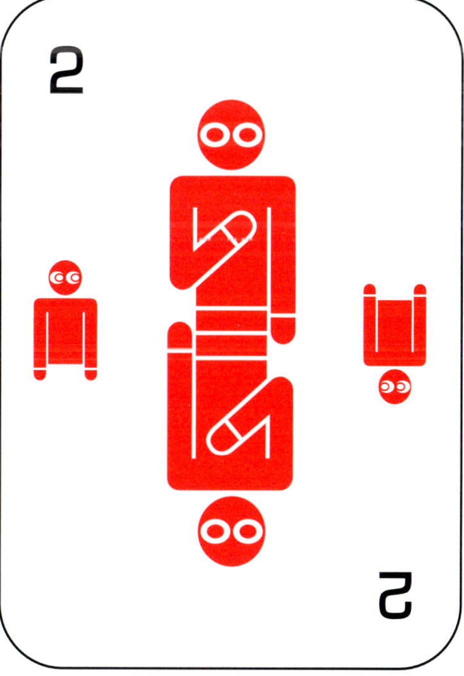

Nature

# Activator

Fire's Activity

Confidence
"I can do that."

Focus on Opportunities
Structures Tactically

Style

## Style 3

### External Attitude

Extraversion

Object Attraction
Expends Energy and Expands
Fascinated by Objective World
Outer Directed and Externally Motivated
"My internal world serves the external world."

### Direct Role

Direction

Directs Action
Instructs Others
Explicit Messages
Commands and Controls
Absolutely Firm Texture

Realm

## Magician of the Known

Variation
Global: The Whole
Simultaneous • Experiential
General to Specific • Whole to Parts
Opens Perception and Refines Decisions
The General Perception and My Specific Rules
What Cannot Be Described nor Prescribed: The Variables
Responds All at Once to the Whole Changing Present Situation

| **Global** | **Most Natural Talents** | **Light** |
|---|---|---|
| L1 | The Actual: Attention | |
| L2 | My Ideas: Precision | |
| L3 | My Ideals: Perfection | |
| L4 | The Novel: Options | |
| *D4* | *My Priorities: Continuation!* | |
| *D3* | *The Methods: Causation!* | |
| *D2* | *The Customs: Relations!* | |
| *D1* | *My Plans: Anticipation!* | |
| ***Local*** | ***Least Natural Talents*** | ***Dark*** |

Compass of Natures

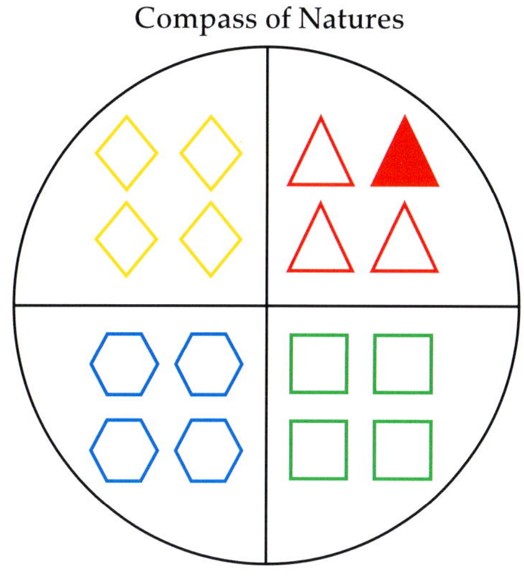

# Activator 3
# Magician of the Known

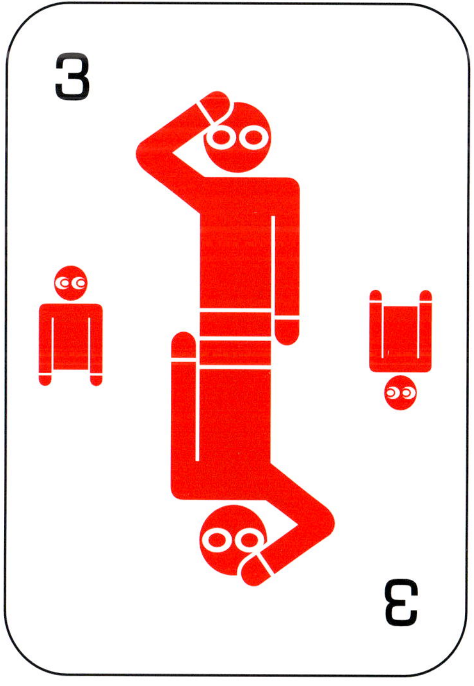


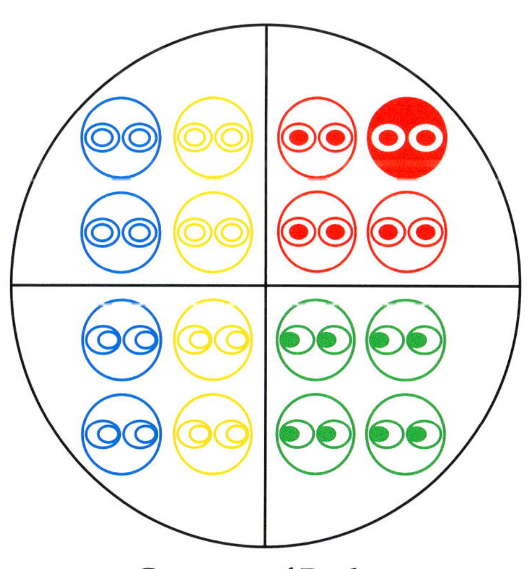

Compass of Realms

Nature

# Activator

Fire's Activity

Confidence
"I can do that."

Focus on Opportunities
Structures Tactically

Style

## Style 4

**Internal Attitude**
Introversion

Subject Attraction
Conserves Energy and Contracts
Fascinated by Subjective World
Inner Directed and Internally Motivated
"The external world serves my internal world."

**Direct Role**
Direction

Directs Action
Instructs Others
Explicit Messages
Commands and Controls
Absolutely Firm Texture

Realm

## Magician of the Known

Variation
Global: The Whole
Simultaneous • Experiential
General to Specific • Whole to Parts
Opens Perception and Refines Decisions
The General Perception and My Specific Rules
What Cannot Be Described nor Prescribed: The Variables
Responds All at Once to the Whole Changing Present Situation

| **Global** | **Most Natural Talents** | **Light** |
|---|---|---|
| L1 | My Ideas: Precision |  |
| L2 | The Actual: Attention | |
| L3 | The Novel: Options | |
| L4 | My Ideals: Perfection | |
| *D4* | *The Methods: Causation!* |  |
| *D3* | *My Priorities: Continuation!* | |
| *D2* | *My Plans: Anticipation!* | |
| *D1* | *The Customs: Relations!* | |
| ***Local*** | ***Least Natural Talents*** | ***Dark*** |

Compass of Natures

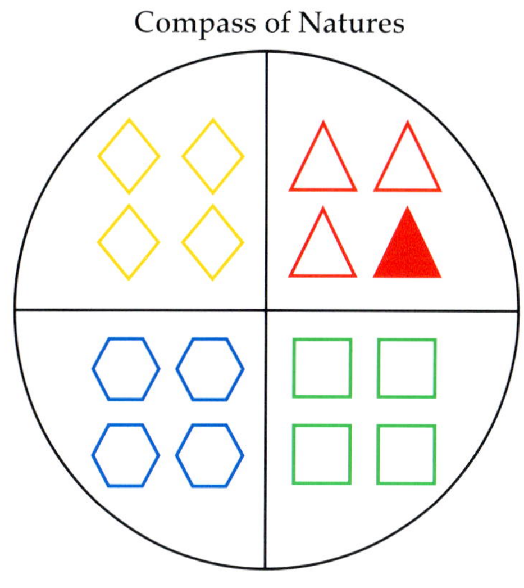

# Activator 4
# Magician of the Known

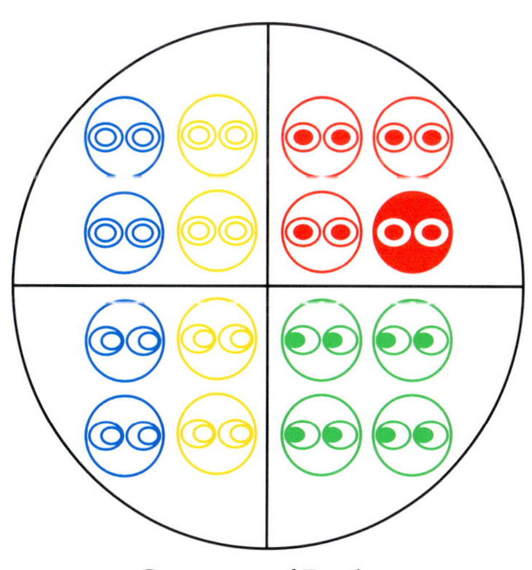

Compass of Realms

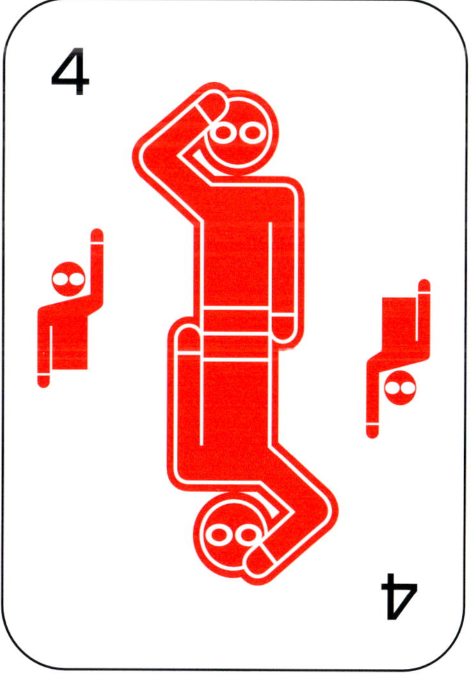

Nature

# Stabilizer

Earth's Stability

Trust, but.
"We can trust others in our group."

Focus on Priorities
Structures Procedurally

Style

## Style 1

### Internal Attitude

Introversion

Subject Attraction
Conserves Energy and Contracts
Fascinated by Subjective World
Inner Directed and Internally Motivated
"The external world serves my internal world."

### Indirect Role

Indirection

Invites Interaction
Informs Others
Implicit Messages
Persuades and Promotes
Relatively Flexible Texture

Realm

## Ruler of the Past

Theme
Local: The Parts
Sequential • Systematic
Specific to General • Parts to Whole
Closes Perception and Confines Decisions
My Specific Perception and The General Rule
What Can Be Described and Prescribed: The Constants
Advances Step by Step, Part by Part, from My Past to My Future

| **Local** | **Most Natural Talents** | **Light** |
|---|---|---|
| L1 | My Priorities: Continuation | |
| L2 | The Customs: Relations | |
| L3 | The Methods: Causation | |
| L4 | My Plans: Anticipation | |
| *D4* | *The Actual: Attention!* | |
| *D3* | *My Ideals: Perfection!* | |
| *D2* | *My Ideas: Precision!* | |
| *D1* | *The Novel: Options!* | |
| ***Global*** | ***Least Natural Talents*** | ***Dark*** |

Compass of Natures

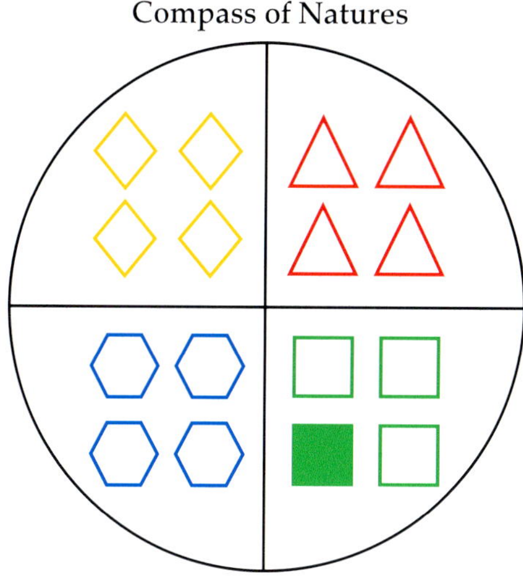

# Stabilizer 1
# Ruler of the Past

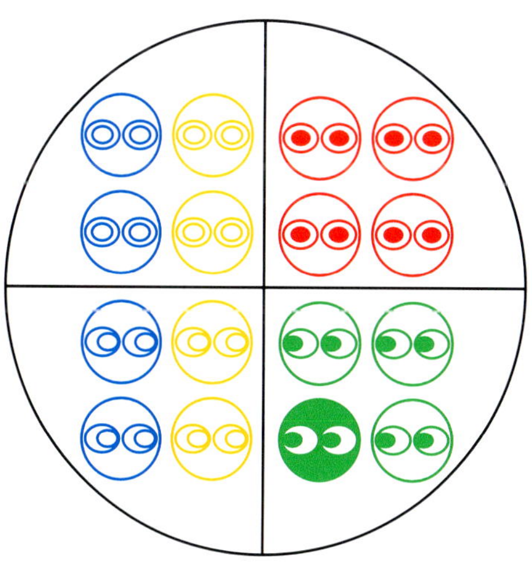

Compass of Realms

Nature

# Stabilizer

Earth's Stability

Trust, but.
"We can trust others in our group."

Focus on Priorities
Structures Procedurally

Style

# Style 2

**External Attitude**
Extraversion

Object Attraction
Expends Energy and Expands
Fascinated by Objective World
Outer Directed and Externally Motivated
"My internal world serves the external world."

**Indirect Role**
Indirection

Invites Interaction
Informs Others
Implicit Messages
Persuades and Promotes
Relatively Flexible Texture

Realm

# Ruler of the Past

Theme
Local: The Parts
Sequential • Systematic
Specific to General • Parts to Whole
Close Perceptions and Confines Decisions
My Specific Perception and The General Rule
What Can Be Described and Prescribed: The Constants
Advances Step by Step, Part by Part, from My Past to My Future

| **Local** | **Most Natural Talents** | **Light** |
|---|---|---|
| L1 | The Customs: Relations | |
| L2 | My Priorities: Continuation | |
| L3 | My Plans: Anticipation | |
| L4 | The Methods: Causation | |
| *D4* | *My Ideals: Perfection!* | |
| *D3* | *The Actual: Attention!* | |
| *D2* | *The Novel: Options!* | |
| *D1* | *My Ideas: Precision!* | |
| ***Global*** | ***Least Natural Talents*** | ***Dark*** |

Compass of Natures

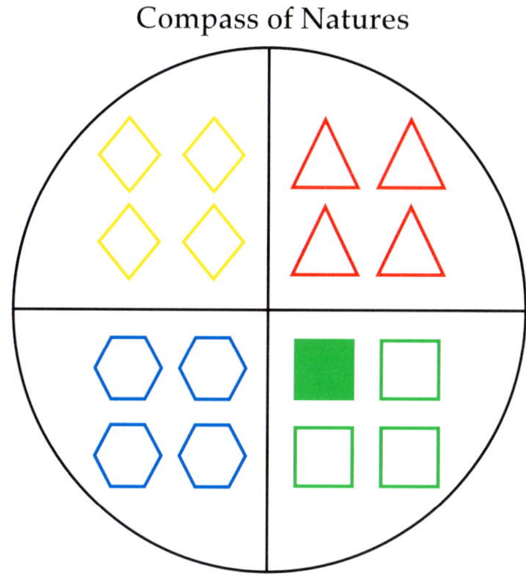

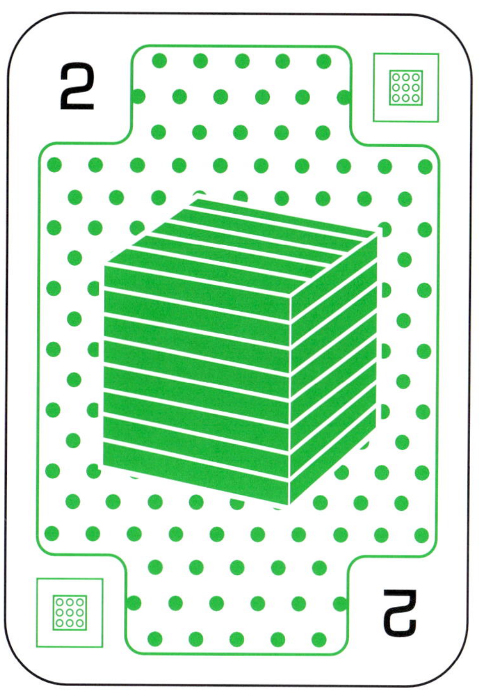


## Stabilizer 2
## Ruler of the Past

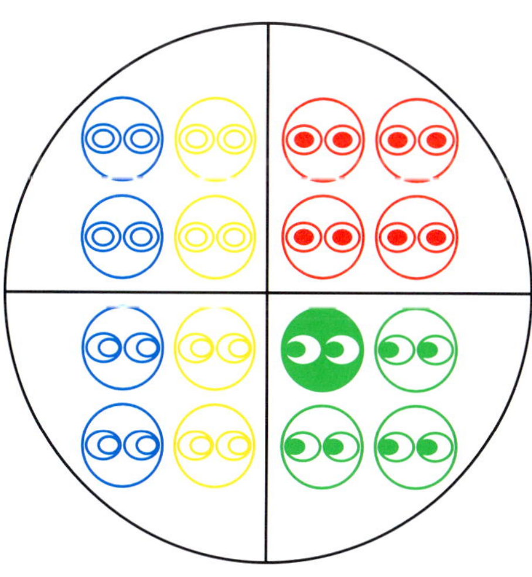

Compass of Realms

Nature

# Stabilizer

Earth's Stability

Trust, but.
"We can trust others in our group."

Focus on Priorities
Structures Procedurally

Style

## Style 3

**External Attitude**
Extraversion

Object Attraction
Expends Energy and Expands
Fascinated by Objective World
Outer Directed and Externally Motivated
"My internal world serves the external world."

**Direct Role**
Direction

Directs Action
Instructs Others
Explicit Messages
Commands and Controls
Absolutely Firm Texture

Realm

## Ruler of the Past

Theme
Local: The Parts
Sequential • Systematic
Specific to General • Parts to Whole
Closes Perception and Confines Decisions
My Specific Perception and The General Rule
What Can Be Described and Prescribed: The Constants
Advances Step by Step, Part by Part, from My Past to My Future

| **Local** | **Most Natural Talents** | **Light** |
|---|---|---|
| L1 | The Methods: Causation | |
| L2 | My Priorities: Continuation | |
| L3 | My Plans: Anticipation | |
| L4 | The Customs: Relations | |
| *D4* | *My Ideas: Precision!* | |
| *D3* | *The Actual: Attention!* | |
| *D2* | *The Novel: Options!* | |
| *D1* | *My Ideals: Perfection!* | |
| ***Global*** | ***Least Natural Talents*** | ***Dark*** |

Compass of Natures

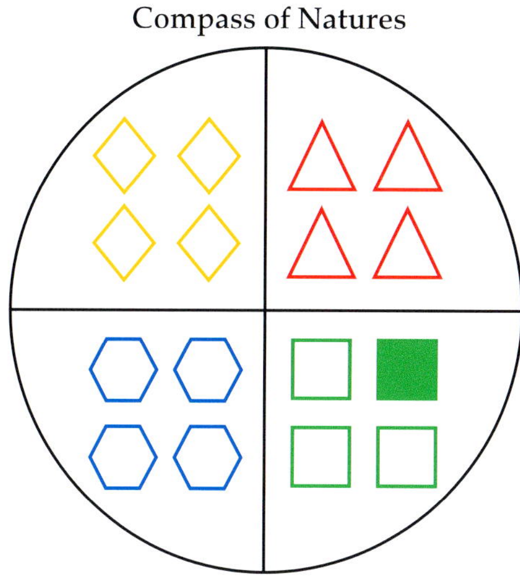

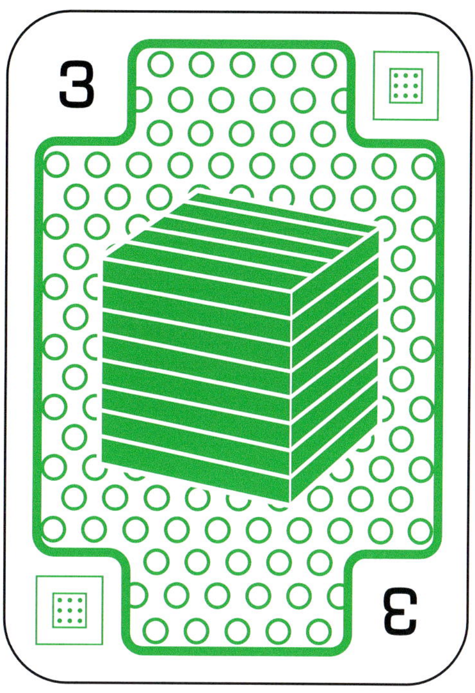


## Stabilizer 3
## Ruler of the Past

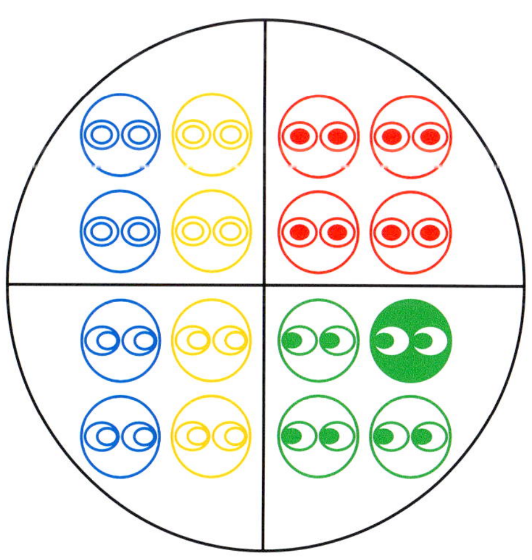

Compass of Realms

Nature

# Stabilizer

Earth's Stability

Trust, but.
"We can trust others in our group."

Focus on Priorities
Structures Procedurally

Style

## Style 4

**Internal Attitude**
Introversion

Subject Attraction
Conserves Energy and Contracts
Fascinated by Subjective World
Inner Directed and Internally Motivated
"The external world serves my internal world."

**Direct Role**
Direction

Directs Action
Instructs Others
Explicit Messages
Commands and Controls
Absolutely Firm Texture

Realm

## Ruler of the Past

Theme
Local: The Parts
Sequential • Systematic
Specific to General • Parts to Whole
Closes Perception and Confines Decisions
My Specific Perception and The General Rule
What Can Be Described and Prescribed: The Constants
Advances Step by Step, Part by Part, from My Past to My Future

| **Local** | **Most Natural Talents** | **Light** |
|---|---|---|
| L1 | My Priorities: Continuation | |
| L2 | The Methods: Causation | |
| L3 | The Customs: Relations | |
| L4 | My Plans: Anticipation | |
| *D4* | *The Actual: Attention!* | |
| *D3* | *My Ideas: Precision!* | |
| *D2* | *My Ideals: Perfection!* | |
| *D1* | *The Novel: Options!* | |
| ***Global*** | ***Least Natural Talents*** | ***Dark*** |

Compass of Natures

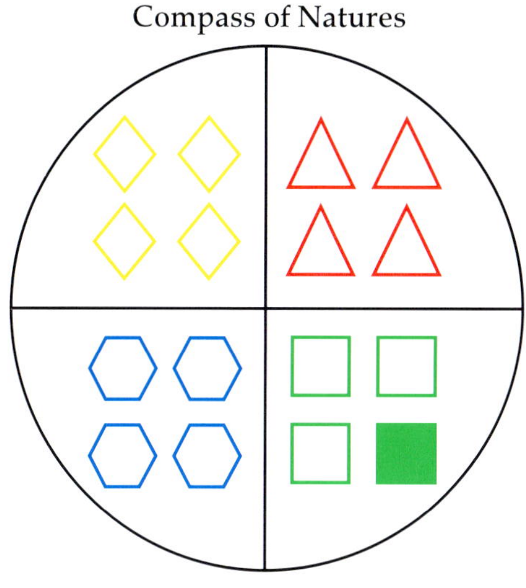

# Stabilizer 4
# Ruler of the Past

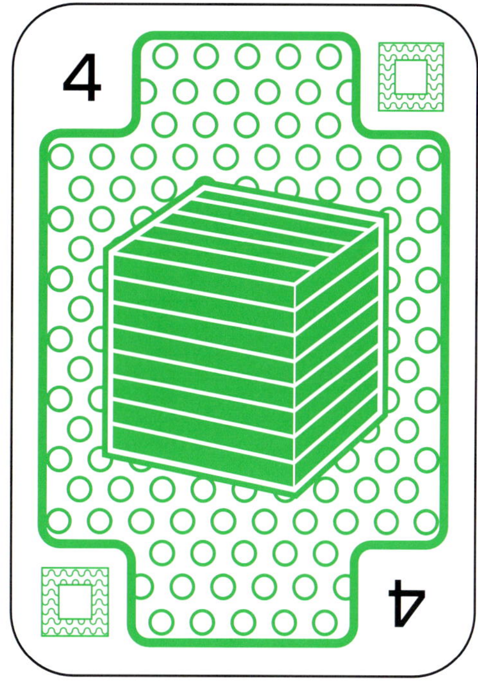


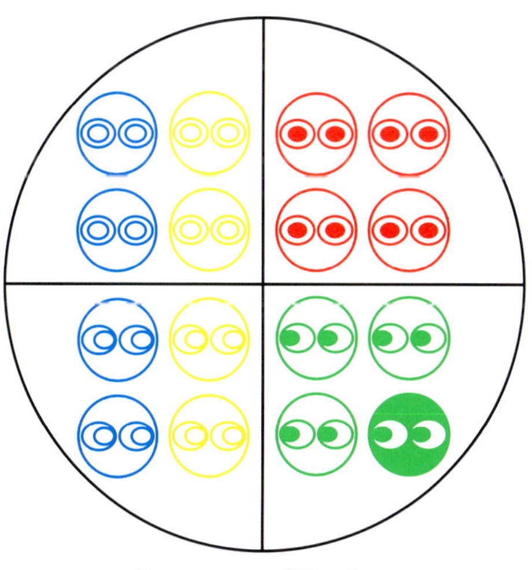

Compass of Realms

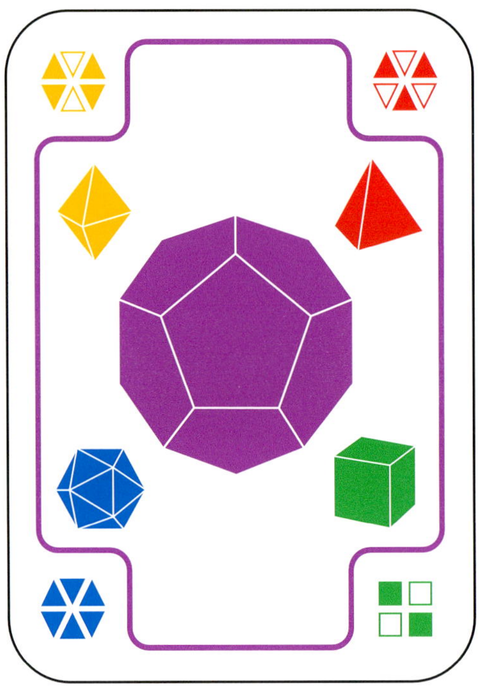

# PART V

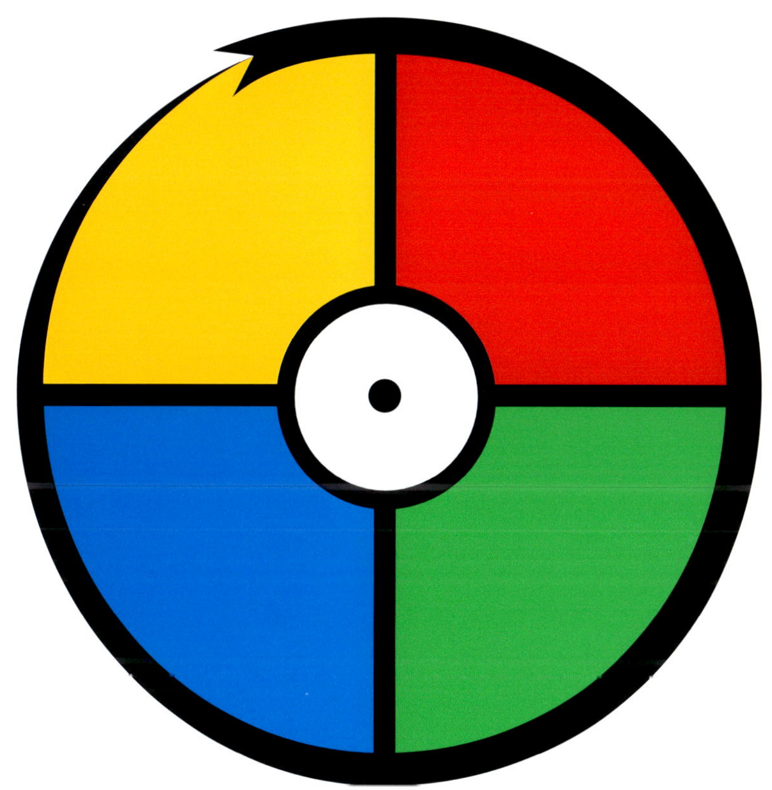

## Full Reference

## The Four Human Natures

| Empedocles 5th Century B.C. | Water Nature | Air Nature | Fire Nature | Earth Nature |
|---|---|---|---|---|
| Hippocrates 5th B.C. | Choleric | Phlegmatic | Sanguine | Melancholic |
| Plato 4th B.C. | Idealist | Rational | Artisan | Guardian |
| Aristotle 4th B.C. | Ethical | Dialectical | Hedonic | Proprietary |
| Galen A.D. 190 | Choleric | Phlegmatic | Sanguine | Melancholic |
| Paracelsus 1540 | Water | Air | Fire | Earth |
| Adickes 1905 | Doctrinaire | Skeptical | Innovative | Traditional |
| Sprãnger 1914 | Religious | Theoretic | Aesthetic | Economic |
| Kretschmer 1920 | Hyperesthetic | Anesthetic | Hypomanic | Depressive |
| Fromm 1947 | Receptive | Marketing | Exploitive | Hoarding |
| Myers 1958 | NF iNtuitive/Feeling | NT iNtuitive/Thinking | SP Sensing/Perceiving | SJ Sensing/Judging |
| Keirsey/Bates 1978 | Apollonian | Promethean | Dionysian | Epimethean |
| Keirsey 1998 | Idealist | Rational | Artisan | Guardian |
| Lopker 2000<br>Pictures of Personality™ | 1<br>Unifier<br>Water's Unity<br>O | 2<br>Clarifier<br>Air's Clarity<br>S | 3<br>Activator<br>Fire's Activity<br>Y | 4<br>Stabilizer<br>Earth's Stability<br>+ |

| The Five Solids | | | | |
|---|---|---|---|---|
| Water 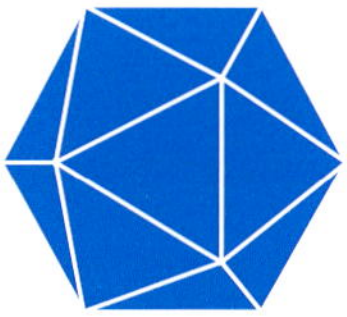 | Air | Fire 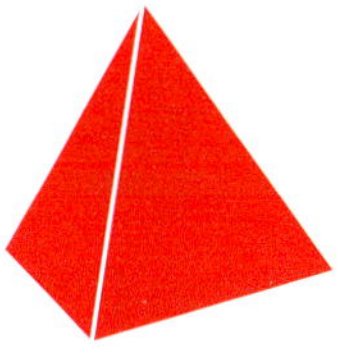 | Earth  | Cosmos 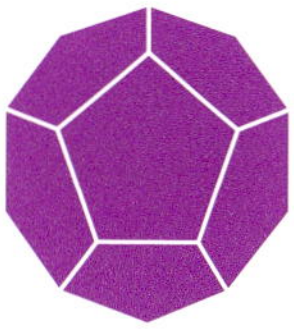 |
| Icosahedron 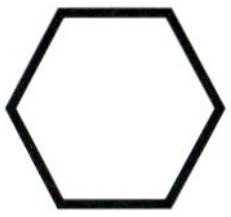 | Octahedron 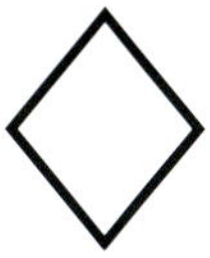 | Tetrahedron  | Hexahedron | Dodecahedron 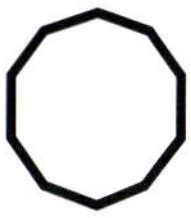 |
| 1 | 2 | 3 | 4 | 5 |

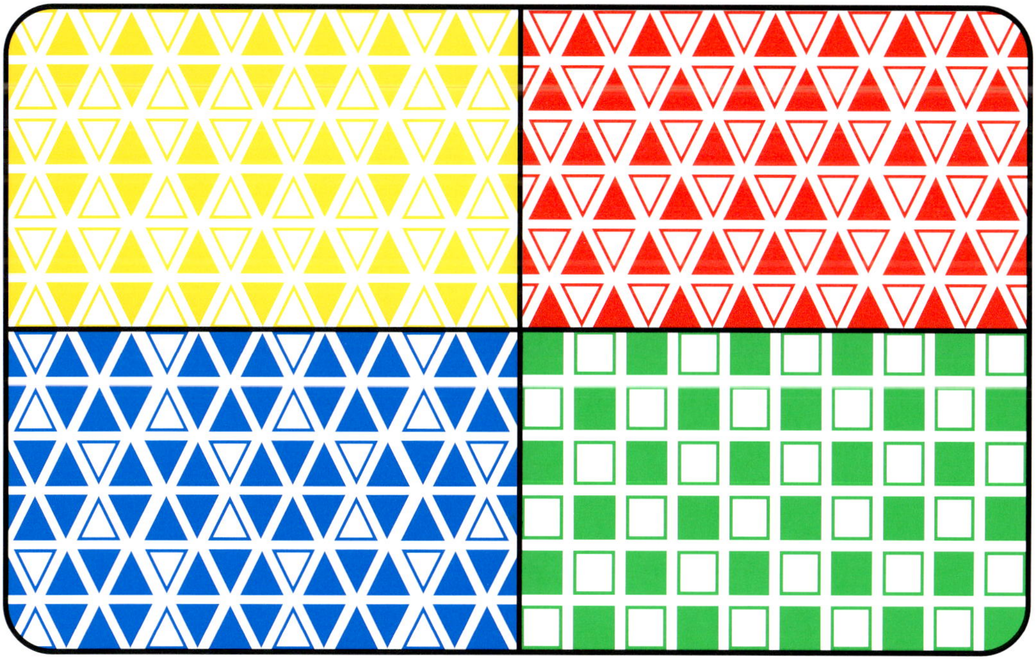

Floor tiles come in only these shapes because they fit together only in this way.

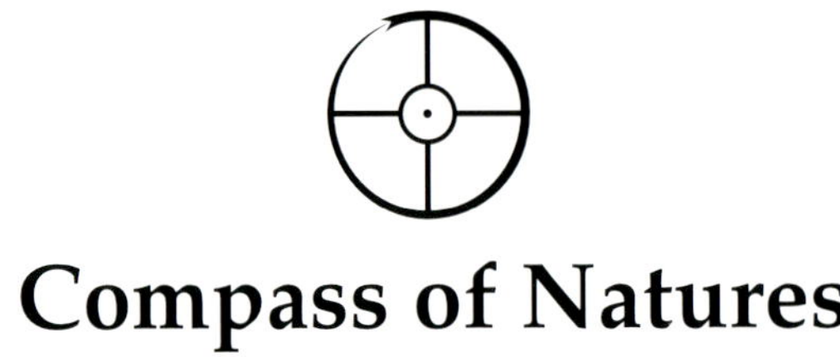

# Compass of Natures

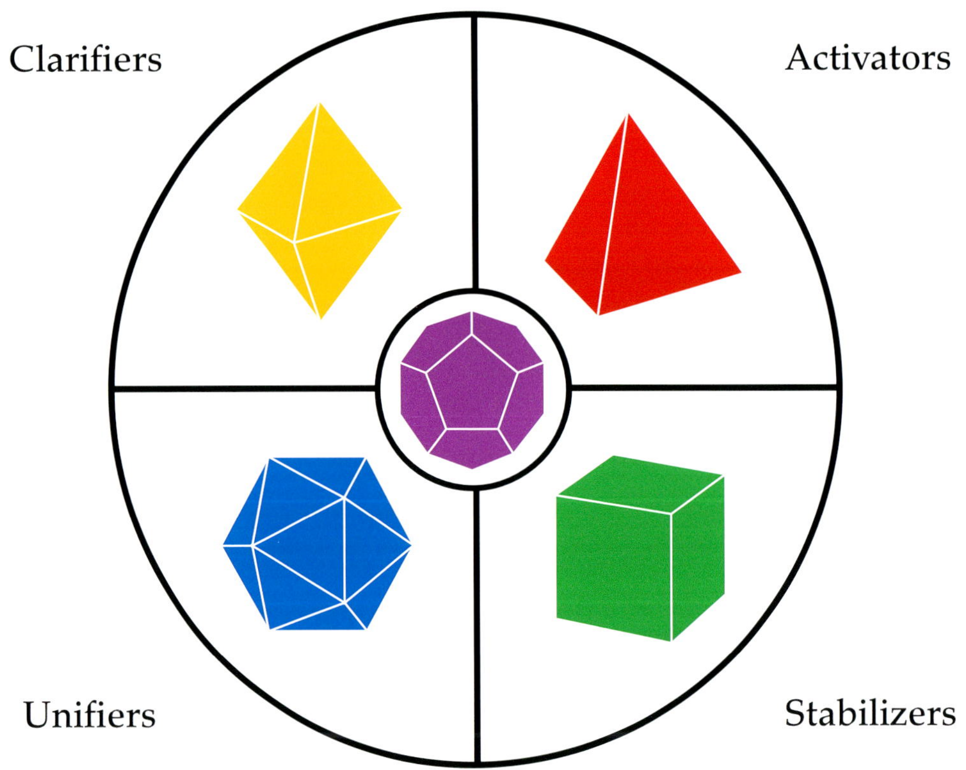

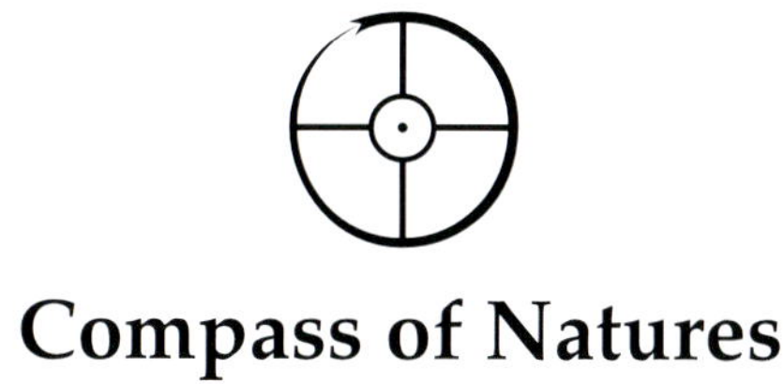

# Compass of Natures

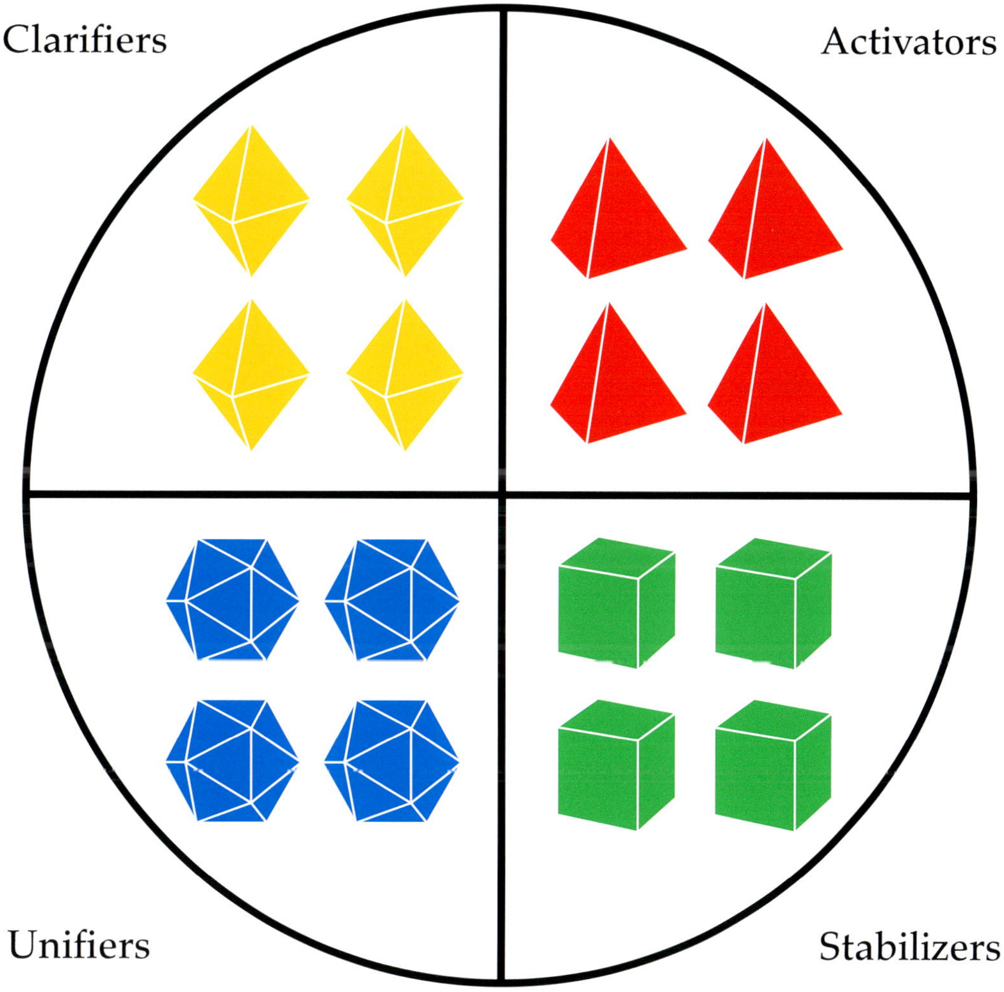

Clarifiers

Activators

Unifiers

Stabilizers

# FAITH

The Vertical Axis of the Compass of Natures

<table>
<tr><th colspan="4">ACTIVATOR</th><th colspan="4">CLARIFIER</th><th colspan="4">STABILIZER</th><th colspan="4">UNIFIER</th></tr>
<tr><td colspan="4">35%</td><td colspan="4">10%</td><td colspan="4">45%</td><td colspan="4">10%</td></tr>
<tr><td colspan="4">Magicians</td><td colspan="2">Rulers</td><td colspan="2">Magicians</td><td colspan="4">Rulers</td><td colspan="2">Rulers</td><td colspan="2">Magicians</td></tr>
<tr><td>A3</td><td>A4</td><td>A2</td><td>A1</td><td>C3</td><td>C4</td><td>C2</td><td>C1</td><td>S3</td><td>S4</td><td>S2</td><td>S1</td><td>U3</td><td>U4</td><td>U2</td><td>U1</td></tr>
<tr><td>External</td><td>Internal</td><td>External</td><td>Internal</td><td>External</td><td>Internal</td><td>External</td><td>Internal</td><td>External</td><td>Internal</td><td>External</td><td>Internal</td><td>External</td><td>Internal</td><td>External</td><td>Internal</td></tr>
<tr><td colspan="2">Direct</td><td colspan="2">Indirect</td><td colspan="2">Direct</td><td colspan="2">Indirect</td><td colspan="2">Direct</td><td colspan="2">Indirect</td><td colspan="2">Direct</td><td colspan="2">Indirect</td></tr>
<tr><td colspan="4">Present</td><td colspan="2">Future</td><td colspan="2">Present</td><td colspan="4">Past</td><td colspan="2">Future</td><td colspan="2">Present</td></tr>
<tr><td colspan="4">Fire's Activity<br>Confidence<br>I can do that.</td><td colspan="4">Air's Clarity<br>Confidence, but.<br>I can do that which I understand.</td><td colspan="4">Earth's Stability<br>Trust, but.<br>We can trust others in our group.</td><td colspan="4">Water's Unity<br>Trust<br>We can trust others.</td></tr>
<tr><td colspan="8">Confidence<br>Faith in Oneself</td><td colspan="8">Trust<br>Faith in Others</td></tr>
</table>

# FOCUS

The Horizontal Axis of the Compass of Natures

| CLARIFIER | | | | UNIFIER | | | | ACTIVATOR | | | | STABILIZER | | | |
|---|---|---|---|---|---|---|---|---|---|---|---|---|---|---|---|
|  | | | |  | | | |  | | | |  | | | |
| 10% | | | | 10% | | | | 35% | | | | 45% | | | |
| Magicians | | Rulers | | Magicians | | Rulers | | Magicians | | | | Rulers | | | |
| C2 | C1 | C3 | C4 | U2 | U1 | U3 | U4 | A2 | A1 | A3 | A4 | S2 | S1 | S3 | S4 |
| External | Internal | External | Internal | External | Internal | External | Internal | External | Internal | External | Internal | External | Internal | External | Internal |
| Indirect | | Direct | | Indirect | | Direct | | Indirect | | Direct | | Indirect | | Direct | |
| Present | | Future | | Present | | Future | | Present | | | | Past | | | |
| Air's Clarity 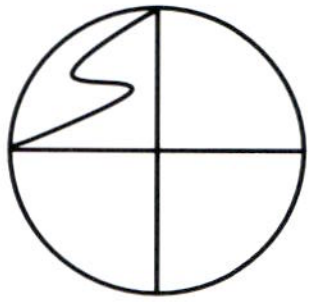 Distinctions Adapts Strategically | | | | Water's Unity 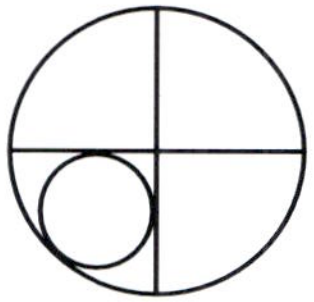 Similarities Adapts Diplomatically | | | | Fire's Activity 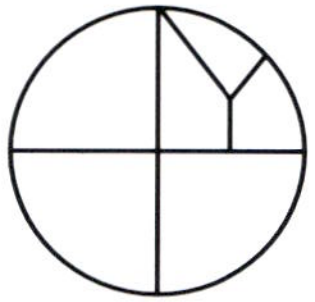 Opportunities Structures Tactically | | | | Earth's Stability 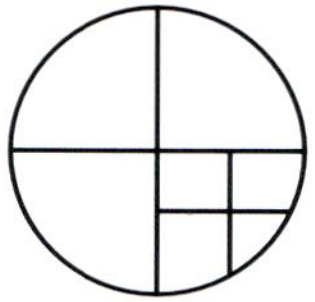 Priorities Structures Procedurally | | | |
| Conceive and Adapt | | | | | | | | Sense and Structure | | | | | | | |
| **Context** To perceive *outside* the container of the five senses. | | | | | | | | **Content** To perceive *inside* the container of the five senses. | | | | | | | |

## The Pictures of Personality™ Universal Symbols

**Map of the Four Natures**

## The Pictures of Personality™ Universal Symbols

Magicians of the Unknown | Magicians of the Known

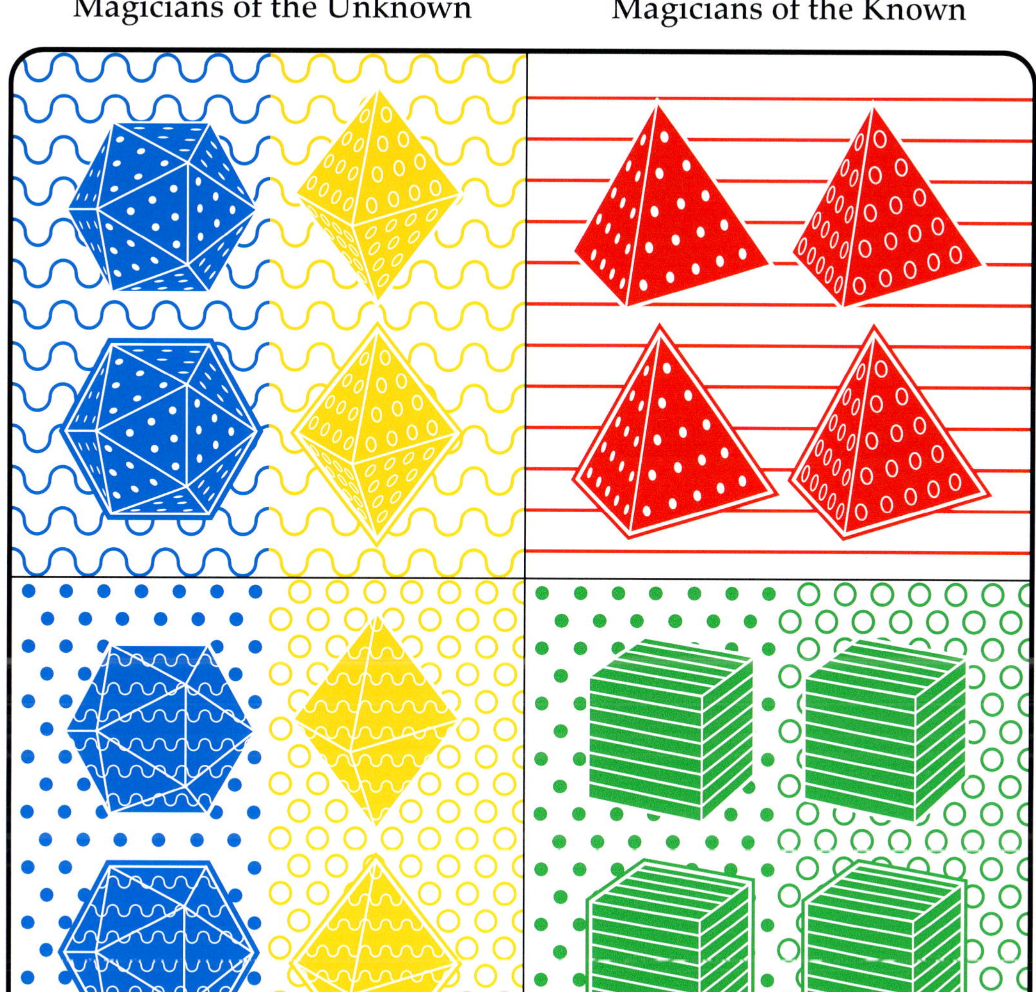

Rulers of the Future | Rulers of the Past

## Map of the Four Realms

# The Pictures of Personality™ International Icons

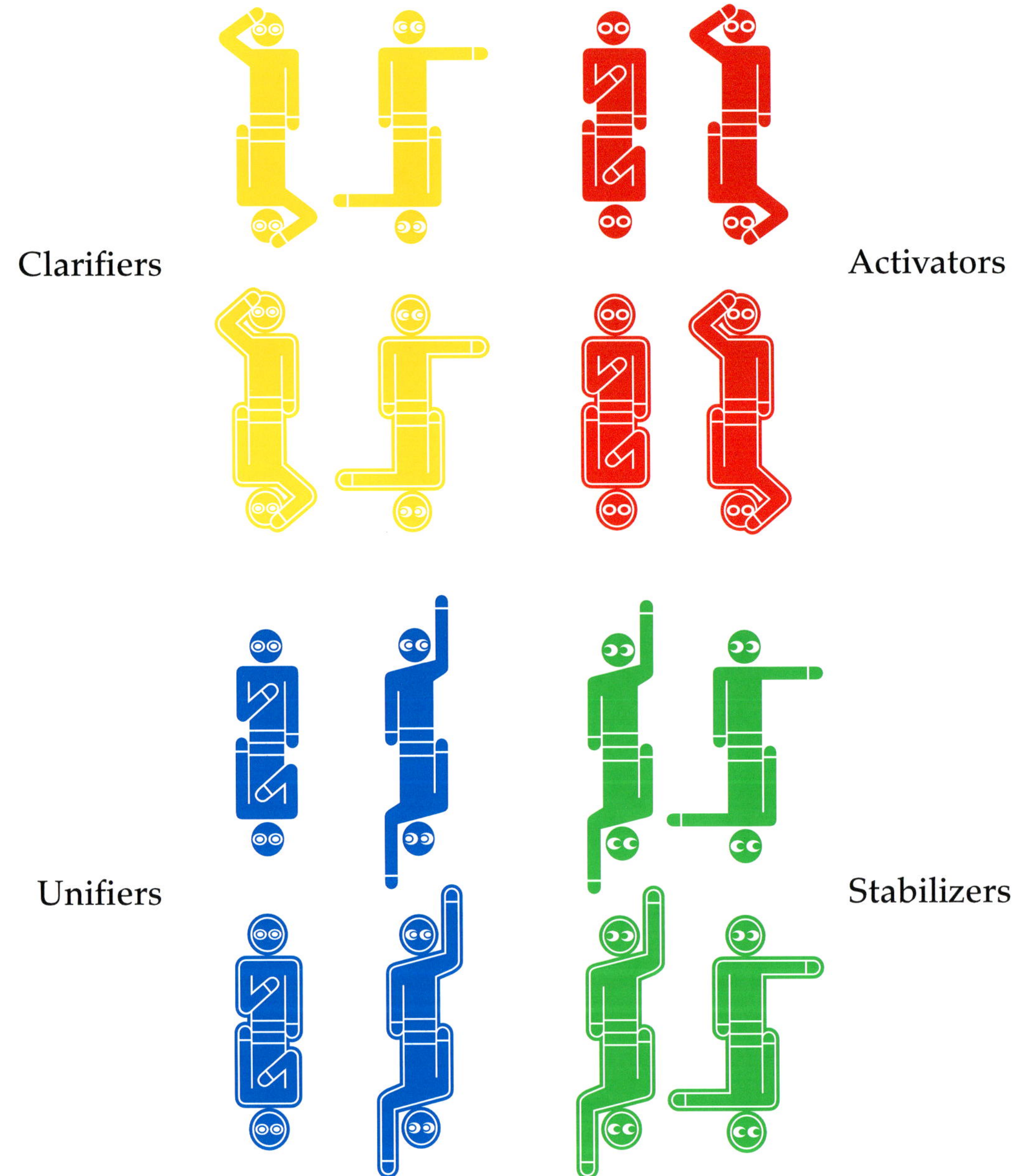


## Map of the Four Natures

# The Pictures of Personality™ International Icons

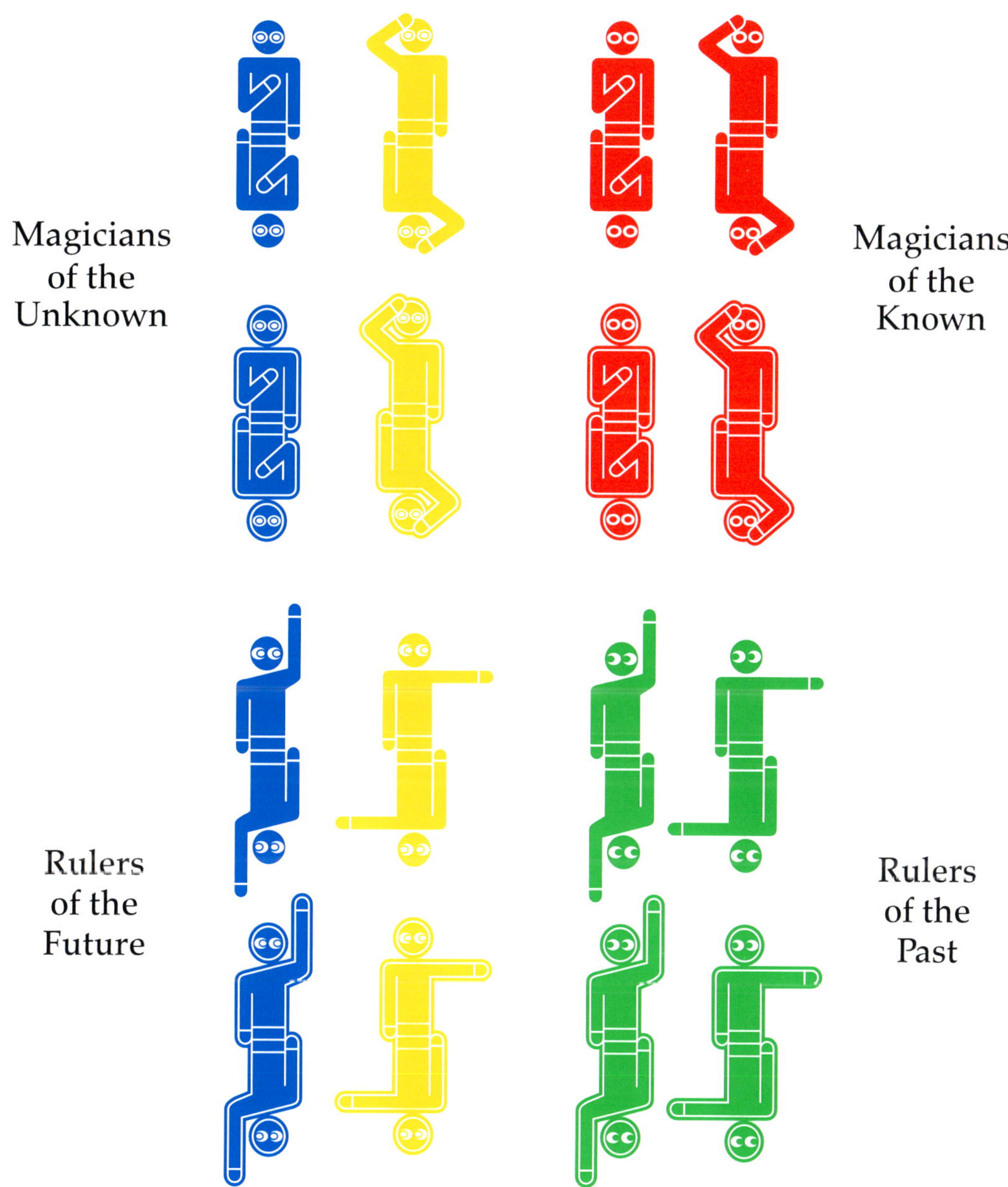


## Map of the Four Realms

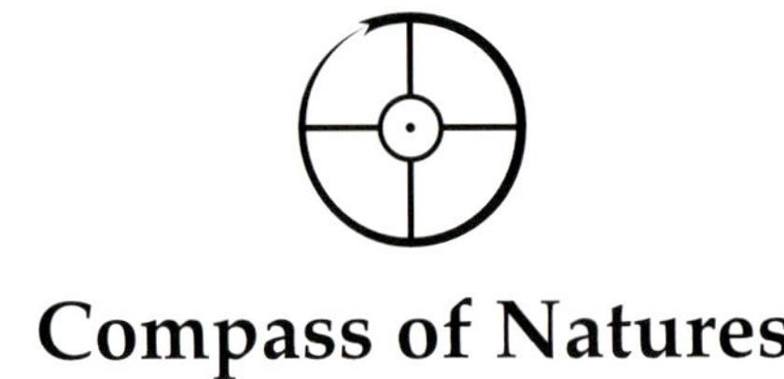

# Compass of Natures

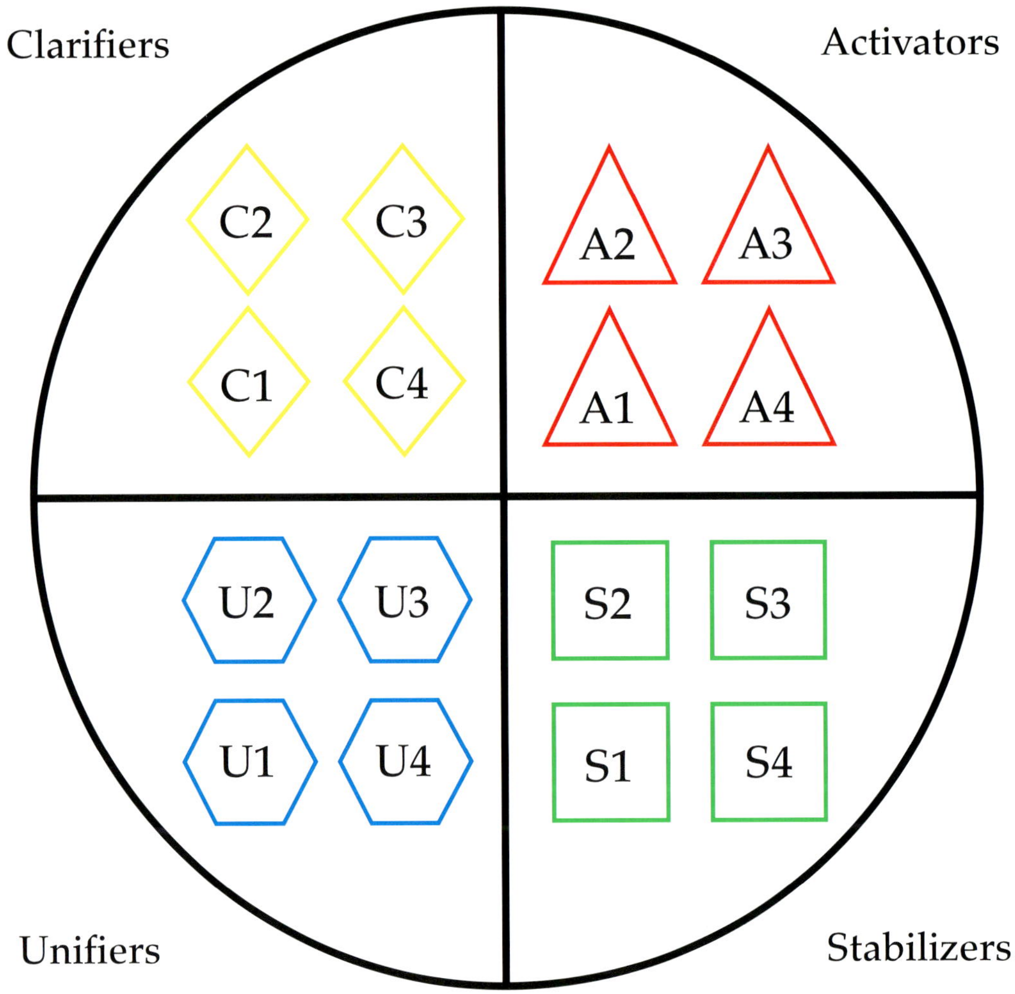

Clarifiers

C2 C3

C1 C4

Activators

A2 A3

A1 A4

Unifiers

U2 U3

U1 U4

Stabilizers

S2 S3

S1 S4

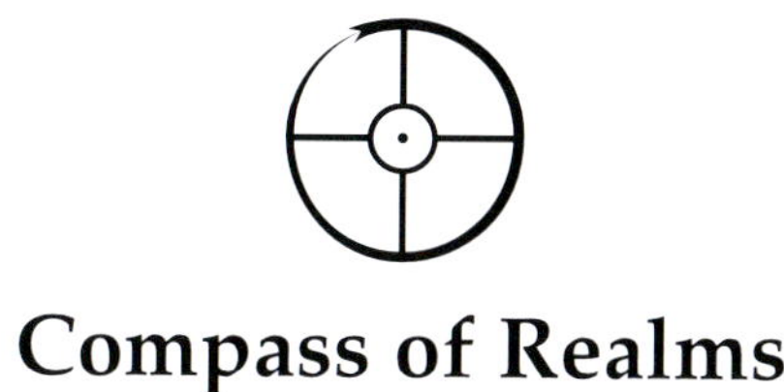

## Compass of Realms

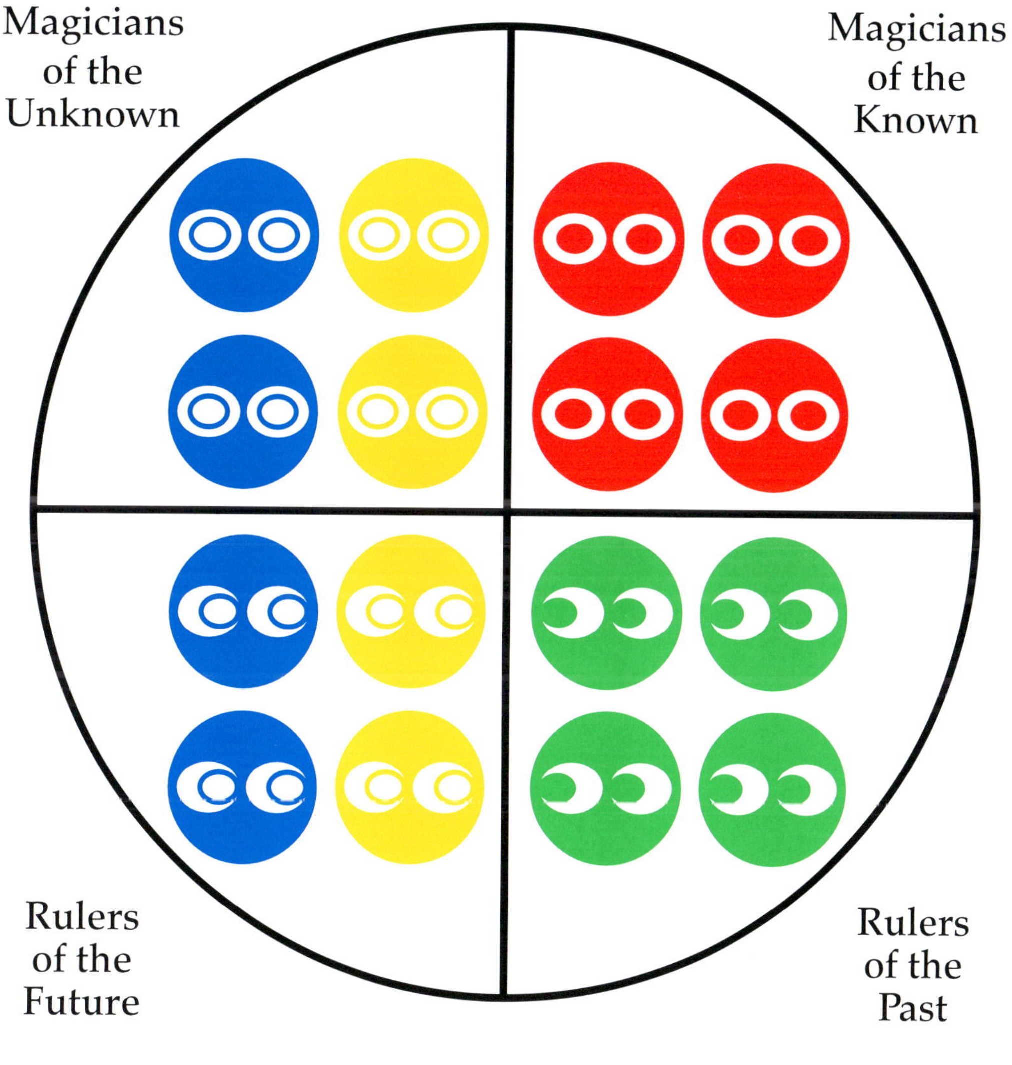

Magicians of the Unknown

Magicians of the Known

Rulers of the Future

Rulers of the Past

Light and Dark,
sparkling nights.

Up and Down,
rounding us.

Rise and Fall,
laughing cries.

Dawn and Dusk,
just yawns.

# Chapter 8
# Our Great Play

## Act I

### Light Rises from Dark

Our Great Play begins in the Middle of the Night, in the dark waters of the womb where we inherit the structures of body and mind. As our body emerges into the world, our mind holds all of the instincts and archetypes that provide the raw materials of human nature – the "10,000 things" that stay with us our entire lives. We can never get rid of anything. We can only shift things from the Dark into the Light and from the Light back into the Dark.

As infants, our internal world blends with the external world in one endless dream. We have not yet made the most basic distinctions. We do not know that we exist. We know "I" but we do not know "I Am." We do not know that others exist. We know "I" but we do not know "Other." We put anything we wish into the Light. Lacking consciousness, we are free of self-consciousness. Detached and uninhibited, we are whole and full of wonder.

Act I ends as we slowly turn toward the Dawn Sky, longing for the Light of Consciousness.

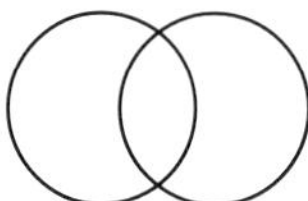

# Act II

## Light Rejects Dark

As Dawn breaks Night into Day, the Light of Consciousness breaks our personality into an unconscious Dark Side and a conscious Light Side. Our Light Side begins its skyward ascent the moment we distinguish between "I" and "Other." After a brief fight, we agree to the definitions of right and wrong that have been agreed upon by our culture. We learn which of the 10,000 things are allowed in the Light, and which things must be kept in the Dark. We begin to realize the power of others, and to appreciate the safe and predictable environment that others have created for us. We accept that some of our best things must remain in the Dark, and some of our worst things may hide under the cloak of collective righteousness.

In Act II, our culture assigns a mask for us to wear. Our mask hides our real identity and shows everyone our role in society. We are rewarded for playing our roles well and punished for not playing well. In playing our role, we naturally favor our Light Talents over our Dark Talents because our performances shine so much brighter when we use our Light Talents. We especially favor two of our Light Talents: one for perceiving and one for deciding; one for the external world and one for our internal world.

In the high drama of Our Great Play, we soon forget our origins. Confused and disoriented, we forget that our Light arose from the Dark. We forget that Our Great Play is not real. We forget that we wear a mask not made by "I" but by "Others."

Act II ends at Noon when our Light Side has reached it zenith. We have survived, so far. Our life is a success, more or less. But we wonder if we missed something. Down deep, something sounds out of tune. Sooner or later, we realize that the fear of Darkness is the fear of our full brilliance.

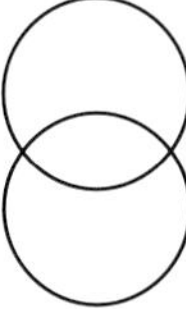

# Act III

## Light Accepts Dark

Noon is the hour of our reversal, and the beginning of the end of Our Great Play.

> From the middle of life onward, only he remains vitally alive who is ready to die with life. For in the secret hour of life's midday the parabola is reversed, death is born. The second half of life does not signify ascent, unfolding, increase, exuberance, but death, since the end is its goal. The negation of life's fulfillment is synonymous with the refusal to accept its ending. Both mean not wanting to live; not wanting to live is identical with not wanting to die. Waxing and waning making one curve. (CW 8, par. 404)

Every human being is also a human becoming. Like pendulums and seesaws, all opposites switch places in search of balance: warm things cool down and cool things warm up; soft things harden and hard things soften; inhale and exhale; day and night; up and down; extreme reverence becomes violent and extreme violence becomes highly revered; the sacred is soon profane and the profane suddenly sacred. Likewise, human nature abides by this primary natural law. Our Dark Side balances our Light Side moment by moment, day by day, and year by year in every Act of Our Great Play.

In the Morning, our Light radiates out from our persona to help us survive in the world. In the Afternoon, our Light glows from our luminous spirit to revive our whole personality and unique individuality. In the Afternoon, Magicians welcome their Rulers hidden in the Dark, and Rulers welcome their Magicians hidden in the Dark. In the Afternoon, Introverts embrace their Dark Extraverts, and Extraverts embrace their Dark Introverts. The energy pouring into our Light Side all Morning reverses direction in the Afternoon to power the exploration of our forgotten Dark Side and find the person behind the mask. And strangely, by discovering our unique individuality we uncover our universal commonality.

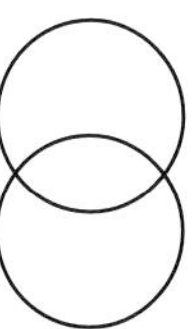

# Act IV

## Light Rejoins Dark

So long ago, when the purpose of life was not so well hidden, we cherished our Dark Side as much as our Light Side. With so few complex inventions, we had plenty of time for simple reflection. We lived lightly and feared not as Midnight neared.

Somewhere along the way, we lost *sophrosyne* (soh-froh-soo'-neh) – the "blended wisdom" behind those famous words of warning: "Know thyself" and "Nothing in excess." Although *sophrosyne* was the overarching ideal of the ancient Greek culture, this word cannot be translated into any one English word because the ideal was lost so long ago.

So many of Our Great Plays have turned tragically small and routinely slapstick as we crawl over ourselves to get more and more of what we do not really want. Billions have come before us, and more will follow, yet we try to escape our own mortality through busyness and distractions. We demote ourselves to units of production and consumption, marketing our fake elixirs to all ages. Consumed by the pain of desire, we fail to see our true needs.

Someplace inside our hubris, present in its absence, rests the seed of *sophrosyne*. Between the extremes of ignorance and excess we will find our blended wisdom buried in the extraordinarily ordinary middle. It is all fate. In the end, what we do in life matters much less than what we do next. The Evening always belongs to destiny. And no matter what happens in Our Great Plays, we all arrive at the beginning, once again, in the Middle of the Night . . . .

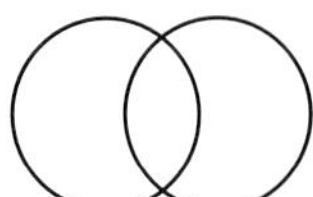

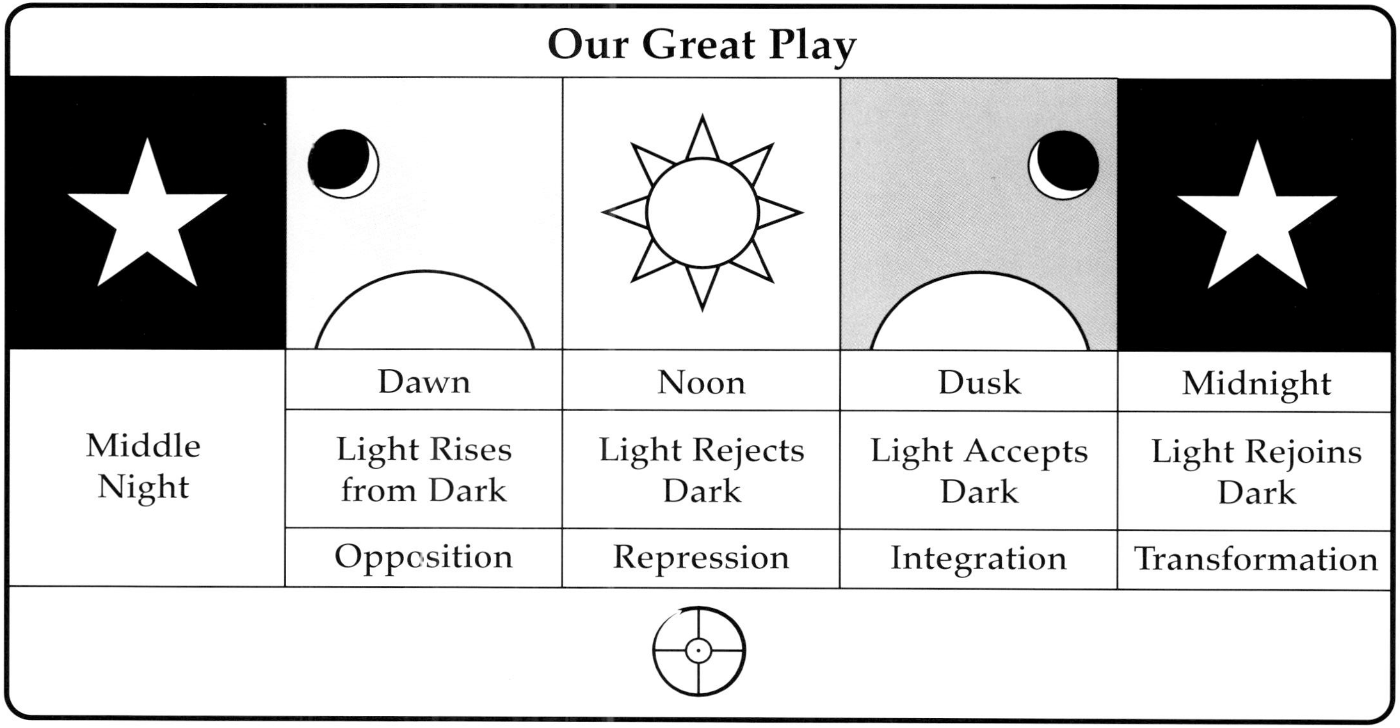

## Our Great Play

| Middle Night | Dawn | Noon | Dusk | Midnight |
|---|---|---|---|---|
| | Light Rises from Dark | Light Rejects Dark | Light Accepts Dark | Light Rejoins Dark |
| | Opposition | Repression | Integration | Transformation |

# THE BAKERY

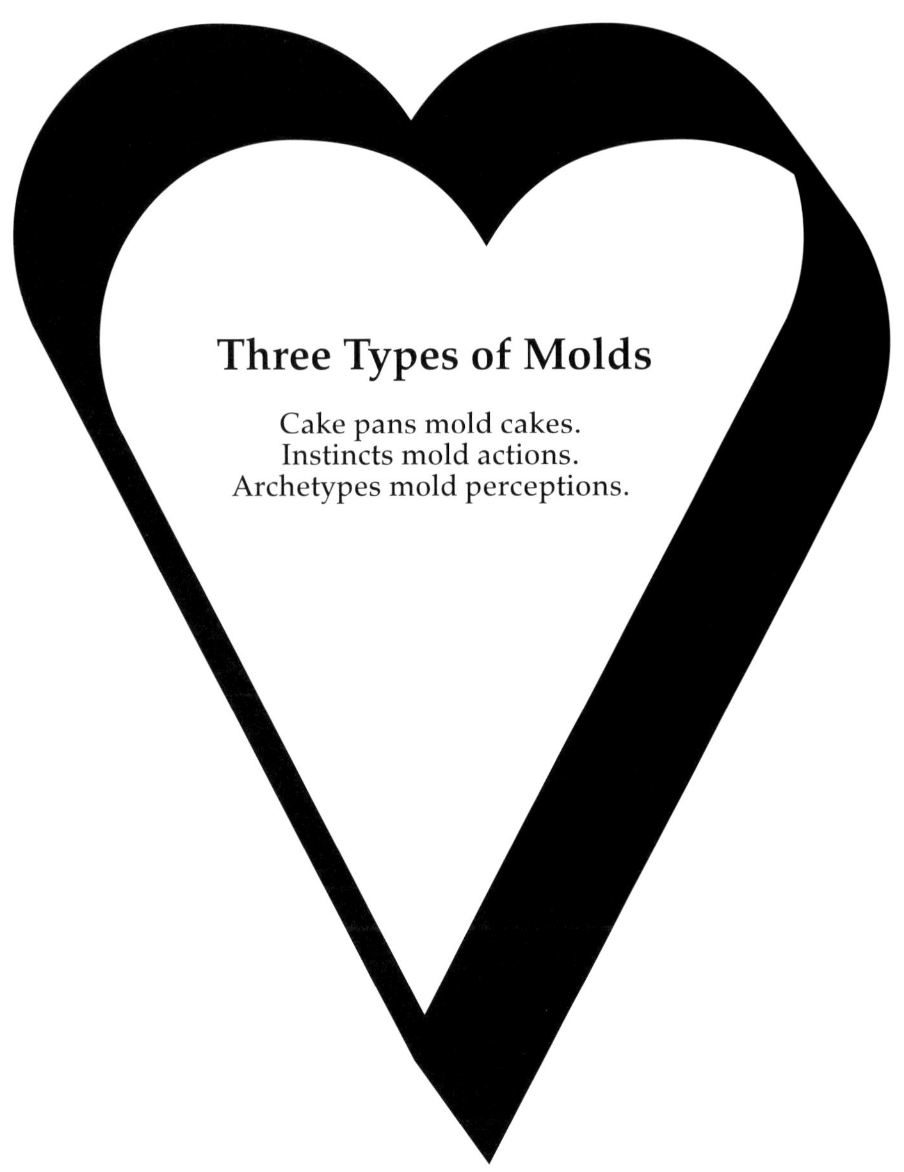
Three Types of Molds
Cake pans mold cakes.
Instincts mold actions.
Archetypes mold perceptions.

**Active Imagination:** the conscious exploration of the unconscious using the Fifth Talent, as if "dreaming with open eyes." Like two children, the Light Side and the Dark Side of the personality play together making symbols for later evaluation and integration.

**Alchemy:** alchemists throughout history openly pursued three goals: 1) transmuting base metals into gold; 2) discovering panaceas; and 3) mixing elixirs of longevity. After the Renaissance and Inquisitions, alchemists revealed their true goal: personal transformation as spiritual beings dwelling in material bodies.

**Anima:** the feminine Soul Image imprinted on the Dark Side of males. Males personify the Anima as a separate personality and project it onto females. The Anima is an archetype and a personal complex. One of the goals of Active Imagination is to transform the Anima from an autonomous adversary to a valuable envoy from the Dark.

**Animosity:** ill will arousing active hostility; deep-seated, mutual hatred. The Anima and Animus have natural animosity.

**Animus:** the masculine Soul Image imprinted on the Dark Side of females. Females personify the Animus as a separate personality and project it onto males. The Animus is an archetype and a personal complex. One of the goals of Active Imagination is to transform the Animus from an autonomous adversary to a valuable envoy from the Dark.

**Archetype:** Original Mold. Archetypes mold our perceptions just like cake pans mold cakes. A cake pan molds one type of cake, and an archetype molds one type of perception. Imagine baking a cake in a heart-shaped pan and saying to a friend: "This cake is typical of the one hundred cakes that I will bake for you." The friend will expect 99 more cakes of that type. Likewise, archetypes produce archetypal perceptions that mold the grand themes of humanity. Humans all inherit the same instincts and archetypes. Instincts mold our actions, and archetypes mold our perceptions. Just as the cake is not the mold, the action is not the instinct, and the perception is not the archetype. Archetypes always remain unconscious, only the perceptions that they mold enter consciousness.

**Bakery:** baking a cake requires all Four Human Natures. First, the baker mixes different ingredients into a cool and moist mixture of concentrated dough. Then, the baker pours the mixture into a rigid cake pan to establish boundaries for the cake. Next, the baker puts the pan and mixture into the hot oven to exhaust the moisture from the mixture and activate the process of leavening which expands the mixture. The cake rises with air as gas bubbles develop from the leavening agent that catalyzes a subtle lightening of the mixture and fills the moist bakery air with a warm aroma. In summary, Unifiers provide the mixture, Stabilizers provide the pan, Activators provide the heat, and Clarifiers provide the catalyst. In the middle is the Baker.

**Blake, William:** (1757–1827) a great English poet, artist, printer, and engraver. A rebel all of his life, he championed innocence and imagination over tyranny and excess.

**Briggs, Katherine:** (1875–1968) the perceptive co-creator of the popular Myers-Briggs Type Indicator®. She devoted her life to the perception and evaluation of personality with the goal of helping us to recognize and respect our individual differences.

**Centrifugal:** center-fleeing; developing outward from the center.

**Centripetal:** center-seeking; developing inward toward the center.

**Chaos:** disorder; the opposite of cosmos; unpredictable behavior in systems that are extremely sensitive to variations in initial conditions. For example, a boulder rolling down a hill is in a state of chaos. Cosmos arises from chaos.

**Collective:** belonging to a collection of people; a group; a culture; the human race.

**Collective Consciousness:** our collective Light Side; the conscious mind of a collection of people. The collective consciousness of any group is always primitive compared to individual consciousness.

> If any considerable group of persons are united and identified with one another by a particular frame of mind, the resultant transformation experience bears only a very remote resemblance to the experience of individual transformation. A group experience takes place on a lower level of consciousness than the experience of an individual. This is due to the fact that, when many people gather together to share one common emotion, the total psyche emerging from the group is below the level of the individual psyche. If it is a very large group, the collective psyche will be more like the psyche of an animal . . . . The group experience goes no deeper than the level of one's own mind in that state. It does work a change in you, but the change does not last. (CW 9i, par. 225f)

**Compensation:** the natural balancing of both sides of the psyche. Like the action of a seesaw, the Dark Side compensates for any and all extremes of the Light Side, constantly bringing the psyche back to the middle. Like a pendulum, we perpetually swing between opposite extremes from Light to Dark and Dark to Light.

> The activity of consciousness is selective. Selection demands direction. But

> direction requires *the exclusion of everything irrelevant*. This is bound to make the conscious orientation one-sided. The contents that are excluded and inhibited by the chosen direction sink into the unconscious, where they form a counterweight to the conscious orientation. (CW 6, par. 694)

**Complex:** the source of all human emotions; an autonomous and emotionally charged group of perceptions that cluster around an archetype.

> [A complex] is the *image* of a certain psychic situation which is strongly accentuated emotionally and is, moreover, incompatible with the habitual attitude of consciousness. (CW 8, par. 201)

> Complexes interfere with the intentions of the will and disturb the conscious performance; they produce disturbances of memory and blockages in the flow of associations; they appear and disappear according to their own laws; they can temporarily obsess consciousness, or influence speech and action in an unconscious way. In a word, complexes behave like independent beings. (CW 8, par. 253)

> Complexes are focal or nodal points of psychic life which we would not wish to do without; indeed, they should not be missing, for otherwise psychic activity would come to a fatal standstill. (CW 6, par. 925)

> Some degree of one-sidedness is unavoidable, and, in the same measure, complexes are unavoidable too. (CW 8, par. 255)

> The possession of complexes does not in itself signify neurosis . . . and the fact that they are painful is no proof of pathological disturbance. Suffering is not an illness; it is the normal counterpole to happiness. A complex becomes pathological only when we think we have not got it. (CW 16, par. 179)

> A complex can be really overcome only if it is lived out to the full. In other words, if we are to develop further we have to draw to us and drink down to the very dregs what, because of our complexes, we have held at a distance. (CW 9i, par. 184)

**Conflict:** tension between opposites. In holding the tension between opposites, a third thing will appear that transcends the opposites and resolves the conflict. The conflict between our Light and Dark Sides is part of the self-regulation of the psyche. Conflict between individuals and groups externalizes the conflict between our Light and Dark Sides.

> The self is made manifest in the opposites and in the conflict between them; it is a *coincidentia oppositorum* [coincidence of opposites]. Hence the way to the self begins with conflict. (CW 12, par. 259)

> Out of [the] collision of opposites the unconscious psyche always creates a third thing of an irrational nature, which the conscious mind neither expects nor understands. It presents itself in a form that is neither a straight "yes" nor a straight "no." (CW 9i, par. 285)

**Consciousness:** arises out of unconsciousness. Consciousness begins with the discrimination between opposites, and grows painfully from the conflict between our Light and Dark Sides.

> Consciousness does not create itself – it wells up from unknown depths. In childhood it awakens gradually, and all through life it wakes each morning out of the depths of sleep from an unconscious condition. It is like a child that is born daily out of the primordial womb of the unconscious. . . . It is not only influenced by the unconscious but continually emerges out of it in the form of numberless spontaneous ideas and sudden flashes of thought. (CW 11, par. 935)

> The conscious mind is on top, the shadow underneath, and just as high always longs for low and hot for cold, so all consciousness, perhaps without being aware of it, seeks its unconscious opposite, lacking which it is doomed to stagnation, congestion, and ossification. Life is born only of the spark of opposites. (CW 7, par. 78)

> There is no consciousness without discrimination of opposites. (CW 9i, par. 178)

**Constructive:** "leading forward" as opposed to reductive which means "leading back." A constructive view (Jung) looks at the internal symbolic meaning for the development of the individual. A reductive view (Freud) looks for external causes.

**Cosmos:** order; the opposite of chaos; from the Greek word *kosmos* meaning beautiful order. The Four Cosmos Attractors reveal how cosmos arises from chaos.

**Dreams:** fragments of the unconscious. Dreams can be viewed constructively as purposeful symbols of the dreamer's internal world, or viewed reductively as caused by external events.

> Dreams are neither deliberate nor arbitrary fabrications; they are natural

> phenomena which are nothing other than what they pretend to be. They do not deceive, they do not lie, they do not distort or disguise. . . . They are invariably seeking to express something that the ego does not know and does not understand. (CW 17, par. 189)

**Ego:** as the "Light of Consciousness," the Ego experiences itself as the center of our whole personality, but it is only the center of our Light Side. The Ego evolves out of the Self, which is the true center of our whole personality.

> Anyone who has any ego-consciousness at all takes it for granted that he knows himself. But the ego knows only its own contents, not the unconscious and its contents. People measure their self-knowledge by what the average person in their social environment knows of himself, but not by the real psychic facts which are for the most part hidden from them. In this respect the psyche behaves like the body, of whose physiological and anatomical structure the average person knows very little too. (CW 10, par. 491)

> There is no form of human tragedy that does not in some measure proceed from [the] conflict between the ego and the unconscious. (CW 8, par. 706)

**Elements:** arising from the Original Compass, the Four Elements of Water, Air, Fire, and Earth are archetypes and form a quaternity. The Elements are each made from two Forces in a 3/1 ratio: Water is Cool/Moist, Air is Moist/Warm, Fire is Warm/Dry, and Earth is Dry/Cool. The Four Elements each have an essential nature and number quality: Water's Unity (One), Air's Clarity (Two), Fire's Activity (Three), and Earth's Stability (Four).

**Empedocles:** (495–435 B.C.) a great Greek philosopher, statesman, and poet. Empedocles was the first person to discover the archetypes of the Four Elements, the Four Forces, and the Four Human Natures. He wrote the *Doctrine of the Four Elements (Tetrasomia)* which formed the framework for many great philosophical and scientific traditions. Aristotle hailed Empedocles as the inventor of rhetoric. Aristotle, and many famous philosophers including the Pythagoreans and Plato, refined our understanding of the Four Elements, Four Forces, and Four Human Natures.

***Enantiodromia*:** the ancient Greek word for a primary natural law: all opposites switch places in search of balance. In the East, this natural law is known as *Yin* and *Yang*.

**Explicit:** "unfolded" as opposed to implicit which means "infolded." Directors (Styles 3 and 4) are naturally explicit and Indirectors (Styles 1 and 2) are naturally implicit.

**Fifth Talent:** a blend of our Four Light Talents, our Fifth Talent connects our Light and Dark Sides just as the horizon joins day with night, and a waterfall joins above and below.

**Five Point Survey.**™ The words *guide*, *survey*, and *wise* all share the same ancient root, *weid: to see*. The Five Point Survey™ shows us our Nature, Style, and Realm. By clearly defining the primal polarities of personality, the Survey takes us to the top of the five hills that overlook our Light Side and our Dark Side. By ascending these five hills, we can see the beautiful contrast between light and shadow. From high above, we survey the Map of the Four Natures and the Map of the Four Realms. If we look over our lives carefully, we can see our birthplace on both maps. And if we observe others fairly, we can see their homelands too. Descending from the serenity of these five hills, we carry with us a new outlook on our innate similarities and differences. Having seen all the parts that make up the whole of humanity, we awaken to a blended wisdom of ourselves and others. By knowing our potential, we develop fully. And by knowing our limitations, we avoid excess. In the middle, we discover the most extraordinary, ordinary lives.

**Five Solids:** beautiful and mysterious, the Five Solids have played a central role in the art, architecture, symbology, and philosophy of many cultures. The Five Solids emerge from a series of uniform divisions of the sphere. They are the only possible straight-sided shapes with equal sides and equal angles (regular polyhedra). Each Solid has external and internal accord: externally, all five unite perfectly in various permutations; internally, all five fit together one inside the next like a magic box. The Five Solids are traditionally known as the Platonic Solids, but Plato did not discover them. The cube and the pyramid were known long before Plato, and the Pythagoreans discovered the remaining three by experimenting with ordinary Greek floor tiles. They found that only three regular shapes of tiles could fit together to cover a flat area completely: triangles, squares, and hexagons. They glued these tiles together into solid shapes to form the Five Solids.

**Forces:** the Four Forces are the archetypes that mold the vertical axis (north–south) and the horizontal axis (east–west) of the Original Compass: Warm north, Cool south, Dry east, Moist west. The Space in the middle is the center point and Original Force (also known as the Fifth Force). The Four Forces each have an essential nature: Cool unites, Moist conforms, Warm separates, and Dry forms.

**Fourfold:** nature shows a fourfold order, for example:

Four cardinal points: east, west, north, south
Four seasons: winter, spring, summer, fall
Four parts of the day: dawn, noon, dusk, midnight

Four chambers of the heart: right/left atria, right/left ventricles
Four dimensions: line, plane, solid, time–space
Four states of matter: solid, liquid, gas, plasma (ionized gas)
Four Elements: Water, Air, Fire, Earth
Four Cosmos Attractors: Point, Cycle, Torus, Strange

**Functions** or **Psychological Functions:** Carl Jung's eight functions are the same as the Eight Talents, just named differently. Jung named the functions using words "current in daily speech, perfectly accessible and comprehensible to everyone." Jung chose words "easily intelligible in current speech" because he was not creating an abstract theory but rather clarifying something so real and obvious that "every language" had "absolutely unmistakable expressions for them." (CW 6, par. 949) In sum, universal intelligibility was Jung's one goal in naming the functions. However, Jung's clear terminology has become confusing because these terms are defined and used in current daily speech differently than Jung defined and used these terms. The Pictures of Personality™ Guide to the Four Human Natures provides the natural synthesis of both sides of Jung's terminology (the clarity that turned into confusion) and remains loyal to Jung's goal to use typology throughout the world so that we may each develop our whole personality as unique individuals and live peacefully with greater understanding and tolerance for others.

> The four functions are somewhat like the four points of the compass; they are just as arbitrary and just as indispensable. Nothing prevents our shifting the cardinal points as many degrees as we like in one direction or the other, or giving them different names. It is merely a question of convention and intelligibility. But one thing I must confess: I would not for anything dispense with this compass on my psychological voyages of discovery. (CW 6, par. 958)

> Classification has little value if it does not provide a means of orientation and a practical terminology. I find classification into types particularly helpful when I am called upon to explain parents to children or husbands to wives, and vice versa. It is also useful in understanding one's own prejudices. (CW 18, par. 219)

Carl Jung saw two basic functions of the mind: perceiving and deciding. He saw that we can perceive what is, or what is not, and he named these two opposite perceiving functions "sensation" (Content) and "intuition" (Context). He saw that we can decide based on logic or value, and he named these two opposite deciding functions "thinking" (Organizing) and "feeling" (Harmonizing). He saw that each function has two sides or "attitudes." One side inclines toward our internal world, and one side inclines toward the external world. He named these two opposite attitudes "introversion" and "extraversion." He saw that every person has one favorite function that naturally arises in one favorite attitude. Thus, Jung described eight Psychological Types according to the function and attitude that naturally dominates the conscious mind (the Light Side). Jung named the most developed function (Talent L1) the "superior function" or "primary function." He saw that every Type has a natural "auxiliary function" (Talent L2) which is the opposite of the superior function in kind (Perceiving or Deciding) and attitude (Introverted or Extraverted). In this way, we naturally develop, more or less, one function for the external world and one function for our internal world; one function perceives and the other function decides. Finally, Jung saw that the more we develop our most natural functions, the more we neglect our least natural functions. The least natural and most neglected function he named the "inferior function" (Talent D1), the superior function's deeply unconscious counterpart.

> One always has to answer people in their main function, otherwise no contact is established. (CW 18, par. 140)

> Experience shows that it is practically impossible, owing to adverse circumstances in general, for anyone to develop all his psychological functions simultaneously. The demands of society compel a man to apply himself first and foremost to the differentiation of the function with which he is best equipped by nature, or which will secure him the greatest social success. Very frequently, indeed as a general rule, a man identifies more or less completely with the most favoured and hence the most developed function. It is this that gives rise to the various psychological types. (CW 6, par. 763)

> Positive as well as negative occurrences can constellate the inferior counter-function. When this happens, sensitiveness appears. Sensitiveness is a sure sign of the presence of inferiority. This provides the psychological basis for discord and misunderstanding, not only as between two people, but also in ourselves. The essence of the inferior function is autonomy: it is independent, it attacks, it fascinates and so spins us about that we are no longer masters of ourselves and can no longer rightly distinguish between ourselves and others. (CW 7, par. 85)

**Gestalt:** something whole that cannot be derived from the addition of its parts.

**Golden Mean** or **Phi:** a mysterious ratio found in nature; an archetype of order and balance. Discovered by the ancient Greeks, the Golden Mean is represented by the Greek letter *phi* and also known as the Golden Ratio, Golden Section, Golden Proportion, and Divine Proportion. *Phi* is an infinite number like *pi* that orders our internal and external worlds. *Phi* divides a line so that the shorter part (A) is to the longer part (B) as the longer part (B) is to the whole (A+B). Put simply, the lesser is to the greater as the greater is to the whole. The Greeks and Egyptians used the Golden Mean in designing their cities, buildings, and monuments. Architects, artists, and musicians throughout history have used the Golden Mean to recreate nature's beauty and proportion. The Golden Mean is found, for example, in the curve of a fern, the spiral of shells and leaves, pine cones and starfish, flowers and plants, the breeding patterns of rabbits, the spirals of galaxies, a bee's genealogy, the behavior of light and atoms, and DNA molecules. *Phi* is the perfect rate of growth for things that grow by adding one unit, and provides the optimum arrangement for packing objects that grow in size. The equation for *phi* has five at the center: $1 + \sqrt{5}$ divided by 2. The result of this equation is an irrational and infinite number: 1.618 repeating (approximately a 10:6 ratio).

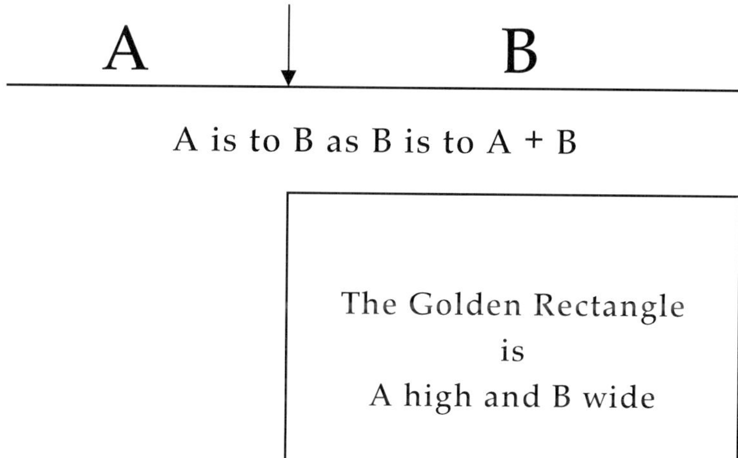


**Graphical User Interface (GUI):** pronounced GOO-ee, the GUI is a universal picture language for computer operation that enables people to communicate with computers through symbols and icons. The GUI replaced the arcane and difficult textual interfaces that prevented the universal use of computers. The GUI makes computer operation easy to learn, fun, and natural. Likewise, the Pictures of Personality™ Guide to the Four Human Natures presents the first universal picture language of personality.

**Haiku:** a form of poetry (two lines of five syllables framing a middle line of seven syllables) that conveys a moment of transcendence in nature captured with pure, innocent perception.

**Heraclitus:** (535–475 B.C.) a great Greek philosopher and one of the founders of Greek metaphysics. He championed the natural law of *enantiodromia* (all opposites switch places) as the central theme of the universe. He saw that everything constantly changes, not only being but becoming. Warm water is not only being warm but becoming cool. Cool water is being cool and becoming warm. Heraclitus saw that every human being becomes wise by respecting this one natural law.

**Hubris:** aggressive arrogance; the opposite of *sophrosyne*; disregard for the natural laws of the universe; overbearing pride and presumption; selfishness; self-indulgence; greed; vanity; lack of self-control. The Greeks regarded hubris as the most tragic human failing and greatest danger to the individual and society.

***I Ching* or Book of Changes:** an ancient book of wisdom that reveals the hidden relationships between humans and the changing universe.

**Icon:** an image in the likeness of something. An icon looks like the thing that it represents. The words *icon* and *like* share the same root.

**Implicit:** "infolded" as opposed to explicit which means "unfolded." Indirectors (Styles 1 and 2) are naturally implicit and Directors (Styles 3 and 4) are naturally explicit.

**Individual:** indivisible; the whole, unique personality; the person that appears when the Light Side and Dark Side are not divided.

> Everything that is not collective is individual, everything in fact that pertains only to one individual and not to a larger group of individuals. (CW 6, par. 756)

> The larger a community is, and the more the sum total of collective factors peculiar to every large community rests on conservative prejudices detrimental to individuality, the more will the individual be morally and spiritually crushed, and, as a result, the one source of moral and spiritual progress for society is choked up. (CW 7, par. 240)

> *Resistance to the organized mass can be effected only by the man who is as well organized in his individuality as the mass itself.* (CW 10, par. 540, Jung's italics)

**Individuation:** the unending process of reuniting the Light Side and Dark Side of the personality to reveal the whole, unique individual.

> Individuation does not shut one out from the world, but gathers the world to itself. (CW 8, par. 432)

> Everything good is costly, and the development of personality is one of the most costly of all things. It is a matter of saying yes to oneself, of taking oneself as the most serious of tasks, of being conscious of everything one does, and keeping it constantly before one's eyes in all its dubious aspects—truly a task that taxes us to the utmost. (CW 13, par. 24)

> The aim of individuation is nothing less than to divest the self of the false wrappings of the persona on the one hand, and of the suggestive power of primordial images on the other. (CW 7, par. 269)

> In this way there arises a consciousness which is no longer imprisoned in the petty, oversensitive, personal world of the ego, but participates freely in the wider world of objective interests. This widened consciousness is no longer that touchy, egotistical bundle of personal wishes, fears, hopes, and ambitions which always has to be compensated or corrected by unconscious counter-tendencies; instead, it is a function of relationship to the world of objects, bringing the individual into absolute, binding, and indissoluble communion with the world at large. (CW 7, par. 275)

**ISOTYPE:** the International System of Typographic Picture Education. ISOTYPE is the universal picture language conceived by Otto Neurath (1882–1945) who believed: "The ordinary citizen ought to be able to get information freely about all subjects in which he is interested, just as he can get geographical knowledge from maps and atlases. There is no field where humanization of knowledge through the eye would not be possible." Likewise, the Pictures of Personality™ Guide to the Four Human Natures presents the first universal picture language of personality.

**Jung, Carl Gustav:** (1875–1961) the great Swiss psychiatrist, philosopher, and founder of analytical psychology. Jung was a wise and practical man. He cared deeply for others and moved easily between his internal world and the external world in a four part process: 1) observation; 2) theory; 3) illustration; and 4) application. Rather than expending his resources trying to prove his theories, Jung preferred to illuminate, amplify, and apply his theories for the maximum benefit of the individuals under his care and for all of humanity. Jung's observation and constructive exploration of tens of thousands of people led to many important discoveries about human nature. In one of his most famous works, *Psychological Types*, Jung explained his perception of human typology from both a personal and historical perspective. Jung's typology forms the foundation for much of the typology shown in this guide.

**Keirsey, David:** the perceptive psychologist who expounds the intelligent roles of the four temperaments. In 1978, David Keirsey and Marilyn Bates wrote the popular book entitled *Please Understand Me*. In 1998, Keirsey updated and expanded the book into the popular sequel entitled *Please Understand Me II*. He has devoted his life to the perception and contemplation of personality with the goal of helping us to recognize and respect our individual differences.

**Mandala:** a circle, often combined with a fourfold design. On the one hand, mandalas symbolize the whole and the transcendence of polarities (the change from many to one). On the other hand, mandalas symbolize fractions of the whole and the conscious awareness of polarities (the change from one to many).

> Roundness (the mandala motif) generally symbolizes a natural wholeness, whereas a quadrangular formation represents the realization of this in consciousness. In the dream the square disk and the round table meet, and thus a conscious realization of the center is at hand. (Carl Jung, *Man and His Symbols* [New York: Dell, 1964], 234)

> When I began drawing the mandalas, however, I saw that everything, all paths I had been following, all steps I had taken, were leading back to a single point—namely, to the mid-point. It became increasingly plain to me that the mandala is the center. It is the exponent of all paths. It is the path to the center, to individuation. (Carl Jung, *Memories, Dreams, Reflections* [New York: Vintage Books, 1989], 196)

> [Mandalas] are used to consolidate the inner being, or to plunge one into deep meditation. The contemplation of a mandala is meant to bring an inner peace, a feeling that life has again found its meaning and order. (Carl Jung, *Man and His Symbols* [New York: Dell, 1964], 230)

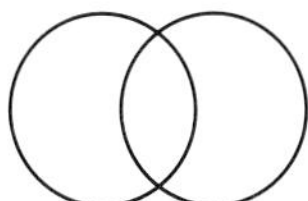

**Mandorla:** the Italian word for almond; the almond shaped center between two overlapping circles symbolizing the union of opposites, and the hidden, enclosed, inviolable, and divine nature of all things.

**Myers, Isabel Briggs:** (1897–1980) the perceptive co-creator of the popular Myers-Briggs Type Indicator® and author of the popular book entitled *Gifts Differing: Understanding Personality Type*. She devoted her life to the perception and evaluation of personality with the goal of helping us to recognize and respect our individual differences.

**Myers-Briggs Type Indicator® (MBTI®):** Isabel Briggs Myers and her mother, Katharine

Briggs, developed the MBTI® to make Jung's typology understandable and useful to people. The MBTI® is a popular personality inventory that is professionally administered to millions of people every year to indicate their preferences on four polarities: Extraversion or Introversion (E or I); Sensing or iNtuition (S or N); Thinking or Feeling (T or F); Judging or Perceiving (J or P). Sixteen Personality Types result from the sixteen possible combinations of the four preferences, each designated by a four letter code.

**Number:** the primary archetype of order. The natural numbers (0, 1, 2, 3, 4, 5, 6, 7, 8, 9) are both signs and symbols. As signs, numbers represent a quantity (measurement). As symbols, numbers express a quality (meaning). The first five numbers symbolize Unity, Polarity, Activity, Stability, and Center.

> There is something peculiar, one might even say mysterious, about numbers . . . [if] a group of objects is deprived of every single one of its properties or characteristics, there still remains, at the end, its *number*, which seems to indicate that number is something irreducible . . . [something which] helps more than anything else to bring order into the chaos of appearances . . . It may well be the most primitive element of order in the human mind . . . we [can] define number psychologically as *an archetype of order* which has become conscious. (CW 8, par. 870)

**Numinosity:** the mysterious "other worldly" energy that we feel in special moments that seems to be beyond our conscious will or understanding. We can view the experience reductively (caused by something external) or constructively (coming from within).

> The main interest of my work is not concerned with the treatment of neurosis but rather with the approach to the numinous . . . [which] is the real therapy.
> – Carl Jung

> The most beautiful thing we can experience is the mysterious. It is the source of all true art and science. – Albert Einstein

**Object:** the opposite of subject. We live in the objective reality of the external world, and the subjective reality of our internal world.

**Original Compass:** a central archetype of order. The Original Compass molds our perception of the Four Elements, the Four Natures, the Four Styles, and the Four Realms. The Original Compass maps the primary polarities of personality. The first five natural numbers mold the Original Compass: One SW, Two NW, Three NE, Four SE, with Five at the Center. The Four Forces also mold the Original Compass. The two Active Forces create the vertical axis (Warm north and Cool south). The two Passive

Forces create the horizontal axis (Moist west and Dry east). The Fifth Force (Original Force) is in the Center.

**Pentad:** a group of five. In Greek philosophy, the Pentad represents the fifth level of cosmic design after the Monad (point), Dyad (line), Triad (surface), and Tetrad (volume). Nature often favors a fivefold design, for example: five-petaled flowers, five-edged leaves, five senses, and five extensions of the body.

**Persona:** Latin for *mask*. Our persona is not our whole personality. Our persona is our public image and social identity. We wear our mask to protect ourselves and survive in the world. We do not create our persona. Rather, our culture assigns our mask to us and rewards us for performing well. Consequently, we strongly identify with our persona and soon forget that we are wearing a mask.

> The persona is that which in reality one is not, but which oneself as well as others think one is. (CW 9i, par. 221)

> It is, as its name implies, only a mask of the collective psyche, a mask that feigns individuality, making others and oneself believe that one is individual, whereas one is simply acting a role through which the collective psyche speaks. When we analyse the persona we strip off the mask, and discover that what seemed to be individual is at bottom collective; in other words, that the persona was only a mask of the collective psyche. Fundamentally the persona is nothing real: it is a compromise between individual and society as to what a man should appear to be. He takes a name, earns a title, exercises a function, he is this or that. In a certain sense all this is real, yet in relation to the essential individuality of the person concerned it is only a secondary reality, a compromise formation, in making which others often have a greater share than he. (CW 7, par. 245f)

> Society expects, and indeed must expect, every individual to play the part assigned to him as perfectly as possible, so that a man who is a parson . . . must at all times . . . play the role of parson in a flawless manner. Society demands this as a kind of surety: each must stand at his post, here a cobbler, there a poet. No man is expected to be both . . . that would be 'odd.' Such a man would be 'different' from other people, not quite reliable. In the academic world he would be a dilettante, in politics an 'unpredictable' quantity, in religion a free-thinker – in short, he would always be suspected of unreliability and incompetence, because society is persuaded that only the cobbler who is not a poet can supply workmanlike shoes. (CW 7, par. 305)

**Personality Type:** the primary polarities of human nature produce the Sixteen Personality Types: U1, U2, U3, U4, C1, C2, C3, C4, A1, A2, A3, A4, S1, S2, S3, S4. The Original Compass maps the primary polarities of human nature into the Four Natures, Four Styles, and Four Realms. No Personality Type is better or worse than any other Type. Both sides of every polarity are equally valid and valuable.

**Philosopher's Stone:** symbolizes the archetype of Wholeness. In alchemy, the Philosopher's Stone is a metaphor for personal transformation as spiritual beings dwelling in material bodies.

> Make a round circle of man and woman, extract therefrom a quadrangle and from it a triangle. Make the circle round, and you will have the Philosopher's Stone. (CW 11, par. 92, quoting from the *Rosarium philosophorum*)

**Polarity:** an intrinsic separation of polar opposites; mutual opposition; polar alignment; the archetype of Two. Typology types personality by primal polarities. (Note: Clarifiers clarify polarities rather than create polarities. Accordingly, the Nature molded by the archetype of Two is named "Clarifier" rather than "Polarizer.")

**Primal:** first; primary; original; not derived from something else.

**Projection:** to thrust out upon the external world (onto other people and things) like a movie projector thrusts a movie upon the screen. We unconsciously project the best and worst parts of our Dark Side, individually and collectively.

> Just as we tend to assume that the world is as we see it, we naïvely suppose that people are as we imagine them to be. . . . We always see our own unavowed mistakes in our opponent. Excellent examples of this are to be found in all personal quarrels. (CW 8, par. 507)

> The effect of projection is to isolate the subject from his environment, since instead of a real relation to it there is now only an illusory one. Projections change the world into the replica of one's own unknown face. In the last analysis, therefore, they lead to an autoerotic or autistic condition in which one dreams a world whose reality remains forever unattainable. (CW 9ii, par. 17)

**Psyche:** the word *psyche* arises from the ancient root *bhes: to breathe.* Like the body, our psyche inhales and exhales to maintain balance between our Light Side and our Dark Side so that we find our center (balanced in the middle between the two extremes).

**Pythagoras:** (580–500 B.C.) a great Greek philosopher and mathematician who found numbers to be the universal language of nature.

**Quaternity:** the union of four in one (just as a trinity is the union of three in one). Quaternity is the sum of 3+1, not 2+2, because one of the four is always of a different quality than the other three. Quaternity is a universal theme found in all cultures, usually symbolized as a mandala. Quaternity forms the foundation of all balanced perceptions and decisions.

> The quaternity is one of the most widespread archetypes and has also proved to be one of the most useful schemata for representing the arrangement of the functions by which the conscious mind takes its bearings. It is like the crossed threads in the telescope of our understanding. The cross formed by the points of the quaternity is no less universal and has in addition the highest possible moral and religious significance for Western man. Similarly the circle, as the symbol of completeness and perfect being, is a widespread expression for heaven, sun, and God; it also expresses the primordial image of man and the soul. (CW 16, par. 405)

**Quintessence:** Fifth Essence or Fifth Element. Aristotle coined the word *quintessence* to describe the ether that permeates the space between matter. The Fifth Element transcends all opposites and provides the medium of exchange between the Four Elements as they spiral around the center. Today, quintessence is the scientific term for the empty space of the universe.

**Realm:** our natural sphere of influence. Above, Magicians reign over the Known and Unknown. Below, Rulers rule the Past and Future.

**Repress:** to press down by force as in "to repress a rebellion." We repress down into the Dark everything that is incompatible with our Light Side.

> Repression is a process that begins in early childhood under the moral influence of the environment and continues through life. (CW 7, par. 202)

> Repression causes what is called a *systematic amnesia*, where only specific memories or groups of ideas are withdrawn from recollection. In such cases a certain attitude or tendency can be detected on the part of the conscious mind, a deliberate intention to avoid even the bare possibility of recollection, for the very good reason that it would be painful or disagreeable. (CW 17, par. 199a)

**Seesaw:** a plank balanced on a central fulcrum so that one end goes up as the other goes down. The seesaw is also known as a teeter, teeterboard, teeter-totter, tilting board, dandle, dandle board, and teedle board.

**Self:** an archetype of wholeness; the center of the whole personality balanced between the Light Side and the Dark Side.

> The self is not only the centre, but also the whole circumference which embraces both conscious and unconscious; it is the centre of this totality, just as the ego is the centre of consciousness. (CW 12, par. 44)

> The self appears in dreams, myths, and fairy tales in the figure of the "supraordinate personality," such as a king, hero, prophet, saviour, etc., or in the form of a totality symbol, such as the circle, square, *quadratura circuli*, cross, etc. When it represents a *complexio oppositorum*, a union of opposites, it can also appear as a united duality, in the form, for instance, of *tao* as the interplay of *Yang* and *Yin*, or of the hostile brothers, or of the hero and his adversary (arch-enemy, dragon), Faust and Mephistopheles, etc. Empirically, therefore, the self appears as a play of light and shadow, although conceived as a totality and unity in which the opposites are united. (CW 6, par. 790)

**Shadow:** as part of our Dark Side, the Shadow hides all of the negative and positive things that we disown and deny. The Shadow is unconscious, tricky, dangerous, and chaotic. Individuals cast personal Shadows, and groups cast collective Shadows. The image of the Trickster, the mischievous troublemaker in stories and myths, personifies the Shadow.

> The shadow is merely somewhat inferior, primitive, unadapted, and awkward; not wholly bad. It even contains childish or primitive qualities which would in a way vitalize and embellish human existence, but convention forbids! (CW 11, par. 134)

> The so-called civilized man has forgotten the trickster. He remembers him only figuratively and metaphorically, when, irritated by his own ineptitude, he speaks of fate playing tricks on him or of things being bewitched. He never suspects that his own hidden and apparently harmless shadow has qualities whose dangerousness exceeds his wildest dreams. (CW 9i, par. 478)

> The shadow is a moral problem that challenges the whole ego-personality, for no one can become conscious of the shadow without considerable moral effort. To become conscious of it involves recognizing the dark aspects of the personality as present and real. (CW 9ii, par. 14)

> This process of coming to terms with the Other in us is well worthwhile, because

> in this way we get to know aspects of our nature which we would not allow anybody else to show us and which we ourselves would never have admitted. (CW 14, par. 706)

***Sophrosyne*:** (soh-froh-soo'-neh) "blended wisdom." The highest ideal of the ancient Greeks, *sophrosyne* is the synthesis (*syne*) of wisdom (*sophia*) that comes from the confluence of the following: knowledge of our limitations; moderation; self-restraint in the exercise of freedom; respect for nature and society; compassion; tolerance; patience; balance; and love of truth, beauty, and excellence.

**Soul Image:** an archetypal image of our inner personality behind the mask of our persona. A male's Soul Image (Anima) is female, and a female's Soul Image (Animus) is male. Extraverts have an introverted Soul Image, and Introverts have an extraverted Soul Image. Yearning for union with our other half, we project our Soul Image onto others of the opposite sex and opposite Attitude. Opposites attract and then repel as the natural animosity between the Anima and Animus surfaces. Jung observed that human pairings result either in tremendous individual growth or total stagnation.

> Wherever an impassioned, almost magical, relationship exists between the sexes, it is invariably a question of a projected soul-image. Since these relationships are very common, the soul must be unconscious just as frequently. (CW 6, par. 809)

**Squaring the Circle:** an ancient mystery and symbol of the union of opposites. Throughout the ages, many have tried but failed to construct a square equal in area to a given circle. Squares are rational, linear, and finite. Circles are irrational, non-linear, and infinite. The alchemists viewed the problem of "squaring the circle" as the equivalent to their search for the Philosopher's Stone. Jung saw the squared circle (mandala) as the central archetype of the psyche.

**Subject:** the opposite of object. We live in the subjective reality of our internal world, and the objective reality of the external world.

**Symbiosis:** a human pairing where one or both persons is a container for the other person's Dark Side projections. Symbiotic relationships commonly form between two persons of opposite Attitudes.

> Either type has a predilection to marry its opposite, each being unconsciously complementary to the other. . . . The one takes care of reflection and the other sees to the initiative and practical action. When the two types marry, they may effect an ideal union. So long as they are fully occupied with their adaptation to the

> manifold external needs of life they fit together admirably. When . . . external necessity no longer presses, then they have time to occupy themselves with one another. Hitherto they stood back to back and defended themselves against necessity. But now they turn face to face and look for understanding only to discover that they have never understood one another. Each speaks a different language. Then the conflict between the two types begins. This struggle is envenomed, brutal, full of mutual depreciation, even when conducted quietly and in the greatest intimacy. For the value of the one is the negation of value for the other. (CW 7, par. 80)

**Symbols and Signs:** a symbol points to something unknown; a sign points to something known. A symbol points to something greater, but a sign is always less than the thing it represents. Something can be either a symbol or a sign depending on our perception of it as symbolic of something unknown or symptomatic of something known.

> A sign is always less than the thing it points to; a symbol is always more than we understand at first sight. Therefore, we never stop at the sign but go on to the goal it indicates; but we remain with the symbol because it promises more than it reveals. (CW 18, par. 212)

**Synchronicity:** "meaningful coincidences." Our internal world and the external world are synchronized, yet independent. Carl Jung defined synchronicity as an "acausal connection between psychic states and objective events."

**Teleology:** purposeful development toward a goal. Our personality develops purposefully towards the goal of balancing our Light Side and our Dark Side.

**Traits:** Typology identifies the polarities of the Sixteen Personality Types rather than measure personality traits. Traits are measured in quantity, and vary in their desirability. In contrast, the Sixteen Personality Types are identified by the primary polarities of human nature, and are all equally desirable. Traits are usually treated as isolated qualities rather than one side of a polarity. In contrast, typology always looks at both sides of a polarity.

**Transform:** to change from one form into another; to transmute; to metamorphose. Caterpillars transform into butterflies, tadpoles transform into frogs, and human beings transform into individuals.

**Typology:** typing personality by primal polarities. The Original Compass maps the primal polarities of human nature into the Four Natures, Four Styles, and Four Realms. All of the Sixteen Personality Types are equally valid and valuable. Typology identifies which side of each primary polarity a person naturally aligns. Typology does not measure a person's abilities.

**Unconscious:** everything that is not conscious. We have a personal unconscious and a collective unconscious.

> The personal unconscious contains lost memories, painful ideas that are repressed (i.e., forgotten on purpose), subliminal perceptions, by which are meant sense-perceptions that were not strong enough to reach consciousness, and finally, contents that are not yet ripe for consciousness. (CW 7, par. 103)

> The collective unconscious contains the whole spiritual heritage of mankind's evolution, born anew in the brain structure of every individual. (CW 8, par. 342)

**Unconsciousness:** a state of high suggestibility and lack of control.

> An extreme state of unconsciousness is characterized by the predominance of compulsive instinctual processes, the result of which is either uncontrolled inhibition or a lack of inhibition throughout. The happenings within the psyche are then contradictory and proceed in terms of alternating, non-logical antitheses. In such a case the level of consciousness is essentially that of a dream-state. A high degree of consciousness, on the other hand, is characterized by a heightened awareness, a preponderance of will, directed, rational behaviour, and an almost total absence of instinctual determinants. The unconscious is then found to be at a definitely animal level. The first state is lacking in intellectual and ethical achievement, the second lacks naturalness. (CW 8, par. 249)

***Unus Mundus*****:** "One World," the union of spirit and matter giving birth to something new which is neither spirit nor matter.

**Whole Personality:** the union of the Light Side and Dark Side.

> Although "wholeness" seems at first sight to be nothing but an abstract idea (like anima and animus), it is nevertheless empirical in so far as it is anticipated by the psyche in the form of spontaneous or autonomous symbols. These are the quaternity or mandala symbols, which occur not only in the dreams of modern people who have never heard of them, but are widely disseminated in the historical records of many peoples and many epochs. Their significance as symbols of unity and totality is amply confirmed by history as well as by empirical psychology. (CW 9ii, par. 59)

> Consciousness should defend its reason and protect itself, and the chaotic life of the unconscious should be given the chance of having its way too – as much of it as we can stand. This means open conflict and open collaboration at once. That, evidently, is the way human life should be. It is the old game of hammer and anvil: between them the patient iron is forged into an indestructible whole, an "individual." (CW 9i, par. 522)

**World View:** our personal point of view.

> It is a fact, which is constantly and overwhelmingly apparent in my practical work, that people are virtually incapable of understanding and accepting any point of view other than their own. (CW 6, par. 847)

**Yin and Yang:** Yin means "shadowy slope" and Yang means "sunny slope." Yin and Yang join in a circle, one half dark and one half light, symbolizing the duality of the universe and the process of eternal change. Each half contains a small circle of the opposite color symbolizing that each side contains its opposite and will eventually become its opposite. These small circles are the "Seeds of Change" symbolizing the "presence in absence." Both sides spiral perpetually, Yin turning to Yang and Yang turning to Yin. Yang is the side of Light, Spirit, Heaven, and Sun. Yin is the side of Dark, Matter, Earth, and Moon. Yang is warm like summer and spring; Yin is cool like winter and autumn.

Yang is high and narrow; Yin is low and flat. A three dimensional Compass of Forces shows the two Yin Elements, Water (O) and Earth (+), resting low and flat like the surface of all bodies of water and like the colorful skin that covers the body of Earth. When viewing the two dimensional Compass of Forces, imagine the Yin images of O and + pivoted 90 degrees (horizontal like a coin and a cross resting flat on a table). In contrast, the two Yang Elements, Air (S) and Fire (Y), are high and narrow like warm air rising above water and like fire flaming up above Earth into the sky. In summary, the two Yin images (O and +) rest below horizontally and the two Yang images (S and Y) rise above vertically.

As with all polarities in nature, both Yin and Yang are equally valid and valuable.

> A living system is a self-regulating system and must be balanced. Neither spirit nor matter is good in themselves, for, in excess, both destroy life. – Carl Jung

| Pictures of Personality™  | MBTI® | |
|---|---|---|
| External | E | Extraverting |
| Internal | I | Introverting |
| Content | S | Sensing |
| Context | N | iNtuiting |
| Organize | T | Thinking |
| Harmonize | F | Feeling |
| Globalize | P | Perceiving |
| Localize | J | Judging |
| Unifiers | NF | |
| Clarifiers | NT | |
| Activators | SP | |
| Stabilizers | SJ | |
| Magicians of the Unknown | NP | |
| Magicians of the Known | SP | |
| Rulers of the Past | SJ | |
| Rulers of the Future | NJ | |
| Direct | NJ and ST | |
| Indirect | NP and SF | |

| Pictures of Personality™ | | Jung | | MBTI® |
|---|---|---|---|---|
| **External Content**<br>Experience the Object<br>The Actual: Attention | Global | Se | Extraverted Sensing | SP |
| **External Context**<br>Decipher the Object<br>The Novel: Options | Global | Ne | Extraverted iNtuiting | NP |
| **Internal Organizing**<br>Subjective Contemplation<br>My Ideas: Precision | Global | Ti | Introverted Thinking | TP |
| **Internal Harmonizing**<br>Subjective Evaluation<br>My Ideals: Perfection | Global | Fi | Introverted Feeling | FP |
| **Internal Content**<br>Subjective Impressions<br>My Priorities: Continuation | Local | Si | Introverted Sensing | SJ |
| **Internal Context**<br>Subjective Interpretations<br>My Plans: Anticipation | Local | Ni | Introverted iNtuiting | NJ |
| **External Organizing**<br>Objective Formulas<br>The Methods: Causation | Local | Te | Extraverted Thinking | TJ |
| **External Harmonizing**<br>Objective Conventions<br>The Customs: Relations | Local | Fe | Extraverted Feeling | FJ |

The Eight Talents

The Pictures of Personality™

# Map of the Four Natures

with **MBTI® Codes**

| | | Context | | Content | |
|---|---|---|---|---|---|
| | | Indirect | Direct | Indirect | Direct |
| Confidence | External | C2 ENTP | C3 ENTJ | A2 ESFP | A3 ESTP |
| | | *Clarifiers* | | *Activators* | |
| | Internal | C1 INTP | C4 INTJ | A1 ISFP | A4 ISTP |
| Trust | External | U2 ENFP | U3 ENFJ | S2 ESFJ | S3 ESTJ |
| | | *Unifiers* | | *Stabilizers* | |
| | Internal | U1 INFP | U4 INFJ | S1 ISFJ | S4 ISTJ |

The Pictures of Personality™

# Map of the Four Realms

with MBTI® Codes

| | | Context | | Content | |
|---|---|---|---|---|---|
| | | Harmonize | Organize | Harmonize | Organize |
| Globalize | External | U2<br>ENFP | C2<br>ENTP | A2<br>ESFP | A3<br>ESTP |
| | | *Magicians of the Unknown* | | *Magicians of the Known* | |
| | Internal | U1<br>INFP | C1<br>INTP | A1<br>ISFP | A4<br>ISTP |
| Localize | External | U3<br>ENFJ | C3<br>ENTJ | S2<br>ESFJ | S3<br>ESTJ |
| | | *Rulers of the Future* | | *Rulers of the Past* | |
| | Internal | U4<br>INFJ | C4<br>INTJ | S1<br>ISFJ | S4<br>ISTJ |

| C | A |
|---|---|
| U | S |

# FAITH

The Vertical Axis of the Compass of Natures
with MBTI® Codes

| 2 | 3 |
|---|---|
| 1 | 4 |

| ACTIVATOR | | | | CLARIFIER | | | | STABILIZER | | | | UNIFIER | | | |
|---|---|---|---|---|---|---|---|---|---|---|---|---|---|---|---|
| A3 | A4 | A2 | A1 | C3 | C4 | C2 | C1 | S3 | S4 | S2 | S1 | U3 | U4 | U2 | U1 |
| ESTP | ISTP | ESFP | ISFP | ENTJ | INTJ | ENTP | INTP | ESTJ | ISTJ | ESFJ | ISFJ | ENFJ | INFJ | ENFP | INFP |
| STP | | SFP | | NTJ | | NTP | | STJ | | SFJ | | NFJ | | NFP | |
| Direct | | Indirect | | Direct | | Indirect | | Direct | | Indirect | | Direct | | Indirect | |
| SP | | | | NT | | | | SJ | | | | NF | | | |
| Confidence | | | | | | | | Trust | | | | | | | |

| C | A |
|---|---|
| U | S |

## FOCUS

The Horizontal Axis of the Compass of Natures
with MBTI® Codes

| 2 | 3 |
|---|---|
| 1 | 4 |

| CLARIFIER | | | | UNIFIER | | | | ACTIVATOR | | | | STABILIZER | | | |
|---|---|---|---|---|---|---|---|---|---|---|---|---|---|---|---|
| C2 | C1 | C3 | C4 | U2 | U1 | U3 | U4 | A2 | A1 | A3 | A4 | S2 | S1 | S3 | S4 |
| ENTP | INTP | ENTJ | INTJ | ENFP | INFP | ENFJ | INFJ | ESFP | ISFP | ESTP | ISTP | ESFJ | ISFJ | ESTJ | ISTJ |
| NTP | | NTJ | | NFP | | NFJ | | SFP | | STP | | SFJ | | STJ | |
| Indirect | | Direct | | Indirect | | Direct | | Indirect | | Direct | | Indirect | | Direct | |
| NT | | | | NF | | | | SP | | | | SJ | | | |
| Context | | | | | | | | Content | | | | | | | |

| C | A |
|---|---|
| U | S |

# FAITH

The Vertical Axis of the Compass of Natures
with MBTI® Codes and Yin Yang Spectrum

| 2 | 3 |
|---|---|
| 1 | 4 |

| ACTIVATOR | | | | CLARIFIER | | | | STABILIZER | | | | UNIFIER | | | |
|---|---|---|---|---|---|---|---|---|---|---|---|---|---|---|---|
| A3 | A4 | A2 | A1 | C3 | C4 | C2 | C1 | S3 | S4 | S2 | S1 | U3 | U4 | U2 | U1 |
| ESTP | ISTP | ESFP | ISFP | ENTJ | INTJ | ENTP | INTP | ESTJ | ISTJ | ESFJ | ISFJ | ENFJ | INFJ | ENFP | INFP |
| +16 | +12 | +12 | +8 | +8 | +4 | +4 | +0 | −0 | −4 | −4 | −8 | −8 | −12 | −12 | −16 |
| External 4 | Internal 0 | External 4 | Internal 0 | External 4 | Internal 0 | External 4 | Internal 0 | External 0 | Internal 4 | External 0 | Internal 4 | External 0 | Internal 4 | External 0 | Internal 4 |
| STP | | SFP | | NTJ | | NTP | | STJ | | SFJ | | NFJ | | NFP | |
| Direct 4 | | Indirect 0 | | Direct 4 | | Indirect 0 | | Direct 0 | | Indirect 4 | | Direct 0 | | Indirect 4 | |
| SP | | | | NT | | | | SJ | | | | NF | | | |
| Confidence 8 | | | | Confidence, but. 0 | | | | Trust, but. 0 | | | | Trust 8 | | | |
| **Confidence + Yang** | | | | | | | | **Trust – Yin** | | | | | | | |

# Natural Order and Usage

List the Forces, Elements, Natures, and Styles in the order of the numbers that mold them:

Cool, Moist, Warm, Dry
Water, Air, Fire, Earth
Unifier, Clarifier, Activator, Stabilizer
Style 1, Style 2, Style 3, Style 4

List the Four Realms clockwise starting either with Magicians of the Unknown or Rulers of the Past (always pairing the two Magicians and the two Rulers).

List the Talents in the order of their related dimension: 1st, 2nd, 3rd, and 4th dimensions.

Harmonizing, Organizing, Content, Context

The Talents may be described generally as:

| | |
|---|---|
| Talent L1 or L1 | Talent D1 or D1 |
| Talent L2 or L2 | Talent D2 or D2 |
| Talent L3 or L3 | Talent D3 or D3 |
| Talent L4 or L4 | Talent D4 or D4 |

The Talents may be described specifically in any of the following ways, for example:

| | |
|---|---|
| LX–Internal Content | *DX–Internal Content!* |
| LX–My Priorities | *DX–My Priorities!* |
| LX–Continuation | *DX–Continuation!* |
| LX–Subjective Impressions | *DX–Subjective Impressions!* |

Note: X is the number of the Talent: 1, 2, 3, or 4. As an option, italicizing and/or adding an exclamation mark to the Dark Talents helps to show the quality of the Dark Talents.

Drawing by William Blake. © The British Museum

# Eve's Awakening

Eve awoke before dawn, suspecting something missing. She detected the faint scent of something real, something sealed between night and day. Was it the wildflowers or the fragrance of fate?

Eve searched for the source of that strange scent of five in the morning. The seasons turned and turned, but Eve found nothing. Her endurance dwindled to a trickle, yet her desire would not let go. Eve's obsession had pulled her inside itself and pushed her out of control. On the edge of despair, Eve collapsed on a massive rock high above the deep lagoon. The pulsing chorus of crickets sifted the night air with a mysterious monotone code as she gazed sadly into the sky shimmering in the still waters far below. Alone and afraid, Eve dared to deliberate her destiny.

Suddenly, her rock dissolved plunging Eve into the dark underworld. A furious whirlpool spun her deeper and deeper into its center. Fighting for her freedom, she spent all of her energy and exhausted all of her air. Finally, letting go, her body sunk calmly with perfect surrender. The crooked moonlight flickered like an old silent movie framing every moment of her descent.

In the darkness, Eve began to see. Her pain mellowed into a full-bodied ache aged in the vault of eternal desire. A white mist fell as Eve began to rise. The night bloomed in every color when Eve softly surfaced somewhere between daylight's obscurity and night-time's distant glow. Eve drifted in peace while the sky bent into the most beautiful red sunrise she had ever seen. As the morning warmed, Eve floated up with the gentle heat, spiraling higher and higher, closer and closer, solid and graceful like a single stone spinning in space. At last, in the death of her fear, the answer appeared.

Eve never found that scent, but she always stayed close to the wildflowers. And she never found anything quite so real again.

# INDEX

**Pictures of Personality™ Guide to the Four Human Natures $25**
See Your Nature, Style, and Realm with the Original Compass.
Discover the Symbols and Icons of the Sixteen Personality Types.
208 Pages, Color, 212 Illustrations, Glossary and Index, 7.5 x 9.25 inches. ISBN 0-9705810-0-9

**Pictures of Personality™ Symbol Cards $12**
Compare and contrast the personalities of two or more persons. Place the cards side by side to see yourself, your partner, family, team, club, company, or organization.
Color, High Quality, Durable, 2.5 x 3.5 inches. ISBN 0-9705810-1-7

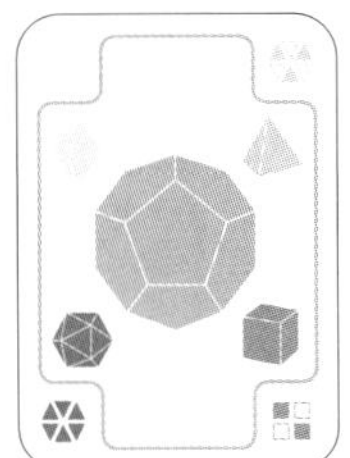

| Set of 55 Symbol Cards exactly as shown in PART IV | | | |
|---|---|---|---|
| 2 Sets of Clarifiers | (8 Cards) | 4 Sets of Activators | (16 Cards) |
| 2 Sets of Unifiers | (8 Cards) | 5 Sets of Stabilizers | (20 Cards) |

**Pictures of Personality™ Icon Cards $12**
Compare and contrast the personalities of two or more persons. Place the cards side by side to see yourself, your partner, family, team, club, company, or organization.
Color, High Quality, Durable, 2.5 x 3.5 inches. ISBN 0-9705810-2-5

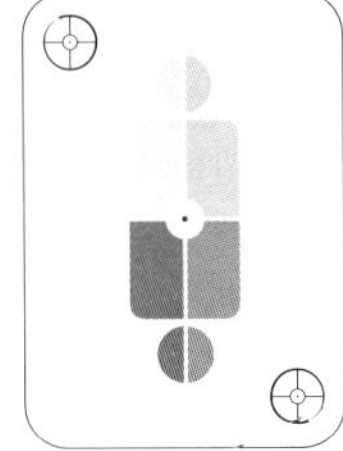

| Set of 55 Icon Cards exactly as shown in PART IV | | | |
|---|---|---|---|
| 2 Sets of Clarifiers | (8 Cards) | 4 Sets of Activators | (16 Cards) |
| 2 Sets of Unifiers | (8 Cards) | 5 Sets of Stabilizers | (20 Cards) |

Name: ______________________________

Address: ______________________________

______________________________

Telephone: ____________________ Email: ____________________

Payment (Circle One): Visa MasterCard AMEX Check Money Order

Credit Card Number: ______________________________

Name on Card: ____________________ Expiration Date: ____________________

How Many? ________ Guides ________ Symbol Cards ________ Icon Cards

**Call 1-800-TYPOLOGY (1-800-897-6564)**
**www.Typology.Net**

| Shipping Rates | Per Order | Per Item |
|---|---|---|
| U. S. | $3 | $1 |
| International | $7 | $3 |

Payable to TYPOLOGY in U.S. Currency. Add 7% tax for items shipped to California.